GR
705
R68

Rowland, Beryl.
  Animals with human faces; a guide to animal symbolism.
[1st ed. Knoxville] University of Tennessee Press [1973]

xix, 192 p. illus. 17 x 27 cm. $10.75

Bibliography: p. 169–177.

1. Animal lore.   I. Title.

GR705.R68   398′.369   70–173657
ISBN 0–87049–136–9   MARC
                                        · 155
Library of Congress   73 [4]

Animals with Human Faces

Animals

with Human Faces

A Guide to Animal Symbolism ∫ *Beryl Rowland*

THE UNIVERSITY OF TENNESSEE PRESS

Library of Congress Catalog Card No. 70–173657
International Standard Book No. 0–87049–136–9
   Copyright © 1973 by The University of Tennessee Press, Knoxville.
   All rights reserved. Manufactured in the U.S.A. First edition.

Library of Congress Cataloging in Publication Data

   Rowland, Beryl.
   Animals with human faces.
   1.   Animal lore.   I.   Title.

   GR705.R68   398′.369   70–173657
   ISBN 0–87049–136–9

Books by Beryl Rowland

Companion to Chaucer Studies (editor), 1968
Blind Beasts: Chaucer's Animal World, 1971
Animals with Human Faces, 1973
Chaucer and Middle English Studies in Honor of
   Rossell Hope Robbins (editor), 1973

Frontispiece:

The Creation of the Animals. Ashmole 1511 f.6b

To Murray

Preface

This book attempts to put between two covers the most meaningful details of animal symbolism. It is a book to be dipped into by anyone wanting to know what an animal stands for and why, and many readers will no doubt be able to add to the examples which I give. My work, in alphabetical sections, with illustrations from manuscripts, traces the history of various animals as symbols from earliest times to the present day in art, literature, and folklore, and shows why certain ideas are still associated with specific animals.

There are, of course, many excellent works partly or wholly concerned with this subject, and their popularity testifies to the perennial interest in the animal and what it stands for in human terms. Among those works are studies of medieval bestiaries by Florence McCulloch, F. J. Carmody, and T. H. White; and studies of individual animals by H. W. Janson, Maria Leach, and Anthony

Dent. There are, as well, various books such as that by Jorge Luis Borges of a more popular nature emphasizing the fabulous accounts of animals transmitted by Pliny, Aelian, and writers of earlier periods.

While I am indebted to many of these works, my book differs from them. It goes again to the primary sources and reinterprets them, tracing the material over the centuries and setting it in a perspective which is subjective and contemporary. The references at the end of each entry are for those scholars familiar with the research materials alluded to, and I hope the citations may be of some use also to students who, especially if they are medievalists, would rather search the stacks forever or immolate themselves in their library carrels in silent frustration than suffer the humiliation of citing a secondary source.

Some explanation is required of the choice of animals. A few considered here are no longer used symbolically, but even these seem relevant. Admittedly, the basilisk, which could kill a man with a look, has ceased to be the stock antifeminist symbol of woman it was to medieval man, even to Petrarch whom we tend to associate with more romantic notions. Nevertheless, the expression "lethal glance" is still current and probably owes something to the devastating characteristic of this fabled reptile of the African desert. Similarly, while the dire amphisbaena has not had much currency since Milton, some poets may yet decide that it is a fitting symbol for outrageous Fortune's slings and arrows or even for modern man himself. I have reluctantly omitted several delightful creatures, such as the yale with its flexible horns, for the simple reason that some animals never had wide currency as symbols. And I confess to including one insect, which should not be here at all, merely for the fun of it. Altogether, I deal with some fifty mammals and a few reptiles which crept in uninvited.

Most of the animals chosen still possess a very immediate kind of symbolism. While this symbolism may be very different from what it was in the past, earlier meanings do not necessarily lose their significance. For example, western Canada is said to fear that the beaver (genus *castoridae*), the famous national symbol derived from the fur-trade, may be replaced by a symbol from eastern Canada, the little green amphibian (genus *ranae*), which hops out of the pool and startles the princess in the folk-tale. Our combined study of unnatural history, folklore, and psychology makes us pause over these figures and speculate on their present-day application. The beaver's behavior is peculiar: to escape the hunter who pursues it for its valuable oil, it castrates itself and flings its testicles (which were thought to contain an oily secretion called castor) in the face of its pursuer who, having got what he wanted, leaves it alone. In terms of medieval symbolism this unnatural creature represents Man trying to save himself by casting off his sins when he is pursued by the Devil. The frog in the folktale provides a somewhat striking contrast, for it is a symbol of sexual initiation: as everyone knows, the princess, after much persuasion, kisses it; it turns into a prince and marries her. One should add, however, that the frog could also represent fraud and as such eventually got its comeuppance. According to the Romulus fable, a frog promises to help a mouse cross a river by tying it to its own foot. Once it has secured the mouse, it prepares to dive into the water in order to drown it. From the sky a hungry kite (a predatory bird which, in Elizabethan England, even used to snatch bread and jam from the hands of children on the London streets), sees the mouse, swoops down, and carries off the frog as well as its prey. As Herman Melville once said in a different connection, "A good thing might be made of this."

On the whole, however, I am concerned with providing

a knowledge of less esoteric symbolism, the kind of knowledge which, I believe, never ceases to be meaningful because it derives from ideas about animals which lie deep in the human imagination in all ages. It is strong stuff and, perhaps, not to everyone's taste. Today I heard some gentlemen who were once associated in various ways with the work of A. A. Milne being interviewed in a radio program on "Winnie the Pooh." In a few words their well-bred English voices bleakly conjured up the solitary, chilly boyhood not uncommon in England half a century ago. Every boy, they said, should have a teddy bear to talk to when he was lonely or unhappy. All their lives they had themselves been ardent lovers and possessors of teddy bears. A certain retired brigadier was planning to hold a rally of teddy bears and their owners in Kensington Gardens. It was a "jolly good idea"; thousands would attend. Such experiences are not apparently shared by today's extraverted North American child. The interviewer laughingly disclosed that her eleven-year-old son adored rabbits; in fact, he loved all small furry stuffed objects and on the last count had at least eighteen, "but some he liked better than others." From our knowledge of animal symbolism the meaning of these diverse objects of human affection is obvious. Numerous tales of women being violated by bears and giving birth to half-ursine and half-human monsters, as well as accounts of tribal bear ceremonies from which unmarried women were excluded, testify to the primitive identification of the bear with male sexuality. The story of Christopher Robin and Winnie the Pooh tells of a homosexual phase, usually relatively brief, in the life of a child. The symbol of the rabbit is similarly unequivocal. Clearly, for reasons other than that Nannies are now scarce and cleaning ladies are seldom single, we are not likely to find the North American child listening to details of Alice's forthcoming wedding to one of the guards or kneeling at the foot of the bed, asking God to bless his parents as he contemplates his blue dressinggown. A study of animal symbolism does, indeed, enlighten us.

Yet, thinking of those gentlemen gathering in Kensington Gardens (surely near the statue of Peter Pan?), clutching dog-eared animals in plush worn down to the canvas, I acknowledge that animals can also have a very precious private symbolism and, to invert a well-known Chaucerian phrase, let us not "maken game of ernest."

Beryl Rowland
YORK UNIVERSITY
TORONTO

Acknowledgments

This book has been published with the help of a grant from the Humanities Research Council of Canada, using funds provided by The Canada Council.

The author wishes to thank:

The British Museum for permission to reproduce photographs of amphisbaena (MS. Harley 3244, f. 62a), antelope (MS. Royal 12F. XIII, f.9b), basilisk (MS. Harley 3244, f.59b), camel (MS. Royal 12F. XIII, f.38a), dragon (MS. Royal 19.B. xv, f.22b), fox (MS. Royal 12F. XIII, f.26b), hedgehog (MS. Royal 12F. XIII, f.45a), Pegasus and nine Muses (MS. Harley 4431, f.183a), leopard (MS. Harley 4751, f.6a), lion asleep (MS. Royal 12F. XIII, f.4a), lion: three panels (MS. Royal 12F. XIII, f.5b), lynx (MS. Harley 3244, f.38b), siren and ape (Add. MS. 24686, f.13a), snake (MS. Harley 22288, f.49b), unicorn (MS. Royal 12F XIII, f.10b), and wolf (MS. Sloane 3544, f.13a).

The Westminster Chapter House Library for permission to use photographs of Adam naming the animals (MS. 22, f.4a), centaur (MS. 22, f.54a), chimaera (MS. 22, f.53b), elephant (MS. 22, f.20b), griffin (MS. 22, f.19b), hare (MS. 22, f.27a), and lion's cub (MS. 22, f.15b).

The Bodleian Museum for permission to use photographs of the creation of the animals (MS. Ashmole 1511, f.6b), animals are only human (MS. Bodley 264, f.181b), ape (MS. Bodley 764, f.16b), asp (MS. Bodley 764, f.96a), aspidochelone (MS. Ashmole 1511, f.86b), ass (MS. Bodley 764, f.44a), bear (MS. Bodley 764, f.22b), beaver (MS. Bodley 764, f.14a), boar (MS. Bodley 764, f.38b), cow (MS. Bodley 764, f.41b), cat (MS. Bodley 764, f.51a), crocodile (MS. Bodley 764, f.24a), dog (MS. Bodley 764, f.31a), goat (MS. Bodley 764, f.20b), hart and young (MS. Bodley 764, f.20a), hart (MS. Bodley 764, f.17b), horses (MS. Bodley 764, f.46a), hyena (MS. Bodley 764, f.15a), lamb (MS. Bodley 764, f.35b), manticore (MS. Bodley 764, f.25), ox (MS. Bodley 764, f.40a), panther (MS. Bodley 764, f.7b), rabbit (MS. Bodley 264, f.62b), rat (MS. New Coll. 130, f.41a), satyr (MS. Ashmole 1511, f.19a), satyrs (MS. Bodley 764, f.17a), sirens and sailors (MS. Bodley 764, f.74b), tiger (MS. Bodley 764, f.6b), vipers (MS. Bodley 764, f.94b), and weasel (MS. Douce 308, f.96b).

THE PIERPONT MORGAN LIBRARY for permission to use photographs of ant (MS. 81, f.31b), mole (MS. 81, f.47a), and mouse (MS. 31, f.47a).

Contents

Introduction

Today we realize that animals behave very much as we do, probably for very similar reasons. They, like us, are interested in acquiring territory and status. Primitive Man also thought that animals resembled him, but he did not know what motivated them. He saw them as exemplifying human traits which he either admired, feared, or disliked.

In time his ideas about animals were confirmed in religious rituals, literature, and art. He worshipped the bull or goat because the qualities which he attributed to them seemed divine. He invented fables in which the fox demonstrated craftiness and the ant industry because he thought these creatures possessed such characteristics. At Nineveh, Khorsabad, and Nimrud he fashioned massive lions or bulls with eagle wings and human heads because these hybrids had a universal significance: the three parts, deriving from the king of beasts or the great fecundator, from the king of birds, and from the lord of creation,

Animals are only human (a group of mummers).

constituted royalty.

Already the animal was a *symbol*, a word which is from the Greek word συμβάλλειν (to throw together). When a concrete object becomes a symbol, it constitutes the semblance of something which is not shown but is realized through its associations: it is transformed into a metaphor or even into a sermon in shorthand. Animals became symbols of qualities possessed by man.

These ideas about animals were well suited to the unscientific and typological mode of thought which subsequently dominated the West. Many of the supposed characteristics of animals were repeated by Greek and Roman writers as facts of natural history, and they passed almost unchallenged into the medieval world, where they were reinforced by Biblical symbolism.

Only the most ritualistically assertive of the earlier folk-beliefs about animals required modification. "What rational person," asked one prelate in the fifth century, "could believe that he would find some people of sound mind who, making a stag [*cervulum facientes*], would wish to change themselves into a wild beast? Some are arrayed in skins of cattle [*pecudum*], others put on the heads of beasts." Metamorphosis or metempsychosis, an integral feature in the development of religions, was relegated principally to "mummings" and *ludi* such as those presented at the court of Edward III, where the original purposes were forgotten.

The Christian Church, although it identified its great figures with animals because of certain traits, refuted ideas of direct transference; its penitentials, especially those from the fifth to the eighth centuries, inveighed against the ceremonial wearing of animal heads and skins. The brute creation, like the world itself, existed solely for the spiritual edification of man. While animals shared in the Fall they had no part in the great plan of Redemption: their purpose was to provide moral lessons that would assist in man's regeneration. "Ask the beasts," Job had said, "and they will teach you; the birds of the air, and they will tell you" (xii.7). The lamb without spot, originally burned and ritualistically eaten so that the celebrants might acquire its purity and expiate their sins, was the Lamb of God, sacrificed and eaten in the Eucharist in order to redeem the world; the lion, an ancient solar deity, was both the symbol of Christ (the "lion of Judah," Genesis xlix.9, Revelation v.5) and of the Devil (the "roaring lion," 1 Peter v.8); for more ingenious reasons, the fish was an early symbol of Christ because the Greek word for fish, $\iota\chi\theta\tilde{\upsilon}s$, provided the initials for "Jesu Christ, Son of God, Savior."

In the Renaissance, when a great many animal symbols were secularized, the basic symbolism usually remained. Despite a growing concern with the concrete and the particular and the popularity of botanical gardens and zoological parks, the conception of nature as allegory persisted. If the fox had been a symbol of the Devil in the medieval bestiaries, it was still the symbol of craftiness; if the snake in the grass was not precisely the Old Serpent beguiling Eve in the Garden, it was still the symbol of deceit, speaking, as it does yet, with forked tongue; similarly, the wolf in sheep's clothing remained the arch-dissimulator, if not the Evil One himself. The moral implication, so characteristic of the Middle Ages, was present even when an animal symbol served an aesthetic purpose as, for example, in Shakespeare's *Timon of Athens*: "Wert thou the unicorn, pride and wrath would confound thee" (iv.iii). In the plastic and graphic arts, also, although animal symbols were no longer confined to ecclesiastical sculpture, embroidery, tapestries, and heraldry, didacticism was usually implicit, whether in a printer's colophon, a watermark, or an emblem.

With the development of science, of fundamentalism in religion, and of new forms of secular art which enhanced the importance of literal rather than figurative expression, animal symbolism ceased to be an established mode of reference. Indicative of a totally different attitude, for example, is a seventeenth-century theory, described by George Boas, which maintained that beasts—like savages —were more "natural" than civilized man and, therefore, superior to him. Even when symbolic expression revived in the romantic reaction to rationalism, F. E. Hulme, writing in the nineteenth century on symbolism in Christian art, lamented that symbolism in general "could never again attain the importance that it had done in the past."

In this century, however, art, science, psychology, and new kinds of mass communication have given rise to what has been aptly called "a monstrous hypertrophic worship of symbols." We live in a new age of symbolism in which every street corner, supermarket, and television set confronts us with images which conceal hidden messages, simple and complex intrinsic meanings.

Animals are important in this symbolism: while many of today's symbols are strictly contemporary and some are esoteric, relying on a private code which only the initiated can interpret, most animal symbols are traditional, belonging to the mythology of everyone, eternally present in the collective unconscious memory and in the dream world where everything is a symbol. They are an inexhaustible repository which novelists, poets, artists, dramatists, film makers, and even advertisers draw on, either consciously or intuitively, when they wish to evoke an immediate yet profound response. They are the source, too, of many proverbial expressions and conventional figurative ideas which we ourselves employ in daily life.

But although we respond to animal symbols intuitively, their meanings, ancient and universal as they may be, are not always fully apparent. To appreciate these symbols and to be able to assess the skill with which they can be used, we need to rethink them as they developed over the centuries.

To discover the lost meanings, I have taken my evidence from a variety of key works: the Bidpai and the Aesopic fables; Greek and Roman natural histories such as Aristotle's *Historia animalium*, Pliny's *Historia naturalis*, Aelian's *De natura animalium*, and Oppian's *Cynegetica*; the *Physiologus*, which moralized traditional zoological beliefs early in the Christian era and proliferated into innumerable illustrated bestiaries in the Middle Ages; accounts of ritual and myth recorded by Herodotus, Ovid, and Plutarch; the Septuagint version of the Hebrew Bible made in the first century B.C., and the Vulgate translation in the fourth century A.D.; patristic writings of Tertullian, Ambrose, and others; Isidore of Seville's *Etymologiarum sive originum*, which repeated much of the earlier animal lore in order to support erroneous etymologies and which was an important source book for medieval scholars.

Also examined are various medieval encyclopedic works such as Alexander Neckam's *De naturis rerum*, Bartholomaeus Anglicus' *De proprietatibus rerum*, which was translated into English by Trevisa in 1397, (Pseudo) Vincent de Beauvais' *Speculum*, Rabanus Maurus' *Allegoria in sacram scripturam*, the sermons of Honorius "d'Augustodiensis," Odo of Ceriton, and John of Sheppey; the medieval Latin and French bestiaries; the *Gesta Romanorum*, a collection of allegorized tales, and *The Golden Legend*, a compilation of saints' lives.

In addition, numerous works of the Renaissance period are taken into account: the popular emblem books which contained short verses, illustrated by engravings, to express a conceit of a moral or philosophical kind; the main sources of such works: Horapollo's *Hieroglyphics* (1505), a work on Egyptian symbolism, originating in the fourth or fifth century and relying on folklore and the Greek and Roman histories rather than on a sound knowledge of hieroglyphics, and the *Physiologus* (1587), wrongly attributed to Epiphanius; Edward Topsell's *Historie of Foure-Footed Beasts* (1607), where the writer, translating Gesner's *Historia animalium* (1551), provided a detailed summation of popular lore, accompanied by vigorous illustrations in which a full-busted lamia and placid Cheshire cat are both equally lifelike and predatory; the works of the Italian naturalist Aldrovandi (1522–1605) and of the Norwich physician Sir Thomas Browne who, in his *Pseudodoxia epidemica: enquiries into very many commonly received tenents and commonly presumed truths* (1646), refuted some vulgar errors but accepted and repeated many traditional ideas about animals.

These are the primary sources most frequently cited, because they belong to periods when animal symbolism was a fashionable mode of literary expression. For more recent examples of usage, a variety of works was examined, including John S. Farmer's *Vocabula Amatoria* (1896), which shows how animal symbols survive in the argot of the streets. Where standard classical texts are cited, editions are not described in the bibliography. Similarly, when Church Fathers are quoted, reference is made to the volumes of *Patrologia Latina* (*PL*) and *Patrologia Graeca* (*PG*), edited by J. P. Migne, without additional bibliographical note. After each section in the text, the most important sources only are given, including secondary sources, for which full details are supplied in the Selected Bibliography. Spellings, especially with regard to *v* and *u* in some titles and quotations, have been normalized.

Animals with Human Faces

Adam naming the animals.

Amphisbaena

No one liked this creature. It was regarded as a venomous serpent. Milton quite rightly put it in hell: at the very moment of their master's triumph, Satan's followers turned into hissing serpents—"complicated monsters, head and tail, / Scorpion and asp, and Amphisbaena dire."

According to an ancient belief, the amphisbaena had two heads, one in the usual place and the other in the tail. By sticking one into the mouth of the other it could bowl along like a hoop—in either direction, as its name from the Greek ἀμφί, "both ways," and βαίνω, "to go," suggests. This singular mode of transport was employed solely for evil purposes. According to Pliny, the animal needed more than one mouth to discharge all its venom.

On the other hand, some writers in antiquity attributed therapeutic value to the amphisbaena. Apollodorus thought that its old skin wrapped round a walking stick gave protection against other reptiles; Nicander recommended it for chilblains; Pliny, as a remedy for the cold shivers and as an inducement for a pregnant woman to miscarry. Even in the sixteenth century it was still prescribed as a cure for chilblains.

Nevertheless, the idea that the amphisbaena was evil persisted, and few paid any attention to the ancient In-

The amphisbaena has two heads.

dian tale of the *Mahabharata* in which an amphisbaena claimed to have once been a wise and upright prince. Aeschylus compared Clytemnestra, who murdered her

3

husband, to the loathsome amphisbaena, and the bestiaries, using a quotation from Lucan—"the dangerous amphisbaena turned both ways by its two heads, and its eyes shine like lamps"—discovered a resemblance to the Devil.

Bestiary illustrations and medieval architecture often show the amphisbaena either looking at the other head or grasping it in its mouth. A misericord at Chichester Cathedral shows another form: two such creatures feed on the head of a corpse, clinging with their legs to the brow and neck of their victim for better suction. Had the carver not ascribed legs to them, one might suspect some genuine zoological knowledge. The real amphisbaena is a tropical lizard some twenty inches long with a tail which is sometimes not unlike a second head when raised in anger, and it does feed on decaying matter. Its eyes, far from being useful or even lamplike, as Lucan supposed, are actually dummies, and it has no legs. The carver at Chichester is clearly concerned with the symbolism of his design, for he places grotesquely evil faces on either side of it; the misericord is a *memento mori*, portraying the consequences of a life of sin. Worms will destroy the sinner's body in the grave, and the fiends will consume his soul for all eternity.

The carver may have been using the decorative motif of two creatures drinking from a cup. Two amphisbaena do indeed confront each other symmetrically over a cup or chalice on one of the twelfth-century capitals in the north tower of the cathedral at Chartres. The original design called for two griffins and was an ancient one among Germanic peoples, dating back to pre-Christian times. The substitutes here probably have no symbolic meaning. The amphisbaena on the lintel of the north portal of the cathedral of Vienne, however, are said to be a symbol of vigilance.

Aeschylus, *Agamemnon*, 1206; Browne, III.xv; Druce, "Amphisbaena," pp. 285–317; Kidson and Parker, p. 6; Lucan, *Pharsalia*, ix.719; McCulloch, p. 81; Mâle, *L'Art . . . XIIe siècle*, p. 360; Milton, *P. Lost*, x.523–24; Pliny, VIII.23–35; Topsell, pp. 151–53.

Ant, Ant-Lion

From earliest times the ant was praised for its prudence and industry and came to stand for these qualities in man. According to Pliny, it prevented the germination of seeds by nibbling them before storing them; it divided larger seeds from smaller; it dried the seeds which were wet.

These observations were repeated for centuries, and the bestiarists added two further traits: ants walked in a line, carrying grain in their mouths and unmolested by other ants that had no grain; they went into the fields at harvest time and, by climbing an ear of grain, they were able to distinguish wheat from barley and refuse the latter. By its actions the ant signified the provident man who chose the true doctrine and rejected heretical dogmas. The ant dividing the seeds into two symbolized the Christian discerning between the spirit and the letter of Biblical truth.

Often repeated was Proverbs vi.6–7: "Go to the ant, O sluggard; consider her ways and be wise. Without having any chief, officer or ruler, she prepares her food in summer, and gathers her sustenance in harvest."

A high opinion of the ant is almost universal, and the Japanese represent its symbolic qualities in their word for it.

The character on the left represents the word *insect*. When it is combined with the three other characters, which represent unselfishness, justice, and courtesy, the whole makes up the Japanese ideogram for *ant*.

No such virtues are attached to the ant-lion, an evil creature born of a father with the face of an ant. It owes its existence to the use of the word *mirmicoleon* instead of *lion* in the Septuagint version of Job iv.2: "the *mirmicoleon* perishes for lack of prey." According to early natural historians, the ant-lion was unable to eat either plants or flesh because its mother ate only the former and its father the latter. Strabo said that this ant-lion, with a lion's face and the fore- and hindquarters of an ant, existed in Arabia. Another ant-lion, described by Herodotus, Pliny, and Aelian, resembled a large dog with lion's feet and dug for gold. Subsequently, some confusion arose between the two kinds, but the ant-lion's hybrid nature continued to be stressed in the bestiaries, where it was likened to the double-minded man who, like Job's *mirmicoleon*, also perished. In some versions the giant ant became a separate species called *formicaleon*, a small cunning animal which solved its dietary problems by hiding in the dust and pouncing on the industrious ants as they came along with their grain. A bestiary of the fifteenth century based on the encyclopedia of Bartholomaeus Anglicus contains one of the few medieval illustrations of an ant-lion, showing eight legs and very poorly developed antennae.

Aelian, ii.xxv, iii.iv; Clausen, p. 108, fig. 20; Druce, "An Account," pp. 347–64; Herodotus, iii.cii–cv; Philippe de Thaon, *Best.*, pp. 92–93; Pliny, xi.30.36; Strabo, xvi.iv.15.

5

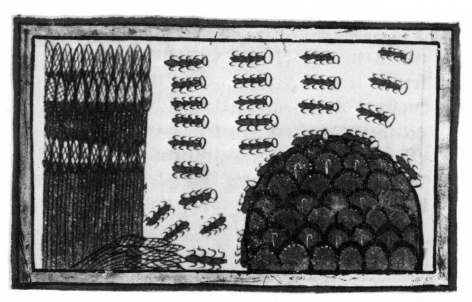

The ant industriously carries grain.

Antelope

The dark, beautiful eyes and the swift, graceful motion of this animal were traditional themes for ancient Arabian and Persian poets. In the East the gazelle was regarded as the image of a tender and gentle woman. The disciple raised to life at Joppa was supposed to be called Tabitha or Dorcas, meaning "the antelope," because of the beauty of her eyes. In Oliver Goldsmith's day, one of the highest compliments which could be paid to a woman in the eastern regions was *aine el lezozel* (you have the eyes of an antelope).

Because of its eyes, which were associated with sharpness of vision, the animal was sacred to Minerva, goddess of wisdom, in ancient Rome. Its acute eyesight probably originally accounts for the fact that among the Egyptians it was a prophetic animal, sacred to Hermes-Anubis. Since the Egyptians depended on the Nile to irrigate their crops, they watched the rise of the river with the greatest concern, and their lives centered on ceremonies regarding it. Some three or four thousand years before the Christian era, the brilliant star of Sirius, the dog star, appeared at dawn in the east about the time of the summer solstice, when the Nile began to rise. The antelope was supposed to be the first creature to know when this star rose, and, according to Aelian, the Egyptians believed

6

that the animal testified to the ascension by sneezing.

The fleetness of the antelope, or the gazelle, was proverbial even in earliest times, and Azahel's speed was compared to it (II Samuel ii.18). Its swiftness was probably the reason for its appearance in the Rig-Veda as the steed of the winds, the leader of the Maruts.

No one knew much about this animal in the West in medieval times, and in heraldry it appeared as a fierce beast, partly resembling a deer and partly some mythical animal with great claws, a lion's tail, and a boar's muzzle and tusks. A Venetian marble relief of the tenth century shows an antelope attacked by a lion. Here the soul is being assaulted by the Devil.

In the bestiaries the antelope symbolized man: man was presented with temptations, yet he was armed with two horns. Such horns represented either the Old and New Testaments or the virtues of abstinence and obedience. Often repeated is a story, unknown in ancient literature, of the antelope that goes to drink in the Euphrates. It catches its horns in the branches of a shrub called herecine, with the result that it is killed by the hunter. Similarly, by hard liquor and women, man is captured by the Devil (Proverbs xxxi.3–5).

Aelian, VII.viii; Goldsmith, I.307–15; Lanoe-Villène, I.119; McCulloch, pp. 84–86.

The antelope is killed when it catches its horns in the bushes.

Ape

Because it resembled man, the ape came to epitomize a variety of human vagaries. Bartholomaeus Anglicus, remarking on the similarity between the Latin *simia* (ape) and *similitude* (likeness), said that the ape was called *simia* because "in many thynges he counterfeteth the dedes of men." In particular, the ape was held to imitate the less admirable deeds of men and as a result symbolized specific evils, such as lust, drunkenness, pride, as well as general follies. Janson and Tervarent cite many examples where the ape appears in sculpture, painting, and engraving as the symbol of various vices ranging from absolute degeneracy to sloth or folly.

In Egypt the dog-headed ape sat on the standard of the scales weighing the souls of the dead and warned Thoth when the pointer reached the middle of the beam. In ancient Greece and Rome the ape typified baseness. Outward appearance was thought to reflect the qualities of the mind. Thus when Socrates conjectured on the form which the ignoble and misshapen Thersites should take in the afterlife, he naturally specified the ape.

In ancient times the ape denoted the inhumanity of a crime. In Rome and in parts of northern Europe, even in the later Middle Ages, a parricide was drowned in a sack along with an ape, a dog, a cock, and a viper. In some areas of Europe in medieval times Jews were hanged with the first two of these animals.

To meet an ape when leaving home was regarded as unlucky, but to dream of one was even worse. The Roman emperor Nero was most upset when he dreamed that the hindquarters of his favorite horse had turned into those of an ape, and he did, in fact, die shortly afterward. Artemidorus Daldianus, the second-century dream expert with whose writings Freud was familiar, was simply summing up a long tradition when he said that to dream of an ape signified misfortune or sickness. The same lore was recorded in the *Talmud* and survived, apparently, even in the Middle Ages. In Chaucer's *Nun's Priest's Tale*, a traveler whose friend has had a warning dream denies that it has any significance. Men are always dreaming of owls and apes, he says. Going heedlessly about his business, he is drowned at sea the next day.

As a symbol of lust the ape also has a long history. Aelian declared that the Indians tried to put the reddish apes to death because they were too fond of women, and the medieval proverb defined a wanton widow as "a dyvell in the kyttchine and a nape in her bedde." This association of the ape and female lasciviousness has some zoological basis in that the female chimpanzee in a phase of her menstrual cycle shows sexual skin changes and enlarged pudendum and presents the hinder end of her body toward her male companions for copulation. In the

Romance countries the she-ape—*guenon, singesse*—came to be an accepted term for a prostitute. In Sebastian Brant's *Narrenschiff* (*Ship of Fools*) (1494), Venus is fashionably dressed in a low-cut gown with leg-of-mutton sleeves, her splendor partially offset by a skeleton with clutching hand who looks over her left shoulder. Before her goes blind Cupid with drawn bow, and on a leash she holds two cuckolds, an ass, a fool, and an ape. The ape sprawls in the foreground, its two rounded buttocks disproportionately emphasized, presumably in acknowledgment of the she-ape's appearance at estrus.

The older symbolic meaning of the ape is, however, male sexuality, and the apes in the controversial phrase "lead apes in hell" must be males: the woman who refuses to mate on earth will be condemned to couple with apes in hell. William Corkine's verse in *Second Book of Airs* (1612), later reproduced by Bullen, is specific:

> Away, away! call back what you have said
> When you did vow to live and die a maid.
> O if you knew what chance to them befell
> That dance about with bobtail apes in hell,
> Yourself your virgin girdle would divide
> And put aside the maiden veil that hides
> The chiefest gem of nature: and would lie
> Prostrate to every peasant that goes by,
> Rather than undergo such shame; no tongue can tell
> What injury is done to maids in hell.

The ape, carrying its children, flees from the hunters.

The ape of lust appears on a leash held by a woman in a design entitled *De fide concubinarium* by Paul Clearius, circa 1505. Sometimes it holds a mirror. In a German en-

9

graving of the late fifteenth century from Nuremberg, a woman strokes the chin of her admirer with one hand while emptying his pocket with the other. Close to the man is a monkey with a mirror, and the motif aptly illustrates the folly of being enslaved by lust.

The persistence of the ape as a more general symbol of sin and sexual license is evident in medieval illustrations and in sculptures of the ape riding on other symbols of lechery: a goat, hound, or pig. Sometimes the ape rides backward, adopting a position which, as I observe in the case of the ass, was assigned to criminals on their way to execution. The ape is also depicted as accompanying Venus and as spying on courting couples. A contemporary commentator of the *Divine Comedy* remarks that the ape is very fond of fornication, especially when he sees a man with a woman. Numerous illustrations support this assertion. The ape appears with Joseph and Potiphar's wife, with Susanna and the Elders, and with many secular lovers.

Of equally ancient origin is the association of the ape with wine. According to rabbinical tradition, Noah and Satan went into partnership to plant a vineyard. Satan killed a lamb, lion, pig, and monkey and made the blood of each in succession flow under the vine. By this means he conveyed what the qualities of wine were: before a man drank it, he was as innocent as a lamb; when he drank moderately he felt as strong as a lion; if he drank more than he could take he resembled a pig; and if he drank to the point of intoxication he behaved like an ape—dancing, singing, talking obscenely, and not knowing what he was doing. A variation of this legend may be seen in the medieval custom at Langres. Local wines were put in four barrels and were offered to persons of rank entering the town. They were called the lion, monkey, sheep, and pig wines in order to indicate the state of mind which they were said to produce—the lion, courage; the monkey, cunning; the sheep, contentment; and the pig, bestiality.

Although the analogies became proverbial, the qualities assigned to the ape varied. In a version in a medieval collection of tales called the *Gesta Romanorum*, for example, the ape denoted curiosity and foolish joy. Here we come close to the popular evaluation of the ape as a foolishly imitative creature because of its unintelligent curiosity, and as an object of ridicule in consequence. This same quality is illustrated on one of the consoles of the north porch of Chartres Cathedral, created in the first half of the thirteenth century, and in emblem books. In the latter an ape is shown throwing gold coins out of the window, and the explanation is that the creature has got at the miser's hoard and dissipated it. The aphorism reads: "Badly gotten, badly scattered." The ape with his foot between wooden blocks also illustrates a similar characteristic: the workman slept; the ape played with the wooden blocks and thereby crushed his foot.

Another fable given by Avianus and others as a fact of natural history was turned into an exemplum by the bestiarists. When the female ape gives birth to twins, she loves one and hates the other. If she is chased by a hunter she carries her favorite infant in front, leaving the other to cling to her back as best it can. Then she becomes exhausted with running on two feet only. She has to drop the preferred child and save the other. This fable in the Aesopian collection simply demonstrates the results of excessive affection. The bestiarists, on the other hand, offer several explanations. The ape symbolizes the seeker after *voluptas* (the preferred child) instead of *bona animae* (the dropped child), or it is the Devil carrying off to hell the wicked people whom he loves while leaving the good whom he hates behind with God. A carving in York Cathedral illustrates the fable, depicting an adult monkey driving a young one in front with a switch. Emblem books show the ape holding a child, with the caption *Calcus amor prolis* (blind love of offspring). The story is an exemplum of the parent who kills his child with kindness.

The fact that the fable really did not lend itself to a consistent allegorical interpretation may account for its gradual disappearance from the later bestiaries and for the emphasis on the ape as primarily the imitator of man. No doubt the performing Macaca ape, a common sight in Europe from the twelfth century onward, stressed the animal's ability to copy man and his capacity to perform tricks. In medieval art and architecture, in the popular subject of the world turned upside down in which animals take human roles, the ape is the star performer. He is a physician inspecting urinals, a teacher instructing pupils with book and rod, a mock bishop wearing a miter and using his crozier as a butter-churner. In marginal illustrations a popular subject is the ancient story, found in Pliny, of trapping apes by means of weighted boots: the illustrators take pains to show how the apes' natural curiosity and imitativeness induce them to put the boots on and how they are then unable to move. In later murals, engravings, woodcuts, and even in a coat of arms and in a ballet, a lively theme is the pedlar and the apes, possibly an extension of the earlier story, in which apes disrobe the man and mischievously plunder his pack while he sleeps. In secularized allegory this ape is equated to the lover hopelessly ensnared by his passion for his mistress. Sometimes the intention is to depict the folly of the dreamer; sometimes the spirit is entirely burlesque.

Popular sayings reflect the illustrations: the animal is revealed as a prankster, grimacer, fool, and a ludicrous imitator. It even symbolizes cowardice, a quality which may have stemmed from Socrates who, in making a distinction between the lion, ape, stag, and bull, seems to imply that the ape lacked courage. Or it may have derived from fact: as Drimmer remarks, in their natural environment where the drive for status and territory is paramount, apes live in troops, and each troop has its leaders and its underdogs.

The persistence of the ape as a symbol of the sense of taste points to a more pejorative analogy. When Sir Thomas Browne, in 1646, remarks that "if common conceit speak true" the ape has a better sense of taste than any other animal, he is obliquely referring to the ape in the Garden of Eden who offered Eve the fatal fruit. The ape, which was regarded as the worst beast (*turpissima bestia*), even in pre-Christian times, was traditionally equated with the Devil, and after its execrable behavior in Paradise it came to represent the sense of taste. Medieval illustrators often depicted the ape munching an apple or squatting vilely by the Tree of Knowledge.

In itself, the equation of the ape to the Devil gave rise to many significances. The writers of the bestiaries and encyclopedias of the Middle Ages, anxious to draw a moral, observed that neither the ape nor the Devil had a tail: in other words, they did not have *finem bonum* (a good end). The possession of a tail meant that the "end" of its owner had been determined by God. The ape, so the learned clerks argued, must have had a tail originally, but he evidently fell from grace. His taillessness indicated his insolence, his hubris, in seeking to emulate man. The animal came to symbolize the sin of pride, which cast

Lucifer from heaven. Tertullian's phrase that the Devil was God's ape was a reminder that the Evil One imitated the Christian deity, having supernatural powers, his own trinity, twelve disciples, and even his own sabbath, a caricature of the holy mass. The Devil appeared as an ape in many illustrations, and in Holbein's *Crucifixion* (1477), the Devil, who carried off the soul of the impenitent thief, was ape-headed. In Chaucer's *Friar's Tale* (1464), the Devil said he appeared on earth sometimes like a man and sometimes like an ape.

The ape was playing the role of the Devil when he was depicted in medieval manuscripts as a hunter. He was ensnaring human souls, symbolized by the small birds fluttering in the trees above him. Frequently he was accompanied by an owl and used the bird as a lure. The owl was a creature that loved darkness rather than light; it was the enemy of all true believers, the worst bird (*turpissima avis*) perched on the Tree of Knowledge. Together the ape and the owl formed a grim partnership, seeking to trap the soul and separate it from God.

The patristic writers not only applied the term *ape* to the Devil but to all enemies of the Christian faith, whether heretics or pagans. In A.D. 391, during the anti-pagan riots at Alexandria, Bishop Theophilus commanded the Christians who were busy destroying heathen temples and idols to preserve the statue of an ape as a testament to human depravity. Not surprisingly, medieval artists often attributed simian features to Christ's persecutors and represented Idolatry as a hairy, monkey-like figure on the façades of the cathedrals at Amiens, Chartres, and Paris.

In Michelangelo's *Dying Slave*, the features of an ape emerge from a mass of stone. Here the ape is probably a generic symbol of slaves as a class, representative of the unregenerate human soul. In medieval art the fettered ape often symbolizes the state of the world before Christianity, and Panofsky cites among other illustrations Lucas Moser's altarpiece at Tiefenbronn, where a fettered monkey and a broken statue denote paganism. In Renaissance art the chained ape seems to have a broader significance. In a work of Robert Fludd, published in 1619, nature is depicted as a woman crowned with stars like the Virgin and with the crescent moon of Diana on her body. She has a chain on her arm denoting her subjection to God, but she in turn holds an ape by a chain. This ape is art and it is sitting upon the terrestrial globe, which it has made its own. The idea of the ape's representing art, an activity which counterfeits nature, is not new. In the *House of Fame*, Chaucer described various famous minstrels playing outside the palace. Inferior harpers were also there, gaping at them and imitating them "as an ape, / Or as craft countrefeteth kynde" (III. 1213). Similarly, Fludd's illustration depicts art as wholly subject to nature and inferior. It also implies that man, for all his skill and knowledge, can never be more than an ape.

In other illustrations the chained ape seems to symbolize subjugated evil. Dürer put chained apes at the foot of the *arc de triomphe* of Maximilian I. He also included the ape in a striking engraving of the Madonna and Child. The vital movement of the illustration is in the child, who strains in his mother's lap to hold a bird, the symbol of the human soul. Below Him, in contrast, sits a motionless, chained simian with some partially eaten nuts. Whereas the bird in the hand is the voluntary captive of Christ, the fettered monkey symbolizes the sinner enslaved by his own bodily lusts. The nuts in evidence in this engraving and in Pieter Brueghel's *Fettered Monkeys* may symbolize the trivial worldly attractions for which the sinner surrenders his soul, or they may be indicative of the ape's sloth, as they are in a work published by Johann Bämler at Augsburg in 1474: just as the slothful man rejects the fruits of eternal life which he should acquire through bitterness, so the ape rejects the best nuts when he finds a bitter rind.

The encyclopedist Bartholomaeus Anglicus stressed only the vileness of the "monstrous brute's unruly nature" when he described the fettered monkey, but theologians such as Berchorius in his *Reductorium Morale* linked this ape to the story of the hunters who captured apes by means of heavily weighted boots. An elaborate allegory was constructed from the fact that the apes were chained to a block, taught to jump and play jokes, and were constantly beaten by their trainers. Such apes were mankind, they said. The hunters were demons from hell; the boots, the goods of this world; and the chains, evil pleasures. The fatuous simians put their feet—that is, their desires—in such boots and were thereby enmeshed in evil habits until the devilish hunters caught them. They were tied to the block, which symbolized the burdensome affairs of this world, and were taught to jump from one sin to another.

In the late fifteenth century the simian was frequently associated with the milder sin of folly. In Shakespeare's *Measure for Measure* (1604), however, proud man in authority is like an angry ape and "plays such fantastic tricks before high heaven / As makes the angels weep" (II.ii). Today the composite figure which has displaced the *imago diaboli* of earlier times is that of a clumsy creature not overgifted with intelligence or looks, yet amiable and possessed of an intriguing resemblance to man.

Aelian, xv.xiv; Artemidorus Dald., II.xii, IV.lvi; Avianus, *see* McCulloch, p. 87; Bartholomaeus Ang., XVIII, "de simea"; Berchorius, x.ix; Brant, p. 34; Browne, VII.xiv; Drimmer, I.175; Ennius cited by Cicero, *De natura deorum*, I.xxxv.97; *Gesta Rom.* (ed. Oesterley), CLIX: Ginzberg, I.168; Haeckel, nos. 136, 164; Janson, *passim*; Lewysohn, *Talmuds*, pp. 66, 68; McCulloch, pp. 87–88; McDermott, *passim*; Needham, pp. 106–19; Oakeshott, pl. 40; Panofsky, *Studies*, p. 195, n. 72; "Physiologus" (ed. F. J. Carmody), p. 122; Plato, *Laches*, 196E; Pliny, VIII.54.80; Rowland, "Owles," pp. 322–25; Rowland, "Chaucer's She-ape," pp. 159–65; Suetonius, *Nero*, XLVI.i; Tacitus, *Historiae*, v.iv; Tervarent, cols. 352–55; Van Marle, II.459; Whitney, pp. 145, 169.

Asp or Adder

The asp is popularly a symbol of death in its dramatic form. The word evokes the image of the thirty-nine-year-old queen of Egypt, unwithered and unstale, dying on her golden bed with venomous twin snakes of the horned variety (*cerastes cornutus*) hanging from her bosom.

Yet the manner of Cleopatra's death is by no means certain. Plutarch did remark that she had made a collection of poisonous drugs and that after daily experiments on criminals concluded that asp poisoning was "the most eligible kind of death because it brought on a gradual kind of lethargy, in which the face was covered with a gentle sweat, and the senses sunk easily into stupefaction . . . those who were thus affected showed the same uneasiness at being disturbed or awakened as people do in the most profound natural sleep." But postmortem accounts are conflicting; some said that she had two pricks in her bosom or arm; others declared that there was not a mark on her. If the first account is true, then only one asp was smuggled in with the basket of figs, because the asp has two teeth and makes a double puncture. Galen, Strabo, and Plutarch, on the other hand, doubted whether there were any asps at all, and Plutarch thought she might have used poison from a hollow bodkin which she carried about with her in her hair.

The natural historian Aelian declared that, contrary to Cleopatra's researches, death by asp poisoning was sharp and violent. When the asp fastened on its victim, its poison did not remain on the surface but penetrated the body. For this reason, there was some doubt about the manner of Cleopatra's death. There were, moreover, at least six different kinds of asp in ancient Egypt, and early natural historians and encyclopedists confused traits and names. According to one bestiarist, an asp drank so deeply of Cleopatra's milk that it sucked out her blood; another authority said that she was bitten by the hypnalis, an asp which killed by causing a fatal sleep. Others claimed that the legend of her death arose because she arrayed herself in all the paraphernalia of royalty to show that she had not compromised her rank. Conspicuous in the royal diadem was the asp, the traditional emblem of Egypt. Inasmuch as no one who was bitten

The asp makes itself deaf by closing one ear with its tail and pressing the other to the ground.

by an asp escaped disaster, the asp was regarded as a fitting symbol of the invincibility of the Egyptian royal house.

15

When hermeneutical writers considered the asp for a moral lesson they turned not to Cleopatra but to Psalm lviii.4, 5: "They are like the deaf adder that stoppeth her ear; which will not hearken to the voice of charmers, charming never so wisely." St. Augustine in a sermon on the feast of St. Stephen claimed that it stopped up both ears, and a misericord at Chichester shows intertwined asps, each with one ear pressed against the ledge while stopping up the other ear with its tail. At the cathedral of Amiens, upon the central pier of the west front, the asp in dragon form has its head laid upon the ground so that one ear is pressed against the earth while the other is stopped up with its tail. The symbolism of the deaf asp, or adder, is explained in a twelfth-century bestiary by Philippe de Thaon:

> *Aspis* is a serpent which signifies people; it is cunning and sly and aware of evil; when it perceives people who want to enchant it and capture it, it will stop up its ears; it will press one against the ground, and in the other it will stuff its tail firmly that it hears nothing of it, and this signifies a great thing. In such a manner do the rich men of this world; one ear they have on the ground to obtain riches, the other is stopped up by sin, by the bad deeds they have performed and by which they are ensnared. By the tail is understood sins. They shall be punished in the day of judgement and shall go to hell.

Another version states that adders stop up their ears in order that they may not hear the voice of the Lord saying unto them: "Who will not renounce all things which he possesses cannot be my disciple or my servant."

Christ is depicted at Amiens as stepping on the asp and upon other creatures of evil. The illustration is from Psalm xci.13: "Thou shalt walk upon the adder and the basilisk, thou shalt trample underfoot the lion and the dragon." In the twelfth century the so-called Honorius of Autun, taking this text for a Palm Sunday sermon, equated the lion with the Antichrist, the dragon with the Devil, the basilisk with death, and the adder with sin. He, too, told of the adder's stopping its ears and claimed it was the image of the sinner closing its ears to the words of life.

In some illustrations there is less emphasis on the self-induced deafness of the asp than on its fondness for music. In the fourteenth-century *Queen Mary's Psalter* the serpent is lulled to sleep by a cacophony of sound coming from a portable organ, a double horn, and various strings and woodwinds. This musical enchantment of the asp is associated with the belief that the adder has a precious carbuncle in its head. There are various myths describing the means whereby the adder might be persuaded to part with it. Solinus declares that a snake charmer needs sweet music to pry this jewel loose because if the serpent dies the stone will disintegrate. This story, in the hands of the moralist, becomes an allegory:

the enchanter is the preacher; the adder, the sinner; and the precious stone, the soul.

The adder is also regarded more generally as a symbol of cunning. A young squire in Chaucer's *Merchant's Tale* who plots to seduce the girl-wife of his elderly employer is described as an adder in the "bosom sly untrewe" (l. 1786). This adder in the bosom does not refer to Cleopatra but comes from a story in the *Gesta Romanorum*. An emperor riding in a forest finds a serpent caught in a tree. He releases it and warms it in his bosom only to be bitten for his pains. Here the serpent is specifically equated with the Devil, and in Chaucer's tale the young squire steals into an Eden-like garden to achieve seduction.

The role of the adder in Eden leads to its association with the sin of envy, for it is said to have envied the happiness of Adam and Eve. So-called natural phenomena are used to enforce the lesson. "The neddur [adder] is fowle and maliciouse," says one fourteenth-century preacher, who declares that the creature pretends to play with the elephant and would "styngeth the elephaunte in the eye" and destroy him. Here the elephant was said to represent the soul and the adder the Devil. As the attribute of envy the adder appears on numerous sculptures and engravings. Envy, personified as a woman eating adders and with adders in her hair, is included on the printer's mark of Pierre de Sainte-Lucie of Lyon (1530–1555). Fortune, depicted as a naked woman, stands on another woman with a snake coiffure in the mark belonging to a sixteenth-century bookseller of Rouen, Théodore Reinsart. The caption is *fortuna domat invidiam* (fortune subjugates envy).

To many writers asps and adders were one, but Bartholomaeus Anglicus made a distinction: "The asp," he said, "is the worst and wickedest of adders."

Aelian, IX.iv; Anderson, *Med. Carv.*, p. 123; St. Augustine, *PL*, XXXVIII, col. 1432; Bartholomaeus Ang., XVIII, "de aspide"; *Gesta Rom.* (ed. Oesterley), CLXXIV; Honorius, *PL*, CLXXII, col. 915; Philippe de Thaon, *Best.*, pp. 102–103; Plutarch, *Lives*, Antony, LXXXVI; Solinus, XXVII.xxxii; Strabo, XVII.i.10.

Aspidochelone

When we see a picture of a sailor drying his stockinged feet beside a fire lit on the back of a sea monster, we may not immediately identify the huge fish with Jonah's leviathan. Yet here is the same creature that swallowed the prophet being turned into allegory to instruct the sinner in the wiles of Satan.

In some versions of the allegory the sea monster is a

The aspidochelone looks like an island to unwary sailors.

giant turtle. In an Old English bestiary poem in the *Exeter Book*, it is a *fastitocalon*:

> I will also tell a poem, a song, about a kind of fish, about the mighty whale. He is, to our sorrow, often found dangerous and fierce to all seafarers. The name Fastitocalon is given him, the floater on ocean-streams. His form is like a rough stone, as if the greatest of seaweeds, girt by sandbanks, were heaving by the water's shore, so that seafarers suppose they behold some island . . . .

In the Middle English bestiary it was named a *cethe-grande* because *cetus* (a sea monster) and *grand* (large) were mistaken for one word by the translator: "Cethe-grandë is a fis / The moste that in water is." One medieval homilist called it a "sea-pig."

But in most versions the central action was the same. Sailors came across what they believed to be a floating island. They gladly disembarked and lit a fire on the sandy surface in order to cook a meal. The island was really the monster fish of ancient legend, and as soon as it felt the heat it dived to the bottom of the ocean, carrying the hapless sailors with it.

The whale here was the Devil; the sea, the world; and the sailors were those who were deceived and put their trust in the Devil and sank with him to hell. In some medieval illustrations only the ship was depicted and in others just the whale. A psalter of Isabella of France, however, showed sailors frantically endeavoring to adjust the mast of their ship in a storm, while, unknown to them, a whale lurked directly underneath.

Another wile of the Devil-whale was to emit a pleasant odor from his mouth when he was hungry and thereby attract little fish into his jaws. Apparently, large fish ignored the smell. Here, according to the medieval theologians, the victims stood for the vacillating Christians; the large fish symbolized those whose faith was too strong for them to succumb to fiendish temptation.

Bestiaries sometimes illustrate the essential features of the whale simultaneously. Sailors cook their dinner under the shadow of trees on the back of the whale, while little fish swim into the extended jaws of the monster. Why the whale should be credited with pleasant breath no one knows, but Florence McCulloch observes that in the oldest Latin texts of the bestiary the aspidochelone follows the chapter on the panther, an animal credited with breath as fragrant as allspice.

The theme of being swallowed and of descending into the depths has its basis in the myth of the trial of the hero. To acquire some special knowledge, the hero goes down into a mysterious and dangerous cavern, and not infrequently, he has to overcome some terrible monster lurking within. In order, initially, to enter the infernal regions, he might die or seem to die, or he might be swallowed by a giant beast and make his descent into the creature's belly. The whale is an emblem of the trials which the hero must face in his progress from death to rebirth.

The story of Jonah and the whale is a specific example of such symbolism. Attempts have been made to rationalize the tale. The great fish Ceto was sacred to Dagon, or Poseidon, and an explanation for the swallowing of Jonah by the great fish is that he was picked up by a Phoenician or Philistine ship bearing the effigy of the whale. Nevertheless, the Jews themselves applied the symbolism to a people as well as to an individual. The tale is of the Israelites devoured by the Assyrian dragon, exiled in Babylon, and then set at liberty by God's grace. When Christ harrows hell after his death and before his resurrection, he is represented in some medieval frescoes as entering, like Jonah, the body of a huge leviathan. Jonah was chosen by Christ as a type of his own resurrection, and it is for this reason that scenes from the life of Jonah are depicted so frequently on the bas-reliefs on the sarcophagi in the catacombs.

The subject retained its symbolical significance throughout the Middle Ages. In some instances the leviathan is depicted as the symbol of the sepulcher, but in a window of Bourges Cathedral, Jonah is depicted as emerging somewhat precariously from the gaping jaws of a whale, his loin cloth apparently still caught in the monster's teeth. The emblematic import of the scene is made clear by the fact that it is one of four illustrations surrounding the picture of Christ rising from the tomb with a double cross in his hand while three soldiers sleep soundly below him. The three other scenes are also symbolic of the same subject: the raising of Jairus' daughter; the life-giving pelican accompanied by King David, who wrote of the Resurrection; and the lion breathing life into his dead cub. In the illustration of Jonah, the divine hand is seen emerging from heaven and sending its rays upon him.

In many medieval illustrations hell itself is portrayed as the gaping black maw of a whale crammed with little devils busy spiking, roasting, or boiling sinners. In the Caedmon manuscript of the tenth century the Devil himself is chained to the tusks of the leviathan.

In the Renaissance, the whale was often depicted playing with a cask. Tervarent quotes the proverb *jeter le tonneau rouge à la baleine* (to throw the red barrel to the whale), a proverb based on the popular belief that if a whale is to be prevented from overturning a ship, some part of the cargo must be thrown overboard to him in order to divert him. Tervarent cites emblem writers Typotius, Camerarius, and others, who used the proverb with the sign *His artibus* (by these means).

The most famous literary whale is, of course, Moby Dick, the baffling multivalent symbol at the heart of Melville's great novel. The overwhelming idea of the great whale himself in all his ferocity and unknowableness is qualified by the ideas of those who seek him. Ahab sees him as the "incarnation" of all evil, Ishmael as a thing of the "wonder-world," a "grand hooded phantom" which seems like a "snowhill in the air" in "endless processions of the whale." As Tindall remarks:

> that whale in context is more than a thing to a man. All things in heaven and earth, unassigned and indefinite, he embodies our feeling and thought when face to face with ourselves and with what surrounds us.

Cook, pp. lxiii–lxxxv; Coulter, *passim*; McCulloch, pp. 91–92; Réau, II.412; Tervarent, col. 40; Tindall, p. 26; Twining, pl. lxxix, figs. 1, 4.

Ass

Some people may still believe that a sandwich of ass's hair will cure whooping cough or that whooping cough can even be prevented entirely if a child is passed over the back and under the belly of an ass in the name of the Blessed Trinity. Since the first superstition decrees that the hair must come from the cross on the ass's back and the second involves the ritualistic breaking and eating of bread by both child and beast, the reason for such practices is not far to seek. A belief in the curative powers of the ass clearly stems from a symbolism given to the ass in early Christian times, a symbolism which, in itself, no longer survives.

In many Eastern countries, where it was domesticated earlier than the horse, the ass was highly prized as the steed of the rich and noble. Balaam's ass was a miraculous, talking animal which was able to see the Angel of the Lord when his master could not (Numbers xxii.21–33). Abraham, Joseph and his brethren, and Moses all rode asses, and Job in his prosperity was said to have one thousand she-asses. The she-ass was particularly valued by the patriarchs because it subsisted on scanty fare and not only carried its rider through barren deserts but supplied him with milk as well. From such a high estimate of the ass comes the proverb "one knows a man by his ass." Vestiges of its former worth remain in myth. Dionysus, Silenus, the Virgin and Child, all escape from their enemies by means of a donkey.

When the victorious king in Zechariah ix.9 was foreseen as riding on an ass, the animal probably symbolized peace rather than humility. Christ used the animal primarily for the same reason. Had He been prophesied as a military leader He would have been mounted on a war steed. He may also have been regarded as typifying the ass because He was the well-spring of eternal life. Both Plutarch and Tacitus remarked that the Jews worshipped the animal because it found water springs in the desert during the Exodus.

The Jews were also said to have immolated a man in a gold head of the animal and worshipped it. Tertullian declared that the enemies of the Gospel imagined that God had the head of an ass. He described a picture of a long-robed creature with the ears and legs of an ass inscribed *Deus Christianorum Onokoths* (The Christian God with the ass's hoof). A mural in the Palace of the Caesars on the Palatine showed a crucifixion of the head of an ass and a figure making a gesture of adoration before it. In Christian times, the unorthodox were accused of harboring similar blasphemies: Epiphanius said that the Gnostics believed that the Lord of Sabaoth had an ass's head.

In medieval times Christ's use of the ass became an illustration of His humility, for among the Western countries the animal was despised. It was the usual mount of malefactors when they were driven through the streets to their death. As a mark of degradation, the prisoner would be forced to reverse the normal riding position, face the animal's buttocks, and hold its tail in his hand. In France, prostitutes were condemned to ride naked through the streets on an ass, head to tail. According to Dulaure, the Duke of Orleans, brother of Louis XIII, gave the celebrated courtesan la Neveu this treatment—*après avoir fait plusieurs fois la débauche chez elle*. Even in ancient times a woman riding an ass often carried a particular implication of degradation. Plutarch in his *Moralia* recorded that a woman taken in adultery among the Cumans was mounted on an ass and lived the rest of her life in disgrace. This use of the animal was not regarded as inconsistent with its religious associations: by choosing this humble mount, said the exegetical writers, Christ showed His willingness to be despised and rejected. Such writers delighted in giving the animal mystical significance and not only likened the animal to Christ but in some curious way saw the body of the ass, particularly its rib cage, as symbolizing the whole structure of the cathedral. In the last century in the ancient French province of Angoumois, children were still using a catechism that compared the anatomy of an ass to the architecture of a church.

Nevertheless, the most popular religious ceremony involving the ass was associated with pagan festivities. For many centuries the Saturnalia of ancient Rome was enthusiastically celebrated in Christian Europe. As late as the eleventh century, Bishop Burchard of Worms inveighed against the excesses committed by the participants. From these revels of the Kalends of the New Year and from the efforts of the clergy to Christianize them arose the Feast of Fools and the Feast of the Ass. In the ninth century the ass had been solemnly introduced into the church to represent the animal of the prophet, of the Nativity, of the Flight into Egypt, or of the Entry into Jerusalem. Now it became part of the ceremonies burlesquing church ritual, in which dancing, feasting, and buffoonery soon provided an occasion for utmost license. At Rouen, Balaam's ass was carved in wood, and inside it a priest danced and uttered prophecies. At Sens, the Feast of the Ass was associated with the Feast of Fools celebrated during the Feast of Circumcision, with two canons receiving the ass at the west door of the church and leading it to the precentor's table, where a medley of vespers was sung in falsetto. Afterward the ass was led out into the church square (*conductus ad ludos*), where the precentor was doused with water. At Beauvais, according to thirteenth-century documents, an ass ridden by a pretty girl with a baby was taken into church to represent the Flight into Egypt. While they were at the altar a mass was sung with each ritual portion ending in a bray. A hymn began:

> Orientibus partibus
> Adventavit asinus
> Pulcher et fortissimus
> Sarcinis aptissimus
> Hez ser Asne, Hez!

(An ass approached oriental countries, beautiful and most strong, most equipped for burdens. Haw, sir Ass, hee-haw!)

22

This *asinaria festa*, or "Feast of Asses," became an occasion for extreme licentiousness, with revellers opening the proceedings with a bout of heavy drinking, wearing women's clothes and garlands of flowers, and carrying their "assing" to remarkable extremes. In such festivities the ass was a complex symbol.

The nature of these rituals establishes their connection with the festivities of the earlier priapic god. One reason for the role of the ass doubtless stems from the fact that the animal was popularly famed for what Iago insinuates was in "foul proportion." Even today in Spain a popular expletive to dispel bad luck is *carajo* (ass's phallus), and this distinctive feature of the ass was used for purposes of sexual imagery from early times. Among the Old Testament prophets, Ezekiel describes how Jerusalem "played the harlot in the land of Egypt and doted upon her paramours there, whose members were like those of asses" (xxiii.19). The Greek poet Archilochus, born seven centuries before Christ, graphically describes how a lover "equipped like a stallion" performs as copiously as a "Prienian [Ionian] ass."

In Egypt an ass cult was superseded by the cult of the goddess Isis, and the ass came to be regarded with abhorrence as the insignia of the god Set (Typhon), the murderer of Osiris. The ass symbolized lust and cruelty, and Plutarch of Delphi, a priest of Apollo, in his essay *On Isis and Osiris*, recorded that at certain festivities asses and men with Typhonic coloring (sandy-red like the coat of a wild ass) were pushed over cliffs in vengeance for the slaying of the new god. In other words, the ass became the scapegoat when celebrants repudiated the excesses that were characteristic of the Saturnalia. A similar idea of punishment attendant on fornication is seen in Apuleius' *Golden Ass*, where a profligate young man is transformed into an ass for rejecting good advice and for involving himself in an erotic witch cult. As an ass he has a variety of extraordinary relationships with women and he is released from the most shameful degradation only when he is accepted as an initiate in the Orphic mysteries. The meaning of the work is graphically expounded by Topsell:

> Apuleius in his eleven bookes of his golden Asse
> taketh that beast for an Emblem, to note the manners
> of mankind; how some by youthful pleasures become
> beasts, and afterward by timely repentant old age are
> reformed men againe. Some are in their lives Wolves;
> some Foxes, some Swine, some Asses . . . . This world
> is unto them an enchanted cup of Circes, wherein
> they drinke up a potion of oblivion, error and ignor-
> ance; afterwards brutizing in their whole life, till
> they taste the Roses of true science and grace enlighten-
> ing their minds . . . .

Much later, the church fathers were to see lustful humanity as behaving like asses and to offer Christianity as the only means of salvation. Yet ironically enough, the ass was also the emblem of the virgin Vesta because it was the animal's unthinking bray which awakened her when Priapus was trying to rape her. The heads of asses surmounted the lamps lit in Roman households in her honor. At the same time, the Roman traveler who went to bed with the maid in a wayside inn would make his payment in very small coins known as "asses," and women who provided such services were known as *asellae*, in token of the animal's libidinous appetite.

The ass was priapic in Hindu mythology, but it was never ignominious. In Greece it was the symbol of the wisdom and prophetic powers of Silenus, who rode an ass, as well as the sacred animal of Bacchus himself. Apollo, it is true, gave ass's ears to Midas in ridicule because the Phrygian king preferred the music of Pan, but Pan himself sometimes wore ass's ears as an emblem of acute perception, of his ability to enjoy the most subtle harmonies of woods and meadows. The myth no doubt reflected a new cult's being superimposed on the old, the Phrygian ass-worship giving way to more humanized modes of worship.

Originally, as Helen Adolf has shown, the ass must have been associated with the lyre as the inventor of music. When the figure passed from Chaldean art to the fable of Phaedrus and to the Greek proverb ὄνος λύρας (ἀκούων), "like an ass listening to a harp (lyre)," it acquired a pejorative meaning which gained wide currency in medieval times because of a reference in Boethius' *De consolatione Philosophiae*. The Pythagoreans had noted a lack of harmony in the ass: the ass in the fable, on the other hand, was perceptive and humble, if inexpert in performance. Boethius was probably responsible for transforming the four-footed Babylonian harpist into the uncomprehending listener. "Do you understand?" Philosophy asks Boethius in a hypothetical dialogue, "or are you like an ass to a harp?" (1.pr.iv). The symbolic meaning was expressed in homilies and in ecclesiastical sculpture, where the ass stood for the sinner who could not understand the things of the spirit, and in tales of chivalry, where the ass became the representative of the uncourtly as opposed to the courtly. No doubt, the ear-splitting quality of its bray contributed to its reputation. Aelian had recorded that its noise was so strident that it could smash the eggs of any blue tit in its vicinity. Centuries later, Alanus de Insulis (Alan of the Isles) compared the ass to a "singer of burlesque perpetuating barbarities on music." Although the proverb ceased to be current in the sixteenth century, Shakespeare's famous clown Bottom bears traces of the ass's peculiar ancestry. No harpist, Bottom nevertheless sings a ditty. Uncouth as well as complacent, to courtly eyes he wears ass's ears even before Puck's magic makes them visible.

In addition to possessing a specialized proverbial sense,

the ass was the popular symbol of Ignorantia, and as such was well suited to medieval comedy. In Nigel Wireker's late twelfth-century satire on ambitious monks, *Speculum Stultorum*, the hero, Burnellus the Ass, ardently desires a tail. The physician Galen, after expostulating on the folly of his wish, gives him an absurd prescription to be filled at Salerno and brought back in glass bottles. Burnellus, typifying the monk who runs after vanities which are both costly and transitory, sets off on a series of unfortunate adventures. After seven years of unsuccessful study at the university in Paris, he has just resolved to found a monastery where every monk can have a mistress when his old master claims him and leads him back to his original condition of servitude. In this work, by the Benedictine precentor at Canterbury, the picaresque hero symbolizes the whole monastic body—quarrelsome, greedy, and vain. "The Order of the Ass" became common satirical property on the Continent. An ass with a rosary, for example, was carved on a stall in the Minorite cloister of Cleves to ridicule the Dominicans, who had introduced a new method of keeping a proper tally of prayers. In Sebastian Brant's *Narrenschiff* the ass became a variety of secular fools. The sinners were often called asses or apes, and in the accompanying engravings they wear the fool's cap with ass's ears.

Boethius not only used the traditional comparison of the ass to the lyre in the fifth century but also declared

The ass is slow and resists commands; with a sack on its back, it stands at the mill-door and refuses to budge.

that the ass stands for all that was stupid and sluggish in man. Not surprisingly, in representations of the Seven

25

Deadly Sins, the ass appeared as an attribute of Acedia. In a fourteenth-century manuscript in the Bibliothèque Nationale, sloth is depicted as riding an ass and carrying an owl, a bird regarded as a prime example of Acedia. In some illustrations the connection between lechery and sloth is emphasized: Acedia is shown riding a donkey and is provided with a pillow brought to her by a little devil. As Erwin Panofsky observes, the pillow, such as often appears in representations of Cupid and Venus, was a common symbol of idleness and lechery. The ass is also a symbol of sloth in medieval homilies and in the books of exempla. Using the Aesopian fable of the lion summoning the animals to the funeral of the wolf, the famous English Cistercian, Odo of Ceriton, indicated the greed of the Cistercians by means of powerful animal comparisons:

> When a rich man dies, the prior of the convent of men living like beasts calls them together. For it commonly happens that in a convent of black or white monks there are none but beasts—lions by their pride, foxes by their craftiness, bears by their voracity, stinking goats by their incontinence, asses by their sluggishness, hedgehogs by their roughness, hares by their timidity . . . and oxen by their laborious cultivation of their land.

The ass is also the symbol for sloth in a similar tale in the *Gesta Romanorum*, and Tervarent cites several examples of the use of such symbolism in art of a later period.

An even more opprobrious symbolism was given the ass by a bestiarist of the thirteenth century. Using another Aesopian fable, the writer declared that of the animals devoured by the lion, the ass was first because it foolishly resisted and brayed. The lion was Christ and the ass signified the Jews, who were very foolish because they never believed until forced to do so.

Similar specific symbolism is not infrequent in medieval illustrations. The presence of the ox and ass at Christ's nativity was a fulfillment of the prophecy of Isaiah i.3, "the ox knoweth his owner, and the ass his master's crib." The meaning attached to these animals was, however, often pejorative. The ox might symbolize the Gentile; the ass, the Jew. Sometimes the symbols were reversed and the ox was the Jew enchained by the Law; the ass, a beast of burden carrying the heavy load of idolatry. The ox and the ass could also prefigure the two thieves between whom Jesus was crucified.

Anti-Semitic symbolism persisted in Elizabethan times, but with a different explanation. According to Topsell, the ass could represent the Jew because the Jewish people "like asses could not understand the evident truth of Christ in the plaine text of Scripture, wherefore our Saviour secretly upbraided their dulness, when he rode upon an asse."

In another representation the ass is equated with the synagogue: the Holy Church or the New Dispensation, symbolized by a woman with cup and banner and mounted on a tetramorph—the four-headed creature signifying the four evangelists—is placed in opposition to the Synagogue, a woman mounted on an ass. The ass, in contrast to the tetramorph, stoops low, and the woman it carries is represented with eyes blinded against the light of Christianity, with the sacrificial goat, knife, and tables of law in her hands, and a banner cast down at the animal's feet. In a similar representation in the Church of Freiburg, the Old Dispensation is not only mounted very precariously on an ass but holds an ass's mask before her. Herrade de Landsburg, abbess of St. Odile in the latter half of the twelfth century, makes use of similar ideas in a scene in the *Hortus Deliciarum*, a compendium of moralized facts and fables of natural history.

Geoffrey Whitney's emblem book of the sixteenth century maintains the ass's association with religion in a rather curious way, and also gives secular meanings. An engraving shows the ass carrying Isis and being beaten while devotees kneel. The emblem is *non tibi, sed religioni* (not for you, but for religion). The verse states that the ass was beaten because he thought men were kneeling to him. The moral is: Let pastors not forget themselves through pride because they are honored. Other illustrations in the same work show an ass laden with fine food eating a thistle, and an ass eating a rope. The one is a symbol of the miser who foolishly eats poor fare; the other, of a wife who wastes the fruits of her husband's toil.

Emblem writers such as Valeriano and Ripa saw the ass as the symbol of folly and ignorance or of sloth. In one spirited sixteenth-century satirical drawing, a friar is depicted riding an ass, with the legend: "He which rydeth on the asse signifieth sloth. . . . The Fryer's weedes and beades signifieth hypocrisie and lothsomness of the truth." Their contemporary, Topsell, on the other hand, was more concerned with past than contemporary significance. To the ancients, he said, the ass symbolized "immoderate riote of stubborne persons," "impudence and shamelessnesse," "a man possessed of the devil, a woman dissembling her pregnancy, and a base fertility, trifling sluggishness, good fortune, tyrants, and fooles." Somewhat similar to Whitney's is his interpretation of a man weaving a cord while an ass behind him bites it. Such figures, he declared, symbolize "a painefull husband and a prodigall wife."

Robert Graves, on what authority or experience it is not clear, considers the ass far more sagacious than the horse. Nevertheless, the hood with ass's ears which was originally the symbol of divinity finally became the insignia of the fool in western Europe, and even today the animal is a symbol of stupidity.

Adolf, pp. 49–57; Aelian, v.xlviii, x.xxviii; Alanus de Insulis, *PL*, ccx, col. 438; Apuleius, iii.xxv ff.; Archilochus (ed. Lasserre), frag. 184; Boethius (ed. Fortescue), p. 11; Brant, *passim*; Burchard, *PL*, cxl, col. 960; Carcopino, p. 276; Dulaure, ii.310; Epiphanius, *see* Evans, p. 271; Garnerus, *PL*, cxciii, col. 89; *Gesta Rom.* (ed. Herrtage), p. 373; Graves, *White Goddess*, p. 289; Lanoe-Villène, 1.97, 104–105; Odo, iv.216; Panofsky, *Studies*, p. 88; Plutarch, *De Iside*, 362F; Réau, ii.228; Ripa, p. 4, s.v. "Accidia"; Tacitus, *Historiae*, v.iv; Tertullian, *PL*, i, cols. 428–29; Tervarent, cols. 28–30; Topsell, pp. 25–26; Valeriano, xii, s.v. "De asino, Ignavia"; Whitney, pp. 8, 18, 48.

Basilisk

King Alexander once disposed of a basilisk by inducing it to look into a mirror. The basilisk's glance, always fatal to others, proved to be self-destroying. The royal warrior took this desperate action because the basilisk was decimating his troops.

The basilisk is actually a harmless species of hooded lizard with a conical crest that it can inflate. In ancient and medieval times it was credited with extraordinary lethal powers. Not only was its glance and touch fatal, but its fiery breath consumed herbs and animals and broke stones asunder. Pliny tells of a horseman who killed a basilisk with his long spear. The venom immediately passed up the spear and killed both horse and rider. Only the weasel could face the basilisk unharmed, provided it ate rue beforehand, and for this reason the magnificent basilisk carved on a misericord in Worcester Cathedral is flanked by two small animals with foliage in their mouths. Translated into terms of Christian symbolism, the basilisk was the Devil from whom humanity, as represented by the weasels, obtained protection only by digesting the Old and New Testaments.

By the mid-thirteenth century it was thought that the basilisk might hatch from the egg of a cock. The actual hatching was done by a serpent or toad, and a fourteenth-century manuscript in the Arsenal Library, Paris, shows a basilisk hatched by a toad. Ansell Robin suggests that the story originated in the Septuagint version of Isaiah lix.5, "They break the eggs of adders and weave the spider's web: he who would eat of their eggs, having crushed the wind-egg (ὄυριο), finds in it a basilisk." *Wind-egg* usually means the unfertilized egg of a hen, but here it might have been taken to refer to a cock's egg, because Aristotle had remarked that substances resembling an egg have been found in a cock. By the fourteenth century the basilisk began to be termed either the *cockatrice*, a word previously reserved for the crocodile, or the *basilicoc*, probably on account of its alleged genesis. A French bestiary describes this creature as having the head, neck, and chest of a cock, and a serpent-like extremity. Wycliffe, in his translation of the Vulgate (1382), used *cockatrice* for *Basilicus* (basilisk), and so did Trevisa in translating Bartholomaeus Anglicus' encyclopedia in the same period. Sir Thomas Browne, the seventeenth-century Norwich physician who devoted a lifetime to investigating popular fallacies, refuted in *Pseudodoxia Epidemica* (*Vulgar Errors* 1646) the belief that the creature could be bred from a cock's egg, calling it "a conceit as monstrous as the brood itself." Nor did he feel that the basilisk and cockatrice should be confused with one another: whereas the basilisk of the ancients was a kind of serpent, the cockatrice was an artistic fantasy with some of the appurtenances of the cock. As for the malignant effect of the basilisk:

> it is not impossible . . . the visible rayes of their eyes carrying forth the subtilest portion of their poison, which received by the eye of man or beast, infecteth first the brain, and is from thence communicated into the heart.

Despite Sir Thomas Browne's distinctions, however, the basilisk and the cockatrice appear to be regarded as synonymous and having similar powers. Shakespeare refers to the death-darting eye of the cockatrice (*Romeo and Juliet*, III.ii), and later Nares, in his glossary, finds that the cockatrice is a popular word for a loose woman, "probably from the fascination of the eye."

The basilisk is frequently depicted in medieval architecture and in manuscripts. There is a splendid basilisk on a misericord in Exeter Cathedral; on the Norman doorway at St. Margaret's, Walmgate, York; at St. George's Chapel, Windsor; at Manchester, Malvern; and at Stowlangtoft in Suffolk. Some carvings merely illustrate stories from Pliny concerning the basilisk, but usually the basilisk is the symbol of evil pitting itself against the faith. At Amiens it appears with the asp below a figure of Christ in illustration of Psalm xci.13: "Thou shalt tread upon the asp and basilisk, and trample underfoot the lion and the dragon." Here it may be regarded as one of the four aspects of the Devil which, stated St. Augustine in giving this interpretation, were trodden underfoot by the triumphing Christ. Such is its significance in an early liturgical hymn to the Virgin Mary. But it may be equated with death itself: Honorius in his *Speculum ecclesiae* regarded the adder as sin, the lion as the Antichrist, the dragon as the Devil, and the basilisk as death.

For Gregory, on the other hand, the basilisk was the Antichrist, whereas the bestiarists regarded it as the Devil which, beautiful in color and form, slipped into Paradise and seduced Eve. A French bestiary extended the allegory by including some precautionary measures which seem to have some connection with Alexander's strategy. The way to defend oneself against the basilisk

The glance of the basilisk is lethal.

was to get a glass or crystal vessel: the venom would be reflected and would recoil upon the basilisk itself. Similarly, Christ chose a vessel clearer than crystal, namely, the Blessed Virgin Mary, who was able to throw back the venom of Satan and render him powerless. The scene is represented on the capital of a column of the Abbey of Vezelai, where a figure holding a conical vessel as a shield approaches a strange reptilian creature. Nearby is an enormous locust, representing the Gentiles who were saved from the Devil by the atonement of Christ.

The good Parson in Chaucer's *Canterbury Tales* relied upon a long clerical tradition when he likened the lustful glance to the lethal regard of the "basilicoc." The first step in lechery, declared the Parson, drawing upon the works of other homilists, was the unchaste look "that sleeth [slayeth] right as the basilicok sleeth folk by the venym of his sighte; for the coveitise of eyen folweth the coveitise of the herte [heart]" (l. 853). Often it was the regard of the female which could be compared to that of the basilisk. "Alas, why do we look at them?" asked a thirteenth-century misogynist cleric called Matheolus, contemplating women dressed up in all their wicked finery; "I tell you that they slay us with a look, like the basilisk." A century later a bogus world-traveler who wrote *Mandeville's Travels* even claimed to have discovered an island where women if "thei beholden ony man with wratthe thei slen [slay] him anon with the

30

beholdynge as doth the Basilisk." In an early fifteenth-century German illustrated compendium of moral allegories, the *mala mulier* (the harlot) was described as a seductress who destroyed her victims like a basilisk, which killed with its malignant breath. An accompanying illustration depicted not only the basilisk as the woman but an ape as the illustration of what man becomes under her influence (*see* Janson). Not surprisingly, in some representations of the Seven Deadly Sins the basilisk sometimes appeared as the symbol of lust. In an encyclopedic treatise *Lumen animae* written by Mattias Farinator, a Viennese Carmelite, Lust had a basilisk on her robe. Wycliffe, the fourteenth-century preacher, on the other hand, equated the basilisk with pride.

The basic symbolism of both the basilisk and the asp are reflected in an incident which occurred in 1376. The French Pope Gregory XI was setting out for Italy when his aged father attempted to restrain him by throwing himself at his son's feet. The Pope, remarking "it is written that thou shalt trample upon the asp and the basilisk," passed over the prostrate body of his father and boarded his ship.

Browne, III.vii; Evans, pp. 163–66, 170; Farinator, *Titulus* 75; Gregory, *see* Evans, p. 167; Honorius, *PL*, CLXXII, col. 914; Janson, p. 115; *Mandeville's Travels*, I.190; Matheolus, I.131; Nares, I.73; Pliny, VIII.21.33, XXIX.4.19; Robin, pp. 85–91, 181–87; *Wars of Alexander* (ed. Skeat), ll. 4837–57; Trevisa, s.v. "cocatrice"; Wycliffe, *see* Robin, p. 90.

Bear

The bear was the majestic and luminous god of storms and sunshine in ancient myth; the gentle friend or prince in disguise in the folktale; the honey-loving dupe in the fable; the docile disciple of saints in legend; the progenitor of the magic hero in saga; the ferocious monster which was chained, baited, and blinded in Merry England. All these aspects contribute to the paradox of the ultimate symbol, to the bear as a huge clumsy creature whose fierce, shaggy exterior usually belies an inner simplicity and faithfulness.

The bear's strength and tenacity made it a symbol of China in ancient times, and it was adopted by Russia in the nineteenth century for the same reason. In Old Norse legend the hero Hialto ate the heart of a bear and drank its blood in order to gain strength and courage. A similar practice persisted in the New World in the last century among the northern Algonkian. The famous hero Beowulf seems to have been the son of a bear, hence his riddling name "bee-wolf," reflecting the bear's love of honey, as well as his courage.

In heraldry the bear denoted the man of power or nobility attacked by underlings, a figure stemming from the popular diversion of baiting the animal with dogs. The bear with the ragged staff was the device of the Warwicks. The Warwicks' legendary ancestor Arthgal, the first earl, was said to have strangled a bear with his hands in the time of King Arthur. Another ancestor, Morvidius, was reputed to have used a club made out of a young tree to defend himself against a bear. The bear was also the badge of Robert Dudley, the Earl of Leicester, and he proudly displayed stone statues of white bears in the garden of Kenilworth Castle. As a symbol of his devotion to Elizabeth, he presented the queen in 1574 with jewelry depicting "a lyon [Elizabeth] ramping with a white moseled bear at his foote." During the Elizabethan period, whenever the bear occurs as an obvious political reference, one can safely assume that Leicester is intended. Such is the case, for example, in a Catholic onslaught written in 1584: "You knowe the Beares love . . . which is al for his own paunche, and so this Bear turneth al to his own commoditie." Whitney wrote verses in praise of Warwick and Leicester beginning, "Two beares there are, the greater, and the lesse."

In medieval times, however, the bear was predominantly a symbol of evil. Even in the pre-Christian era the bear seems to have been a symbol of male sexuality: tales of bears kidnapping and raping women and of bears becoming secret paramours of willing wives are widely disseminated in European folklore. Angelo de Gubernatis cites Danish and Russian tales of women who were violated by bears and gave birth to half-human, half-ursine monsters. It is interesting to note that in the New World there are many similar stories in which the bear is also regarded as male and called "grandfather," and that in certain tribal bear ceremonies women are excluded. By the end of the twelfth century, the bear had become established as a pictorial motif to signify male sexuality. It also accompanied the ape, the representative of female sexuality, and just as the hound and the hare appeared with amorous couples as a commentary on their intentions, so did the bear and the ape. Even as late as 1550, as Janson notes, Virgil Solis uses the bear and the ape in an ornamental engraving: a nude man and woman recline at the upper corners of a tablet displaying the Roman alphabet while a bear and an ape emerge from the lower corners. The presence of the ape makes it clear that the bear is to be associated with impure love. Sometimes the ape is depicted as riding the bear and the two are contrasted with the unicorn, the symbol of chastity. Janson remarks that the bear as a symbol of male pruriency can be seen in such proverbial expressions as *den Bären treiben* (to pander).

The church made the equivalence clear and saw the bear as the symbol of lust. According to the well-known story quoted by St. Peter Damian and others, Pope Benedict in afterlife acquired a bear's head and an ass's tail as a punishment for his dissolute life. In a poem by the thirteenth-century German mystic Mechthild of Magdeburg, the four sins which the soul overcame were represented by animals, and the bear represented fornication. In the next century the Swedish mystic St. Bridget castigated the sins of her listeners by an extension of the image. The bear, she said, represented both the lusts of the flesh and greed of worldly goods.

Among the authorities cited for regarding the bear as a symbol of lust is the Bible itself. David boasted to Samuel that he had slain a lion and a bear and was therefore able to slay Goliath. According to Cornelius a Lapide, some Church Fathers interpreted the action as a defeat of temptation as well as a victory over the external assaults of the Devil. The bear typified fornication. A similar analogy was made by Rabanus Maurus in interpreting Kings. In the same century the encyclopedist Mattias Farinator showed Luxuria riding on a bear when he depicted the Seven Deadly Sins as riding in a procession, and Luxuria has the same mount in some of the late Gothic cycles of the virtues and vices. In an engraving by Heinrich Aldegrever (1502–1558) with the inscription, "Lascivia, 1549," the bear is the attribute of Luxuria.

The late fourteenth-century Wycliffite Bible declares that men are called bears because of greediness or gluttony, and another work of the same period refers to the "bere of glotonie." In an early fifteenth-century manuscript of Chaucer's *Canterbury Tales*, an illustration to *The Parson's Tale* shows Gluttony riding a bear. This symbolism stems from a fable in the Reynard Cycle, and some moralists actually cite the fable to illustrate their point. The bear intended to bring Reynard to court to answer for his crimes. Reynard, knowing of the bear's weakness for honey, led him to a huge oak. The trunk of the tree was split and the cleft held open by wedges. Inside were delicious honeycombs. As soon as Bruin reached for the honey, Reynard removed the wedges and caught him fast. Thus does the Devil catch those who pursue the sweets of this life. A similar idea is expressed by the homilist Odo of Ceriton: when he likens the inmates of a convent to various beasts, he makes the bear the symbol of voracity.

Sometimes the bear appeared as a more general symbol of craft and violence. "For no beest hath so grete sleyghte to do evyll dedes as the bear," remarked the encyclopedist Bartholomaeus Anglicus. The twelfth-century compendium *Hortus Deliciarum* depicted the bear as the representative of brute force, and legends concerning St. Godric of Finchdale, who died in the same century, told of a cunning fiend who sometimes appeared in the shape of a bear to torment the saint. In the Renaissance the bear often depicted anger. Tervarent cites engravings of

The bear licks its cubs into shape.

Georg Pencz, Aldegrever, and Hendrik Goltzius, in which an ugly hag who symbolizes wrath is accompanied by a bear.

The bear as a type of Satan appeared in illuminated manuscripts, missals, carvings on caskets, shrines, and other objects. On the bronze doors of the cathedral at Hildesheim, reliefs dating from early in the eleventh century depicted the history of sin and redemption. In one of them a bear stood behind Pilate and appeared to whisper in his ear. St. Augustine declared that the Devil was typified by the lion and the bear and supported his contention by observing that the lion's strength was in its mouth, the bear's in its paws. An early fifteenth-century mural on the east wall of the chancel of Gawsworth Church, which was destroyed in 1851, showed the bear in hell.

Of considerable persistence is the association of the bear with laziness, an association which perhaps stems from the bear's habit of hibernating. The twelfth-century *Ancrene Riwle*, a conduct book for nuns, refers to the bear of "heavy sloth," and the medieval compilation *Secreta Secretorum* terms the man who is like a bear "wayk [weak] and sleuthfull." Sebastian Brant some three centuries later draws a moral. The bear sucking its paws in company with the idle grasshopper becomes the symbol of improvidence, with the caption *nit fursehen by zyt* (not providing in time):

34

Who'll never glean in Summer's heat
In winter he'll have naught to eat.
                              (tr. Zeydel)

On the other hand, the emblem writers sometimes put the bear in a more estimable light. The bear's affection for its young was recorded nearly three thousand years ago in II Samuel xvii.8. The idea that its blind cubs are formless at birth and have to be licked into shape is repeated by bestiarists, by pseudo-naturalists, and by Alexander Pope:

> So watchful Bruin forms, with plastic care
> Each growing lump, and brings it to a bear.

Emblems delineated by Boissard and engraved by Théodore de Brie in 1596 show the bear licking her whelp. Here it is a symbol of the inborn forces of nature being brought into shape and beauty by instruction. Crispin de Passe adds Cupid to the scene in *Tronus Cupidinis* or *Emblemata Amatoria* (1596) and adopts the sentiment *Perpolit incultum paulatim tempus amorem* (little by little time perfects uncultivated love). Using the same myth, Horapollo, whose works greatly influenced the Renaissance emblem writers, claims that the Egyptians used the bear to symbolize the man who is born deformed but later acquires his proper shape. As Aldrovandi remarks, Titian took the she-bear as his emblem with the motto *Natura potentior ars* (art more powerful than nature). This identification of the artist perfecting his creation with the bear molding her cub was common in the Renaissance.

Aldegrever, *see* Hollstein, I, fig. p. 57; Aldrovandi, p. 136; *Ancrene Riwle* (ed. Day), pp. 89–90; Bartholomaeus Ang. xviii, "de urso"; Bloomfield, pp. 247–49; Boissard, no. 43; Brant, p. 180; Cornelius a Lapide, ii.326; Evans, p. 88; Farinator, *Titulus* 75; Green, pp. 348–49; Gubernatis, ii.117 ff.; Highet, p. 562; Horapollo, ii.lxxxiii; Janson, pp. 262–66, 248–80n; Odo of Ceriton, iv.216; St. Peter Damian, "Opusculum," xix.428–29; Petti, pp. 76–80; Rabanus Maurus, *PL*, cxii, col. 1086; *Secreta Secret.*, i.104; Tervarent, cols. 291–93; Whitney, p. 106; Zeydel, no. 70.

Beaver

Although not a popular symbol, the beaver had one trait which was useful for allegory. According to Pliny, it castrated itself when pursued by the hunter. Since the hunter wanted it only for its testicles containing valuable medicine (castor), the animal then escaped. Should another hunter pursue it, it showed its incompleteness and was left unmolested. This story was repeated in the bestiaries:

> There is an animal called *castor*, excessively gentle,
> whose testes are useful as a remedy in various illnesses.

The beaver bites off its testicles to escape the hunters.

Physiologus explains its nature by saying that when the hunter shall have found its tracks, he follows in pursuit.

The beaver, when he looks back and sees the hunter coming after it, at once tears off its testes with one bite and casts them before the hunter and fleeing thus, escapes. The hunter, advancing, gathers them up, and pursues no further, but retires. If, on the other hand, the beaver ventures forth again so that another hunter, searching eagerly, should come upon and pursue it, the animal, seeing that it cannot escape, rears upright and reveals its genitals to the hunter.

No satisfactory explanation of the basic fable has yet been given, although Bartholomaeus Anglicus did observe that the veracity of the story had been questioned. *Castoreum*, an oily secretion still used in medicine and perfumery, is not, of course, situated in the testicles, which are hidden, but in a different gland.

The bestiarists thought that the Christian should behave like the beaver. He should sever himself from his sins and throw them in the face of the Devil, who would then depart. Although a church father, Rabanus Maurus, remarked that the beaver could symbolize the eunuch, in general the medieval symbolism was favorable. The beaver was a symbol of the saint triumphing over the lust of the flesh; it was also, as Réau observes, a symbol of chastity, like the bee, the elephant, and the unicorn.

The emblem writers such as Alciatus and Camerarius saw the beaver as an example of how the prudent man

36

should behave. Topsell also maintained that it was better to give one's purse to thieves than one's life. Engravings show a hunter and two dogs in the background, a beaver biting off its testicles in the foreground. Whitney used the emblem *aere quandoque salutem redimendam* (safety must sometimes be bought for money), and stated:

Thus, to his paine, he doth his life preserve
Which teacheth us, if foes do us pursue,
Wee shoulde not care, if goodes for life maie serve
Although we give our treasure to a jewe.

Aldrovandi remarked that God might be called "Castor Divinus," but he also stated that the Egyptians were said to use the same emblem for a man weakened by adultery. Sometimes the beaver was associated with the halcyon, the bird reputed to nest on the seashore when tranquil days are imminent. A woman cherishing a halcyon, while the beaver performed its usual act, denoted peace.

Because of its association with the fur trade, the beaver became a symbol of Canada. It appears on the coat of arms granted by Charles II to Sir William Alexander, who had been given tenure of Nova Scotia by James I, and as the emblem of the Hudson's Bay Company when the animal became the standard item of barter. The beaver was also included in the coat of arms of Montreal upon that city's incorporation in 1832, and the first Canadian postage stamp, issued in 1851, was the "three-penny beaver" of Sir Sanford Fleming.

Alciatus, clii; Aldrovandi, pp. 285, 286; Bartholomaeus Ang., xviii, "de castore"; Camerarius, xciii; McCulloch, p. 95; Philippe de Thaon, *Best.*, p. 94; Pliny, vii.30.47; Rabanus Maurus, *PL*, cxi, col. 22; Réau, i.101; Topsell, pp. 40–41; Whitney, pp. 35–36.

Boar

"The pig in sheer gluttony," remarked Aelian, "spares not even its own young, and if it comes across a man's body it does not refrain from eating it." Here, the early Greek natural historian was emphasizing what was regarded as the most deplorable characteristic of the pig, its voracity. In the Middle Ages pigs were frequently arrested, formally tried, and condemned to death for eating other animals and human beings; and even in 1820 Leigh Hunt, the poet, in his short-lived newspaper *The Examiner*, reported an inquest on an eighteen-month-old girl who was partially eaten by a pig in a field in the little Devonshire village of Newton St. Cyres. A pig actually stood trial for murder as late as 1864 in Yugoslavia. The human ear seems to have been particularly tasty, and it was not uncommon for persons whose ears had been eaten by pigs to seek legal confirmation to that effect to avoid the accusation that their disfigurement was the result of punishment for some criminal offense.

From early times the pig symbolically exemplified the unfortunate trait which it exhibited in life. A judgment scene in the tombs of the Egyptian kings shows Osiris condemning a glutton to be transformed into a hog.

When Claudian, the last poet of classical Rome, celebrated the death of Rufinus, a tyrannical praetorian prefect who was torn to pieces by the mob, he placed him in hell where men guilty of venery, sloth, and gluttony assumed the bloated carcasses of filthy swine. Clement of Alexandria, explaining why Moses forbade the eating of pork, associated the animal with boundless lust, greed, and aggressiveness.

Such comparisons continued throughout the Middle Ages and even later. The Italian poet Dante puts the gluttons in a kind of garbage dump in the third circle of hell and includes among them a Florentine acquaintance whom he actually calls the Hog. He also compares Gianni Schicchi, who once impersonated a dead man in order to acquire a highly prized mare, to a hungry swine emerging from its sty, ravenous and rabid, and sinking his tusks into another unfortunate shade. In medieval processions of the Seven Deadly Sins, in which the sins are depicted as people riding various animals, the boar is the mount of Gluttony and an attribute of Sloth. The Renaissance emblem writers such as Valeriano and Ripa make similar references, and Tervarent cites an engraving of the Fontainebleau school which depicted Gluttony as an old woman riding on a boar.

Often the boar was associated with lechery because this quality was commonly regarded as the most vicious kind of sensual greed. In this respect its reputation was no doubt enhanced by the fact that the particular indiscretion of the beautiful woman whom Solomon likened to a gold ring in a swine's snout was usually regarded as sexual. When the stews were licensed in Southwark in 1162, one of the early signs was a boar's head. "The lascivious," remarked the encyclopedist Pseudo-Vincent de Beauvais in his *Speculum Morale*, "are like the swine which would prefer to have its nose in dung than in flowers." In ecclesiastical sculpture the pig playing the Devil's instrument, the bagpipes, was a symbol of lust. As Marcelle Thiébaux observes, the illuminator of the medieval hunting treatise *Livre de la Chasse par Gaston Phébus* was impelled to portray the boar, alone of all animals, *in coitu*. Venus, medievalized as the queen of lechery, rode a huge boar—a mount especially appropriate inasmuch as the pig, as a symbol of fertility, was one of her ancient attributes, and was, moreover, sacrificed to her on Cyprus in memory of her lover, Adonis, who was slain by a boar. The form which Circe's victims took was usually that of swine. Alciatus and Whitney have an engraving of Circe transforming men into animals with her wand, and Whitney used the motto *Homines voluptatibus transformantur* (men are transformed by lust). Another emblem writer, Reusner, taking the same myth, interpreted it as signifying Sloth turning men into swine.

To dream of a boar presaged misfortune, usually associated with lust. In the romance of *Merlin*, the emperor dreamed of a huge sow which was embraced by twelve young lions. He subsequently discovered that the sow represented his own lascivious wife. In Chaucer's *Troilus and Criseyde*, the Trojan hero, Troilus, dreamed that, while he was walking in a forest weeping because his mistress had been forced to join her father in the Greek camp, he saw a boar with huge tusks sleeping in the sunshine:

> And by this bor, fast in his armes folde,
> Lay, kissyng ay, his lady bryght, Criseyde.
> (v.1240–41)

Here the symbol of the boar had an additional significance in that Diomede, the Greek who escorted Criseyde from Troy, descended from the slayer of a famous boar. As Troilus feared, his lady had betrayed him.

Equally ancient, both in the East and in Europe, is the concept of the boar as a symbol of divine essence. As the incarnation of Vishnu, the boar destroyed demons and raised the submerged earth from the sea; as a Vedic thunderbolt, it was red, bristling, and terrible; as a gleaming creature with bristles of gold, it drew a suncart across the Scandinavian skies and provided meat for heroes in Valhalla. As a symbol of might, it appeared on the helmets of Scandinavian warriors, and some vestiges of its golden divinity can be seen in the description of such helmets in *Beowulf*, an Old English epic based on history and legend brought over from Europe by the Teutonic invaders:

> The Boar images shone over the cheek armor,
> decked with gold. Gay with color and hardened
> by fire, they gave protection to the brave men.

Because of its sacredness, the boar was widely associated with ritualistic eating. The Greeks, who regarded swine-keeping as an honorable profession, even δῖος (divine), rationalized such eating as vengeance on the slain god of vegetation, Adonis—the same god as the Phrygian Attis, the Persian Mithra, the Egyptian Osiris, the Babylonian Tammuz, the Roman Virbius, and also, according to Plutarch, the Jehovah of the Feast of the Tabernacles. They identified the boar with Mars who, according to legend, slew Adonis out of jealousy. On coins, Mars often wore a boar's skin.

An ancient fragment preserved by Plutarch on the subject of love refers to the animal as representing the anti-generative attribute:

For blind, oh, blind, women, is he that perceived not
that Ares in the form of a boar sets all evils in commotion.

In psychological terms, of course, this myth represents the punishment of the son by the father for his incestuous impulses, and parallels the symbolic killing of the son in tribal puberty rites by the totem animal (the father). All the lovers of the great mother deities of the West did penance for incest committed and died an unnatural death. Afterward they were resurrected and, having expiated the primordial sin, they were worshipped as redeemers. Representations of the lion-killing boar on very ancient coins of Acanthus in Macedonia and of a dead boar being carried in solemn procession probably meant the ultimate triumph of Adonis in the destruction of his enemy at the return of spring. The boar was thus identified both as a god and as slain, as the destroyer and the destroyed.

This identification continued, according to Frazer:

The very freedom with which the boar ranged at will through the corn led people to identify him with the corn-spirit, to whom he was afterwards opposed as an enemy.

As the embodiment of the corn spirit, the pig is the focus of rites which are sometimes enacted in Europe even today, not only at harvest in such ceremonies as "carrying the pig," but at the winter solstice in eating the Yule boar or cakes representing the boar. The anthropomorphic and eucharistic significances of such rituals are succinctly illustrated in a remark of John Brand, a recognized antiquarian in the late eighteenth century. In trying to Christianize what he feels to be a primitive pagan custom, he calls such cakes "Yule-Dough, (or Dow) a Kind of Baby" and concludes, more accurately than he realized, that they were probably intended as an image of Christ.

The well-known Hebrew evaluation of swine as unclean animals may stem from taboos which often arise in connection with a sacred beast, but it was subsequently reinforced by Biblical precept and legend. Two symbolic values are conspicuous. Christ cured the insane by expelling devils from them and allowing them to enter the Gadarene swine. Therefore, swine could represent either madness or wrath, a quality closely associated with madness in medieval times—hence such proverbial expressions as "wod [mad] as a wild boar," "bristly [enraged] like a boar." The boar became the steed of Wrath in John Gower's procession of the Seven Deadly Sins and the subject of religious satire in a woodcut published by John Day in 1569. In the latter, the boar is the mount of a soldier in Roman costume who has a banner displaying the pope, and it "signifieth wrath, and the man on his backe mischief . . . ."

The other symbolic value was less abstract. Although the pig represented baseness in general in representations of the virtues and vices in Romanesque sculpture, it also came to be identified specifically with Christ's persecutors. There were numerous stories of children being turned into swine because they mocked the boy Jesus. One curious tale of "the pigs in the oven," graphically illustrated in a fourteenth-century book of hours, told of a father who concealed his five children in a disused oven because he was afraid of the mysterious power of the Christ child.

"What have you got in that oven?" asked the Divine young visitor.

"Pigs," retorted the man.

"Pigs they be!" declared the Christ-child, and when the oven was opened, out rushed five little pigs. As Christ's persecutors, the Jews thus came to be identified with the animal which, in accordance with Mosaic law, they abhorred. A popular medieval anti-Semitic joke was to show Jews being suckled by a sow, and it was illustrated in ecclesiastical carvings at Bale, Magdeburg, Ratisbon, and Freising. A painting of the thirteenth century, formerly

The hunt of the boar is hazardous for both man and dog.

on the lower part of the tower of the bridge across the river at Frankfort, showed an elderly Jew riding backward on a sow while a young Jew suckled at the animal and another received its excrements into his mouth. In

41

the same city in the fourteenth century, Jews were required to take the oath standing on a sow's skin, perhaps a survival of the old Germanic custom of swearing the truth of any statement by invoking Gullinbursti, the boar sacred to the sun god. One representation of the sow and little pigs, carved on the northeast corner of the lofty choir of the parish church of Wittenberg, was approvingly explicated by Martin Luther. He drew special attention to the rabbi who accompanied the Jewish sucklings and was represented as holding up the sow's right leg and inspecting her pudendum. Symbolically, Luther declared, the rabbi was searching the *Talmud, als wolt er etwas scharfes und sonderliches lessen und ersehen* (as if he wanted to read and see something acute and unusual).

The chase of the wild boar in ecclesiastical sculpture is often symbolic, the huntsmen signifying the priests who must destroy the sins which the boar exemplifies. Such symbolism seems to be apparent on the panel of a baptismal font at the parish church of St. Marychurch in Devon, and the fact that the boar exemplifies uncleanness makes its presence especially appropriate. Here a hunter-priest holds the Tree of Life in one hand and winds his horn with the other against his porcine quarry, thereby illustrating the baptismal vow: "I renounce the Devil and all his works." In a misericord in the Henry VII chapel of Westminster Abbey the boar is accompanied

by two serpents and a dragon with a satyr-like head. Porcine grotesques, on the other hand, might illustrate Innocent III's remark, probably apocryphal, that the rules of the Order of St. Francis were more fit for swine than for human beings. Franciscans achieved the sensual paradise of the land of Cokaygne by doing penance in *swineis dritte* (pig's dung), and on the back of the choir stalls at the collegiate church of St. Victor at Xanten on the Rhine, begging friars were depicted as monsters with porcine feet and bodies.

In contrast, a black pig at the feet of St. Anthony is simply a reflection of a valuable privilege: monks of the order were allowed to feed their pigs at public charge and the animals could steal and even kill with impunity. "Antony-pig" came to designate a favorite, and "to follow like a Tantony pig" meant to follow close at heel.

In heraldry, the boar continued to be the powerful symbol that it was in *Beowulf*. King Arthur was referred to in flattering terms as a boar and was depicted in romances as having a boar's head on his shield. In the time of Henry III it appears to have been the only beast, apart from the lion and the leopard, on the English coat of arms; and the cognizance of Richard III was a rose supported on the dexter side by a bull, a badge of the house of Clare, and on the sinister by a boar, a badge of the house of York.

As for the sow, its fruitfulness made it emblematic of

the generative principle, and the sow accompanied Diana in her function as Lucina, goddess of childbirth. Martial described one of the great Roman spectacles in which Diana was represented hunting wild animals. A pregnant wild sow was killed in the arena in honor of the goddess. Conversely, Diana's boar reflected her attribute as the destroyer. It was a reminder of the boar—the same boar later slain by Diomede's ancestor—which she sent to ravage the fields of Aetolia to punish Oeneus, the king of Calydon, for his neglect of her. In the late sixteenth century Zucchi included the boar in his fresco of Diana on the ceiling of the Palazzo Ruspoli.

In England in the same century, according to Topsell, the word *sow* was applied to a prostitute and *boaring* to a woman who "Never resteth to shew her desire till she come to a bore (a man)."

The Boar's Head Tavern in Cheapside offered appropriate accommodation for Shakespeare's profligate comedian, Falstaff. Today the boar is still a familiar inn sign, keeping its heraldic colors certainly but having no further significance. It is the domestic pig which retains the pejorative symbolism. The Pig and Whistle, however, refers not to a musical animal but to a small bowl (pig) and spiced ale (wassail), which went in it.

Aelian, vii.xix, x.xvi; Agnel, pp. 7–12, 15; Alciatus, lxxvi; Brand, p. 163; Claudian, ii.ii.483–87; Clement of Alexandria, *PG*, ix, col. 81; *Cokaygne*, p. 150; Dante, *Inf.*, vi.49, xxx.22–34; Frazer, pp. 31, 327, 347, 471–72; Gower, i.i, l. 879; Gray, p. 5; Holbrook, pp. 173–74; Hunt, p. 608, no. 664; Martial, *De Spectac.*, xv.12–14; *Merlin*, p. 421; Plutarch, *Amat.*, 13; Reusner, iii.xxiv; Ripa, p. 192, s.v. "Gola"; Sillar and Meyler, *Symb. Pig*, *passim*; Seznec, p. 300; Tervarent, col. 335; Thiébaux, p. 296; Topsell, p. 670; Trachtenburg, *Devil*, p. 26; Valeriano, ix; Vincent de Beauvais (Pseudo), iii.ii.20; Whitney, p. 82.

Bull

A bull with horns, ears, and tail cut off, its nostrils filled with pepper and its entire body smeared with soap, used to be sent in lieu of rent by the prior of Tutbury, Staffordshire, to the minstrels of John of Gaunt every August 16. The bull was turned loose with the minstrels giving chase, and whoever succeeded in holding it long enough to cut off a lock of its hair won the animal. This inhumane custom continued until 1788. A more common British pastime, that of "pinning the bull," in which trained dogs attacked the tethered animal and fastened their teeth on its snout, lasted until the nineteenth century. In Spain and Mexico similar ancient sports continue to this day; their persistence and their ritualistic content point to ancient religious orgies.

The bull seems to have been worshipped almost universally from prehistoric times both for its powerful fighting ability and for the exceptional amount of fertilizing power, or *Zeugungskraft*, which it was believed to possess. "Address your prayers to the excellent bull," says an ancient Persian hymn "to the principle of all good, the source of all abundance." In phallic statues the reason for the disproportion of the phallus is that although the statue may appear to be that of a man, the phallus is that of a bull.

In Babylonia, bull-like forms, as symbols of strength, guarded the entrance to public and private buildings. Here and in northern Syria the bull often represented the heavens in their most fiery aspect, and in the latter country the storm god was represented as standing on a bull. In some monuments the bull seems to be striking at something with his horns. Payne Knight suggests that the act is similar to that in Japanese iconography in which the deity at creation is sometimes represented as a bull breaking an egg with its horns and animating the contents with its breath.

In mythology, the bull depicted at the center of a labyrinth is the monster begotten on King Minos' wife Pasiphaë by the white bull of Poseidon. Sometimes the story of the Minotaur is represented by an axe and bull because the labyrinth was the palace of the double-headed, sacrificial axe called *labrys* in Lydian Greek. The Minotaur with his horned bull head and tail and his shape of a man was probably once identified with the king, the source of power. The identification of royalty with the bull was common: in Egypt the king was referred to as a strong bull and the queen as the cow that had borne the bull. As a symbol of royalty, the bull appears on many coins, and the Cretan myth of the Minotaur may illustrate a transition from the ritual sacrifice of the king to that of an animal surrogate. The use of the bull's blood for purposes of divination may have similar associations. According to the *Irish Book of the Dun Cow*, the seer partakes of the sacrificial blood in order to have a vision of the man designated to be the next king and to identify him for the community.

Not surprisingly, modern-day psychiatrists have noted the frequent occurrence, in anxiety dreams of their patients, of the bull as the father figure whom the dreamer wishes to kill. In antiquity the black bull was itself a psychopomp, and on an Egyptian coffin in the British Museum, Osiris is so depicted, bearing away the prostrate body of an embalmed worshipper.

The idea of the bull as the life force is most clearly seen in representations of Mithra, the Persian god of light. In Mithraic sanctuaries are reliefs of a young god in Persian costume with a conical cap kneeling on the bull and plunging his dagger into its neck. A scorpion attacks the animal's genitals, a serpent drinks its blood, and a dog springs toward the wound. From the tail of the dying bull emerge germinating ears of wheat, and the blood gives life to the vine. Here the sacrificial blood creates terrestrial life and has the same mystic potency as the blood-drenched earth which Indians used for their altars. The scorpion in this representation is sent from the lower world to try to defeat its life-giving purpose; the serpent is the symbol of the earth being made fertile by the blood of the sacrificial animal; and the dog is venerated as the companion of Mithra. The initiators of Mithraism enacted the sacrifice of the mysterious bull every spring and probably drank the sacred beverage.

Another grimmer ceremony of blood, the Taurobolium, seems to have been incorporated into the rite by the latter part of the fourth century of the Christian era. In this ceremony the initiate stood in a pit beneath a grating. Above him the bull was stabbed to death with a consecrated spear, and the initiate emerged saturated with blood but mystically reborn and cleansed of every impurity. Since Mithraism also commemorated the winter solstice, December 25, as the sun god's birthday, it is small wonder that the early Christian fathers such as Tertullian and Justin Martyr regarded the cult as some devilish parody of their own ritual.

As a lunar and solar god the bull symbolized the power residing in both astral bodies, and the horns and disc were assimilated into almost every mythology to express divinity. The early culture hero had a bull head and a snake body to denote that he possessed all the creative power of the natural world. The horned Moses with his serpent standard expressed this idea, and his descent from the Mount in Exodus xxxiv.15, when he is described as horned, indicated that the spirit of God was still upon him. In Hebrew literature the horn is equated with power, and the Assyrian kings often adorned themselves with horns for the same reason. Raising the horns of the people symbolized victory; breaking them, defeat. In the Old Testament, the phrase "his horns shall be exalted" meant that the man in question would be raised to power or pre-eminence.

The bull with a human face represents Bacchus, or Dionysus. A Neapolitan medallion shows Victory placing a wreath on him in this form. Such an association is natural: this god with his vineyards is the personification of the sun as the ripener. The Bacchanals of Thrace wore horns in his honor, and the Cretans at their biennial festival tore a live bull to pieces with their teeth. The latter was a re-enactment of the god's dismemberment at the hands of the Titans, an allegory similar to that of the death of Adonis and Attis by a boar, and Osiris by Typhon. A vestige of the ceremonies probably survives in the custom of rewarding an outstanding torero, at the death of the bull, not simply with the ears but with the foot and tail of the animal, for *Dionysus* meant the "lame god," either from *nysos*, the Syracusan word for "lame," or from shrines associated with lameness and called Nyse, Nyssa, or Nysia in Thrace, Asia Minor, and Arabia. Traditionally, the sacred kings appear to have affected a limp, usually regarded as having an erotic significance, and tragic actors imitated it on the Greek stage by wearing the buskin in honor of Dionysus. It was for this reason that when the women at Elis evoked a visitation from the god, they called for him to come among them with his bull-foot, the symbol of sexual potency.

The bull was often regarded as the moist principle in nature. The seas and rivers, and Poseidon himself, were symbolized by bull horns, either alone or with the bull, or with an anthropomorphized bull, in conjunction with waves or between two dolphins. Representations on vases of the solar lion overcoming the bull have been interpreted as illustrating the solar eclipse.

According to Horapollo, the Egyptians used the bull for secular as well as religious symbols. A healthy bull denoted manliness combined with temperance. The ear of a bull was a symbol of hearing because when the cow lowed loudly, the bull even far distant would recognize that she was in heat and would hasten to her. A bull inclining toward the left symbolized the woman who produced males. A reformed rake was symbolized by a bull bound with a wild fig branch.

As an animal which performed such great service to agriculture, the bull was naturally placed under the protection of Ceres; as an astrological sign it heralded the period of growth. Corn stalks issuing from the body of the bull in some of the monuments to the Mithraic cult, and the grains of wheat accompanying the animals on some medallions, testify to the animal as a vegetation spirit. This significance has persisted until recent times. According to Frazer:

> When the corn is thick and strong in one spot, they say in some parts of East Prussia, "the bull is lying on the corn . . . ." At Arad, in Hungary, the man who gives the last stroke at threshing is enveloped in straw and a cow's hide with the horns attached to it. At Pessnitz, in the district of Dresden, the man who gives the last stroke with the flail is called Bull.

In sacred art the bull is the attribute of St. Sylvester. Crouching at his feet, it is a reminder of a miracle which the saint performed in a contest with Zambri the magician. By whispering the secret name of the Omnipotent in the ear of a fierce bull, the magician caused it to drop dead, but when St. Sylvester challenged him to restore it to life, he was unable to do so. The saint, however, made the sign of the cross and raised up the bull as tame and gentle as though it had been under yoke since birth.

The bull appears to have been particularly active among martyrs. The virgin martyrs St. Marciana of Tortosa

46

(January 9) and St. Thecla of Seleucia (September 23) were torn by wild bulls, and St. Blandina (June 2) was tossed by one. A brazen bull found both in colored glass windows and in ecclesiastical sculpture usually represents the martyrdom of St. Eustace in the second century of the Christian era. For refusing to deny his faith, he was incarcerated with his family in such a bull by the Emperor Adrian and was burned to death. A similar fate was accorded to St. Victor of Milan (May 8), St. Pelagia of Tarsus (May 4), and St. Polycarp of Smyrna (January 26).

The cow was a flattering designation for Egyptian gods and royalty. Herodotus tells of a ceremony at the grave of Osiris at which the mourners carried an image of a cow, made of gilt wood, with a gold sun between its horns. This cow was Isis, wife and sister of Osiris, to whom the cow was sacred and whose cult proved most popular with many Greek-speaking lands even before the Hellenistic age. Hathor, or Isis, was the personification of the primeval, feminine creative principle, a cow-headed woman with a lotus-entwined scepter, symbolizing creation. Her head was frequently reproduced on capitals, friezes, and cornices. Isis, or Io as she was also called, was turned into a white cow by Zeus and seduced. Ovid in his *Art of Love* advises young bloods of Rome to pick up a girl at her shrine, the shrine of the heifer, because the goddess makes many a maid follow her ex-

The cow is a symbol of fecundity and love.

ample; *multas illa facit, quod fuit ipsa Iovi* (she [Isis] makes many maids what she herself was to Jove). To Lucius Apuleius, a native of North Africa but of ancient Greek stock, she is the great earth mother, and in his novel *The Golden Ass* he remarks that she is venerated under many names. Among these is Aphrodite; and while the Greeks anthropomorphized the son of the goddess as Cupid, the Egyptians, not unpredictably, repre-

47

sented this personification of animal desire in the form of a calf, the offspring of the cow-goddess. The golden calf set up by Aaron in the absence of Moses can be identified with it. After sacrificing and feasting, the devotees indulged in play, or, more specifically, in sexual play, which was the proper conclusion of the worship of Cupid.

The cow as a symbol of love did not survive into the Middle Ages. The animal was, however, the attribute of St. Bridget (February 1), a fifth-century abbess of Kildare who gave milk and cheese to the poor and was popular in Italian votive tablets, those highly colored illustrations commissioned by the devout for favors received. In Renaissance emblem books the cow sometimes appeared drinking its own milk, while a hen beside it ate its own egg. Sambucus and Whitney regarded the cow as an emblem of selfishness and took the opportunity to declare that man's powers and opportunities were given him to develop for the general welfare, not for the purpose of selfish enjoyment.

As a symbol of virility allied to temperance—a symbol which had been given wide currency through Horapollo —the bull was used in the secular art of the Renaissance. The animal's reputation for temperance was enhanced by the belief that it never had sexual relations with a pregnant cow. Dürer, in an engraving of the Emperor Maximilian I, put a bull on the right of his subject as a compliment to him.

A curious disparity also occurred. Whereas emblem writers such as Valeriano and Ripa saw the bull as a symbol of labor, the bull which draws the chariot of poverty in an allegory by Holbein symbolizes laziness. The latter evaluation stemmed from Horace.

Apuleius, XI.v; Ciarrocchi, xvii; *Encycl. Brit.*, 11th ed., III.575; Frazer, pp. 457–58; Guillim, xiv.121; Herodotus, II.xli; Horace, *Epist.*, 1.14, 43; Horapollo, I.xlvi, xlvii; II. xliii, lxxvii–lxxviii; Knight, *Symbolical Lang.*, p. 123; Ovid, *Ars Amat.*, 1.78; Valeriano, s.v. "Opus et labor"; Ripa, p. 145, s.v. "Fatica estiva"; Whitney, p. 64.

Camel

Although the camel was subjected to many kinds of misrepresentation in medieval art and sculpture, its habit of kneeling down to receive heavy loads seems to have been well known. This animal might be depicted with wart-like projections, horse's hooves, or cloven feet, but it always bowed humbly to the earth and allowed a man to brandish a whip beside it. Most writers followed Isidore, the seventh-century bishop of Seville, who in his *Etymologies* suggested that the word *camel* may have come from *chamai* (χαμαί), an adverb meaning "on the earth," and implied that the camel was a humble beast of burden. Not surprisingly, it was the symbol of humility and of the humility of Christ in particular, stooping to take on the load of the world's sin. As such, the camel appeared on bench-ends and misericords.

The Western world was able to adopt this symbolism because it was relatively unfamiliar with the animal. In actual fact, the camel is a most disagreeable brute, and in the East its obstinacy is proverbial: "the camel curses its parents when it has to go up hill, and its Maker when it has to go down." The camel's stubbornness may explain why the Egyptians, according to Horapollo, made the animal a symbol of a man who is slow on his feet. J. G. Wood remarks that the camel is so accustomed to grumbling that even if a stone no larger than a walnut is placed on its back it will immediately begin to remonstrate, "groaning as if it were being crushed to the earth with its load."

Occasionally, qualities more firmly based in natural history seem to be reflected in the symbolism. In 1330 in a procession of the Seven Deadly Sins described by Mattias Farinator, the camel is the mount of Wrath. It was also the attribute of Prudence. Among the vices and virtues depicted on the central porch of the façade of Notre Dame, the circular disc of Prudence displays a camel. The cycle depicted at Amiens Cathedral gives Prudence the same attribute.

But the camel's most conspicuous role was sexual: it was a medieval nymphomaniac. Alan of the Isles stated that the camel ministered to the wants of men like a bought slave (*quasi servus emptitius*), and this idea may have contributed to a belief in the camel's passion for sexual intercourse. In the Old Testament the camel in heat was a metaphor for Israel whoring after foreign gods (Jeremiah ii.23). Albertus Magnus passed on the remark of Aristotle that camels often spend the whole day in copulation. The monk Bartholomaeus Anglicus, as translated by Trevisa in the fourteenth century, stated that "the female camel boweth herself and goeth on her knees, when she will be coupled with the male and her talent and desire is strong and fervent in time of love," and that it was the "most hottest beast of kind." The remarks of these cloistered medieval encyclopedists are oddly at variance with an observation of the traveler Pallas, quoted by Briffault:

> As soon as impregnation has taken place the female, with a vicious snarl, turns around and attacks the male with her teeth, and the latter is driven away in terror.

Chaucer, with the Wife of Bath in mind, urged women to fight their husbands like camels. Whether he was thinking of the animal as a martial or lascivious or, ironically, as a humble beast of burden we cannot tell. But the association of the camel with lust persisted: in an engraving by Aldegrever, luxury is personified as a woman

49

The camel prudently stores water.

sitting on a camel; Farmer in his *Vocabula Amatoria* (1896) gives *camel* as a slang term for *prostitute*:

Suivre la folie
Au sein des plaisirs et des ris,
Oui, voilà la vie
Des chameaux chéris
A Paris

(Justin Cabassol)

Paradoxically, the temperance of the camel is also proverbial, and in an engraving by Reverdino, Temperance is depicted as having a camel at its feet. This reputation for self-denial may account for Spenser's use of the animal as a symbol of Avarice; he may, on the other hand, simply have associated it with oriental wealth or with the camel's famed ability to hoard water for its long trips across the desert.

Alanus, *PL*, ccx, col. 437; Albertus Magnus, v, fol. 63v; Aldegrever, *see* Hollstein, 1.61; Bartholomaeus Ang., XVIII, "de camelo," "de lacte cameli"; Briffault, 1.119; Farinator, *Titulus* 75; Horapollo II.c; Isidore, XII.i.35; Katzenellenbogen, p. 76, n. 1; Reverdino, *see* Tervarent, col. 70; J. G. Wood, *see* P. S. Robinson, p. 151; Spenser, *FQ.*, I.iv.27.

Cat

In ancient Egypt the cat was sacred. Its fertility, its peculiar ability to see in the dark and to widen or narrow

50

its glance at will, its strange aloofness—all contributed to making it what it has been since, a magic animal. Households went into mourning and shaved their eyebrows as a token of respect when a cat died. When a Roman visitor in Egypt accidentally killed a cat, a mob stormed his house and lynched him despite the fact that an important peace treaty was being negotiated between the Egyptians and the Romans at the time. The Egyptian goddess Bast was feline, and her chariot was drawn by cats. As a symbol of the moon, the cat sat in the middle of the sistrum, which represented the lunar orbit; as the variable power of the sun, it cut off the head of the Serpent of Darkness in the presence of the Sacred Three: Ra, Osiris, and Horus.

Because it was sacred the cat could not be exported, and commissioners were sent out periodically to purchase and repatriate such cats as had been smuggled overseas. This embargo caused the weasel rather than the cat to be domesticated in ancient Greece and Rome to keep down mice. As a result, the cat's role in folklore was not conspicuous. When it did appear, it was as the concomitant of supernatural evil: Hecate, goddess of the underworld, transformed herself into a cat according to Ovid; the witches in Apuleius' *Golden Ass* became cats.

A similar value was given to the cat in the Christian world. Heretics were accused of worshipping the Devil in the form of a cat. According to Gregory IX in 1233, it was a black tom. The devotees kissed the Devil's feline posterior and then proceeded "to the most abominable fornication with no regard for shame or relationship, and if more men than women were present they would satisfy their shameful lust together." The Waldensians and the Knights Templars were denounced for the same crime. Alanus de Insulis thought that another group of heretics, the Catharists, derived their name from their worship of Lucifer as a cat in obscene rites: *Vel Cathari dicuntur a cato, quia, ut dicitur, osculantur posteriora catti, in cujus specie, ut dicunt, apparet eis Lucifer*. Folk etymology in Germany actually traced the world *Ketzer* to *kater* (tom cat); *Ketzerie* in Middle High German means "sorcery" as well as "heresy."

Witches were charged with having a familiar in the guise of a cat or indulging in carnal copulation with the Devil in the form of a cat. Through constant association, the cat became their symbol. A fearsome cat with symmetrical, porcupine-quill markings and an owl-like face decorates the title page of a contemporary tract (1579) on the Chelmsford witches, reproduced in Rossell Hope Robbins' *Encyclopedia of Witchcraft and Demonology*. Psychologists might make something of this cat's striking similarity to some of the later cats of Louis Wain, who died in 1936. Wain is still famous for his animated cats, which appeared in the 1920s in comic cartoon series in children's annuals. When he suffered from schizophrenia,

The cat is so called because she catches things
*(*a captura*), like the cat on the right, or*
*because she lies in wait (*captat*),*
like the cat on the left.

his amiable, rather sentimental creatures suddenly became pointed and vicious, like the one in the sixteenth-century pamphlet on the Chelmsford witches.

Although the cat's predominant association was with wickedness, darkness, and the occult, its symbolism varied, particularly when used didactically: to medieval preachers the cat was either Satan seeking to catch the mouse (the soul), or the wicked priest who wished to devour his parishoners.

Secular writers, especially those concerned with emblems, saw the cat as a symbol of freedom. Paradine remarked on the fact that the Alani (the Sarmatian nomads of ancient times) had a cat for their standard and stressed the animal's love of liberty. Whitney used the cat, as Chaucer had done earlier in the *Manciple's Tale*, to illustrate the maxim that one ultimately reverts to one's real nature; one cannot hope therefore to alter mankind:

> The foole, that farre is sent some wisdom
>   to attaine:
> Returnes an Ideot, as he wente . . .
> The catte, in countries kepte, where are
>   no myse for praye,
> Yet, being broughte where they doe breede,
>   her selfe shee doth bewraye.

There was also another symbolism which has persisted to the present time. Aristotle, stated that the female cat was peculiarly lecherous and wheedled the male on to sexual commerce. Misogynist clerics in the Middle Ages frequently repeated this evaluation, seeing man as the mouse and woman as the sleek, enticing, and predatory cat. Sebastian Brant in his *Narrenschiff* made the same implication:

> The cats pursue the mice in haste
> When once they've had a little taste.
> Women who try out other men
> Become so bold and shameless then.
>
> (tr. Zeydel)

The same value is still current. Instead of having a magical aura, the cat's symbolic qualities are mundane and circulate mainly in the argot of the streets. In such remarks as *la fille a laissé aller le chat au fromage si souvent que l'on s'est aperçu qu'il fallait relargir sa robe*, the expression *laisser aller le chat au fromage* is proverbial. As in "cat-house," the reference is specifically sexual. In politer circles, the cat has degenerated into an epithet for a spiteful woman.

Alanus, *PL*, ccx, col. 366; Aristotle, *Hist. animal*, v.ii (540a); Brant, p. 83; Conger, *passim*; Herodotus, ii.lxvi; Jennison, p. 129; Lanoe-Villène, iii.103–107; Necker, *passim*; Ovid, *Metam.*, v.330; Paradine, *see* Aldrovandi, p. 575; Robbins, *Witchcraft*, p. 91; Spies, *passim*; Whitney, p. 178; Wright (ed.), *Contemp. Narrat.*, pp. 1–3, 32; Zeydel, no. 70.

The centaur shoots his arrow.

Centaur

This creature, half-man and half-horse, has always symbolized lust. He was an archer, and traditionally, as may be seen in the Pentateuch, the bow and arrow (*keschess*) was often used as the symbol for the normal male act of *ejaculatio seminis*. Representations of centaurs on Thracian coins stress the sexual characteristics and, in all, the action is the same: the centaur embraces a large and attractive woman.

When the centaur took to hunting game, its quarry was often the hart, an animal which, from its associations with Psalm xlii, the bestiaries, and the legends of St. Eustachius and St. Hubert, represented virtue. Fortunately, although the centaur as hunter represented the Devil, it might be quelled by a man of God. St. Anthony met a centaur as he was vainly looking for the hermitage of St. Paul. While the saint anxiously made the sign of the cross to ward off any diabolical influence, the strange, hybrid creature uttered a harsh, whinnying sound and meekly pointed in the right direction.

The Sagittarius is the zodiacal representation of the centaur-archer and appears in various allegorical senses. Confronting another centaur, it appears with two mermaids on a border of an illustration in the Manuerius Bible (circa 1175). The illustration itself depicts Christ healing the demoniac, and the presence of the two symbols of lust seems to imply some perception of a connection between mental and sexual disorders.

On the other hand, Philippe de Thaon implies that the Sagittarius is Christ: He is to punish the Jews and harrow hell. The bow "signifies . . . when he was hanged on the cross and wounded in his body, the Holy Spirit departed from him to those whom he loved, who were in hell and awaited his help."

Evans, pp. 317–18; Knight, *Symbolical Lang.*, pp. 77–79; Manuerius Bible, *see* Nordenfalk, pt. ii, p. 174; Philippe de Thaon, *Livre*, p. 44; Van Marle, ii.108–109, figs. 125, 126, 127.

Chimaera

Homer described this creature in the *Iliad* as a fire-breathing hybrid animal with the head of a lion, the body of a goat, and the tail of a serpent. Isidore gave a similar description—*ore leo, media caprea, postremis partibus draco*—and said that each part had its own head. Milton twice called the chimaera "dire" and put it in hell, along with Gorgons and Hydras.

Its use as a symbol of evil in medieval times was infrequent. Specifically, it was associated with lust or *amoris fluctatio*. A Vatican mythographer said its three parts illustrated the three steps of casual love "which invades us ferociously in adolescence like a lion. Then follows the fulfillment of love, designated by the goat because that animal is most prompt in lechery. . . . In the posterior parts it is like a dragon, because after the act, the prick of penance goads the mind."

More recently, the conquest of the chimaera by Bellerophon, described in the sixth book of the *Iliad*, has been variously interpreted. Graves sees it as an allegory of an Achaean capture of the White Goddess's shrine on Mount Helicon; Lanoe-Villène regards it as symbolizing an initiation.

Bode, *Mythogr.,* iii.14.4–5; Graves, *White Goddess*, p. 384; Homer, *Il.,* vi.179; Isidore, xii.iii.36; Lanoe-Villène, iii.166; Milton, *Comus,* 517 and *P.Lost,* ii.628; Réau, i.115.

Crocodile

Polarities in the symbolism of the crocodile existed in ancient times. As Herodotus noted, the crocodile was venerated as a god in some parts of Egypt but was treated as an enemy in others.

In particular, the crocodile's sexual characteristics caused some confusion, and as a result it was endowed both with absolute impotence and with the maximum of generative power. Such ideas, according to Ernest Jones, probably had some physiological basis inasmuch as the crocodile has no visible genital organs since they are

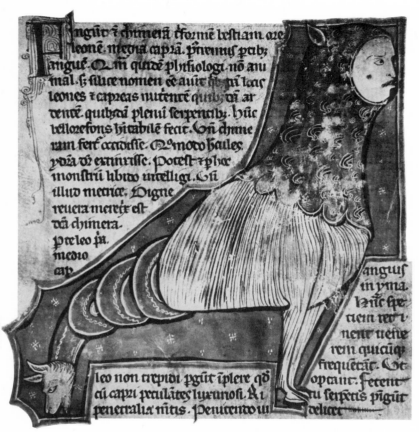

The chimaera is part lion, part goat, and part serpent.

55

The crocodile was renowned for its hard skin and powerful jaws; neither man nor fish could survive its attack.

normally concealed within the cloaca. The male organ is, however, unusually large, and copulation is exceptionally vigorous and of long duration.

The ancient Egyptian text of the Unas, written in the Sixth Dynasty, contains passages expressing the wish that the dead person may achieve the virility of the crocodile in the next world and so become "all-powerful with women." Still current in this century are beliefs that crocodile eaten with spices is a means of increasing sexual vigor.

Where the crocodile's phallic power was glorified, the creature became the object of worship. Further attributes were added. It did not use its tongue and was therefore a symbol of silence and wisdom. It had the habit of veiling its eyes, commonly regarded as the mark of the Supreme Deity.

Horapollo appears to have been drawing on both favorable and unfavorable traditions when he remarked that the crocodile represented a rapacious, furious, or prolific man, and this ambivalence in the symbolism is frequently evident.

Hypocrisy is the quality most persistently associated with the crocodile. In Elizabethan times the Reverend Topsell was simply summing up a long tradition when he observed:

The common proverbe . . . *Crocodili lachrimae,*
the crocodiles teares, justifieth the trecherous nature of

56

this beast, for there are not many bruite beasts that can weepe, but such is the nature of the Crocodile, that to get a man within his danger, he will sob, sigh & weepe, as though he were in extremitie, but suddenly he destroyeth him. Others say, that the crocodile weepeth after he hath devoured a man.

The story of the crocodile's tears was given wide currency by the medieval bestiarists, but it occurred as early as A.D. 400 in a sermon by Asterius, bishop of Amasia. Innumerable medieval illustrations show a crocodile either devouring a man or holding him in his claws, and some of the bestiaries state that "when it devours a man, it weeps." Druce has suggested that the story arose because the crocodile had large lachrymal glands.

Pliny made a statement which further contributed to the animal's reputation for deceit when he said its excrement cured eye diseases and facial blemishes. The story was seized upon by the moralists. Aged prostitutes, according to the bestiarists, used crocodile dung as a rejuvenating cosmetic with good effect until their sweat washed it off and they appeared as withered as before. This apparently genuine illustration of low life was curiously allegorized:

> Whereas of its dung an ointment is made, so evil men are generally praised by the unlearned for their evil deeds; and are glorified by the praise of this world, as it were with an ointment. But when the judge, separating the evil from the good, moves forward in his wrath to strike the evil down, then all that glory and praise vanishes like smoke.

In medieval symbolism, the crocodile also signified hell. According to the bestiaries, a water-snake called the hydrus covered itself with mud and then glided easily into the jaws of the crocodile and later emerged from its side unharmed. The hydrus' initial act represented Christ's incarnation, the second His descent into hell. A hymn in the *Analecta Hymnica* stated the theme allegorically:

> *Hydrus intrat crocodillum,*
> *Extis privat, necat illum.*
> *Vivus inde rediens.*

(The hydrus enters the crocodile, strips him of his organs, kills him. Returns alive from that place.)

Druce suggested that some representations of the jaws of hell derive from the crocodile.

Besides emphasizing the beast's hypocrisy, Topsell remarked that crocodiles "are exceeding fruitefull and prolificall, and therefore also in Hieroglyphics they are made to signify fruitfulness." Some of the emblem writers, in representing luxury, depicted a nude, curly-headed girl sitting on a crocodile, fondling a partridge, and they explained that the crocodile signified fecundity. The crocodile's teeth, tied to the right arm, were said to excite lust.

Whitney, on the other hand, possibly drawing upon Hadrian Junius' *Emblemata* (1565), used the crocodile as a symbol of providence, on the grounds that it prudently laid its eggs in a place where the Nile would not harm them.

Further Renaissance emblems made use of traditional fictions. Camerarius, with the motto *gratis servire iucundum* (it is pleasant to serve free), saw a moral lesson in the bestiary tale of the little bird called the trochilus which entered the jaws of a crocodile unharmed in order to pick its teeth. Like these two creatures, said Camerarius, men should exchange their services. But he and others also made use of more pejorative symbolism deriving from the old fable of the crocodile's hypocrisy. As Aldrovandi stated, the cruelty of the crocodile might be compared to that of Cupid or, under the inscription *Plorat, et devorat* (she weeps aloud and devours), to a woman who had a pious exterior but inwardly was so cruel as to appear to devour her lover.

Aldrovandi, pp. 687–88; *Anal. Hymn.*, xxi.36; Asterius, *PG*, xl, col. 388; Camerarius, xcviii; Druce, "Crocodile," p. 316; Horapollo, i.lxvii, lxviii; Jones, p. 348; McCulloch, pp. 106–108; Pliny, viii.25.37; Topsell, p. 135; Whitney, p. 3.

Dog

The dog appears as mount, messenger, companion, guardian, and manifestation or symbol of innumerable gods in both the Old and New World. The animal was sacred even in India, where it is often thought to have been abominated. Siva rode upon a dog and in some of his aspects was worshipped as a black dog. According to W. Crooke, the nineteenth-century Hindus were never certain whether a dog was a dog or a manifestation of some local deity. Even the corpse-eating hounds of the north were said to incarnate the spirits of those they devoured. It is not surprising that Maria Leach entitled her exhaustive and fascinating account of the folklore of the dog, *God Had a Dog*.

This role of the dog in mythology means that from the earliest times it was regarded as a magic animal, with power over life and death. It was the symbol of the Semitic healing and protecting mother-goddess Gula, and of Hecate, the life-giving, life-taking Greek death-moon goddess. Indeed, probably any representation of a goddess standing on a dog denotes the White Goddess, the Mother of All Living.

As a magic animal its actions were very carefully observed by ancient seers such as the Chaldeans. A red dog entering the temple signified that the gods had left the people; a grey, that the temple would be plundered; a white, that the temple would last a long time. Such cynomancy has been practiced even recently among Czechoslovakian immigrants in the United States, according to L. V. Ryan. People gather in a room and each lays a slice of bread on the floor. Then they call in the family dog. The one whose bread is eaten first will go on a journey within a year or, in some instances, will die.

Its reputation as a magic animal may account for the hatred which the Jews had for the dog. The Haranians, sometimes termed "heathen Semites," who were violently castigated by Isaiah, burned live dogs as offerings and sacrificed to dogs. Their priests associated with dogs and, it seems, practiced sodomy in their temples. The contemptuous reference of the Old Testament patriarchs to outcast, hostile, or erring people as dogs may owe something to the howling pariahs which scavenged around their camps. But their attitude may also reflect a reaction to their own earlier tribal practices, not to those of their Egyptian masters, as is often supposed.

In ancient Egypt, of course, the dog was so highly respected that families even went into mourning when a dog died, and among the Amratians the dog was buried with its master to guide it to the next world. Anubis, the messenger and servant of the gods, was dog-headed. He was said to be the son of Osiris, and he conducted souls to the promised land. The horizon was sometimes depicted in the form of a dog and was called Anubis because, like the dog, it viewed both night and day. A similar idea of the function of the dog may be seen in the Indian epic, the *Mahabharata*, in which the hero Yudhishthira refused to enter India's heaven unless his faithful dog accompanied him. The famous guardian of Hades, Cerberus, seemed originally to have been something of a pet, behaving fiercely only to those trying to escape or to the living trying to get in. Hesiod was the first to give him his monstrous appearance. In Elizabethan times, Topsell remarked that the three heads "signified a multiplicity of Divels" and belonged to a lion, a wolf, and a fawning dog.

Although the Greeks and Romans praised the dog's loyalty and sagacity, they also used the word κύων and *canis* as terms of abuse, as did the Hebrews. The Greek cynics of the third century B.C. took their name from Diogenes, who was called "the Dog" because of his independent thinking and rejection of society. They were also said to have trained in the gymnasium in Athens called Cynosarges, set apart from those who were not of pure Athenian blood. But while the cynics were ascetics and regarded virtue as consisting in the avoidance of physical pleasure, the dog as a symbol seems to have been particularly associated with sexual offenses. In Greece κύων and related words were applied to prostitutes, and in the Middle Ages canine copulation seems to have provoked the imagination. Encyclopedists, such as Bartholomaeus Anglicus, frequently drew attention to canine promiscuity and pointed out the appropriate symbolism:

> Aristotle saith that hounds both male and female use lechery as long as they be alive, and give them the uncleannesse of lechery. They take no diversitie betweene mother and sister, and other bitches touching the daede of lecherie: and therefore the offering of the price of an hounde or of a Bitch was accounted as uncleane by the law of Moses, as offering the price of a common woman: for such wretched persons serve in al lechery as hounds doe.

Medieval priests, taxed with the burden of regulating the sex life of their flocks, found the dog's sexual habits a useful kind of yardstick whereby to elicit information of a most intimate kind. At confession the priest would bluntly ask the penitent before him whether he had copulated with his wife like a dog. The penalty for such an offense, according to Burchard, bishop of Worms early in the eleventh century, was ten days on bread and water: *Concubuisti cum uxore tua vel cum alia aliqua retro, canico more? Si fecisti, decem dies in pane et aqua poeniteas.* Other details concerning the canine mode of copulation were deemed to be appropriately retributive: a typical afterlife punishment for illicit lovers was for them to be joined *quomodo canis* and to whirl around hell for all eternity.

Various notions concerning canine sexuality have persisted through the centuries, particularly with regard to fertility and lasciviousness. The folk ritual of presenting newlyweds with a dog in a cradle and the nineteenth-century nursery rhyme of a young lady who took her "father's greyhound and laid it in a cradle" illustrate a belief in fertility magic, coupled with the idea that canine power can be transferred to humans. *Elle n'est pas jolie, mais elle a du chien* has a particular significance according to J. S. Farmer's *Vocabula Amatoria* (1896). *Avoir du chien* denotes a woman whose eyes, demeanor, and general aspect were sexy. A less commendable symbolism arising from the animal's habit of public copulation persisted among the ancient Maya and the Aztec Indians, to whom the dog stood for fornication and syphilis, and in India where the brand or mark of a dog's foot was the symbol of lust.

In medieval times the dog was the Devil, the hound of hell. The writer of the *Ancrene Riwle*, the twelfth-century conduct book for nuns, urged the nuns not to be passive when the "dogge of helle kumeð snakerinde mid his blodie vlien (flehes) of stinkende þouhtes" (when the dog of hell comes sneaking [?] with his bloody fleas of corrupt thoughts.) Somewhat curiously—since his audience was composed of daughters of the nobility—he recommended the good sisters not only to raise the cross against the "dogge-deovel," but to spit at him in the middle of his beard. The Devil actually appeared as a dog before a young cleric on his way from Astley to Arley to visit a prostitute, and asked for his sword. Bravely the young man refused, swearing "by the death of Christ." Whereupon the Devil vanished, unable to endure the power of the glorious death of Christ even in the mouth of a sinner. Similar appearances were made to St. Dunstan and St. Waltheof, and about 1140 a lesser devil in the shape of a black dog was released from a man named Walter through the intercession of St. Cuthbert, bishop of Lindisfarne.

Black dogs usually denoted evil, and in the Middle Ages they were frequently seen in the company of witches and agents of the Devil. The ancient idea of the dog as psychopomp persisted in the legends of the baying hounds riding over the misty moors at the heels of ghostly huntsmen led by King Arthur, Charlemagne, Odin, Hecate, John Peel, or Dando (the Cornishman who hunted on Sunday) and to meet them meant death. Even today the dog is credited with sinister supernatural powers. There is scarcely a country that does not possess a superstition associating the howling of the dog with impending death, and it is most unlucky for a dog to jump over a coffin.

The dog was also emblematic of a variety of sins. Not only was it the general sinner, the proverbial dog returning to its vomit being likened to the wicked man reverting to his evil ways after confession, but it was the symbol of the litigious, of the cupidinous, and of the deadly sin of envy.

Brief allusions to fables underlined the central symbolism. The dog with the bone looking at its reflection in the stream was the fool who loses what little he has through greed and discontent, and the dog baying at the moon was the fool bawling at learned men. The emblem writers of the sixteenth century, Alciatus, Whitney, Camerarius, and Beza, all used the last device and showed a full moon and a large dog baying. Alciatus and Whitney had the motto *inanis impetus* (a vain attack); Camerarius, *despicit alta canis* (the dog despises higher things). Beza used the device as an emblem of the scoffer of the faith: *Sic quisquis Christum allatrat Christive ministras, / index stultitiae spernitor usque suae* (so whoever barks at Christ or his Ministers, the scorner is the pointer-out even of his own foolishness).

Long before Shakespeare used it in his dog-licking-candy clusters to illustrate deceitful, fawning courtiers, the dog was the symbol of detestable obsequiousness. In a collection of sermons called *Jacob's Well*, the flatterer was compared to a dog which "lyckyth an-oþer hound . . . behynde in the ers [arse], in that unclene membre." The fifteenth-century poet Lydgate likened fraud to a dog that fawns on his master but barks as soon as his back is turned. The backbiter, in the sermons just re-

Faithful dogs rescue their king who was captured by his enemies.

ferred to, is a butcher's dog with bloody mouth "full of synfull defamynges" and, like a dog, "he lyckyth the woundys and the sorys [sores] of another man."

At the same time the dog continued to be a symbol of vigilance and guardianship, just as it had been in Egypt, ancient Greece, old China, and Japan. The favorable symbolism obtained wide currency through the stories of Pliny and other early natural historians, and in the Middle Ages tales of faithful dogs rescuing their beleaguered masters or dying of grief on their demise were widely repeated. In Italy itself the dog as protector of the home is depicted, chained and belled, in the mosaics at entrances to Roman dwellings. The museum at Valencia contains medieval door locks illustrative of the same idea. They are devised in the shape of dog heads, and some have a great ring as a handle in the dog's mouth.

In the Renaissance the dog as guardian appears in emblem books, and the accompanying engravings show the animal with a flock of sheep or at the gate of a church. The dog was also interpreted as a symbol of fidelity in Whitney's emblem *Medici Icon*, which represented Aesculapius seated on a throne with a scepter in one hand and a staff in the other, and a cock, a dragon, and a dog at his feet. It denoted "faithfulness and love," which physicians should show in their profession. This meaning does, in fact, obscure a more ancient one. The animal was sacred to Aesculapius, who was said to have been reared by a bitch, and his cult may originally have been a dog cult. Sacrifices were offered to dogs in Aesculapius' temple. To dream of a dog signified the cure of the suppliant, and its tongue was credited with healing properties.

Another emblem associated with the watchdog occurs in the ancient proverbial expression "let sleeping dogs lie," which was transposed by Francesco Sforza (1401–1466) after he had put down the popular disturbances in Milan and had taken over the city. On his surcoat he had an elaborately embroidered emblem of a dog sleeping under a tree and over the motto: *Quietum nemo ne impune lacessit* (when at rest, no one shall safely provoke me).

The dog at the feet of a recumbent effigy is a feature of medieval sculpture. The position of the animal appears to derive from the figure of Christ trampling on a lion, an adder, or a dragon, as He triumphed over the powers of hell. Reclining at the feet of a man, the dog came to symbolize strength and courage; at the feet of a woman, undying love. In certain fourteenth-century illustrations the dog is given a pose appropriate to its master's reputation. In the case of Charles the Bad, the dog is gnawing a bone; in the case of Philip the Good, it lies patient and submissive at its master's feet. Symbolizing fidelity, the dog sometimes accompanies a widow. Tervarent refers to a portrait of Marguerite d'Angoulême as a widow, at

the Bibliothèque Nationale in Paris, in which she is depicted with a dog in her arms. A contemporary tribute to the faithfulness of the dog is cited by Leach as occurring in the terrible dog covenants observed by certain tribes of Africa, Assam, Burma, and China. At a peace treaty a live dog is cut in half, the two parties swearing to be faithful to their bond as a dog is faithful.

Yet another symbolism is illustrated by the disturbing dreams of mothers of saints. The mother of St. Bernard dreamed that she carried a dog in her womb. The animal was white with red on its back and it barked. A holy man interpreted the dream as signifying that she would bring forth a noble preacher who would utter great barkings against the enemies of the church. Such an interpretation was symbolically appropriate, for medieval exempla termed preachers the little barking dogs of the Lord. The mother of St. Dominic dreamed before her son was born that she saw a black and white dog emerge from her womb carrying a flaming torch, which set the whole world afire. Such a dream was prophetic, for her son (1170–1221) founded the Dominican order, which was to instruct both clergy and laity to fight the heretical doctrines of the Albigenses. The Dominicans were called "hounds of the Lord," and this title was reinforced not only by their task, which was to keep the flock from straying into heresies, but by the pun, *domini canes*. The saint is often portrayed in Dominican habit with a star on his forehead, a lily, a rosary, and a book, and he is accompanied by a dog. The dog alone with a torch in its mouth is also a symbol of St. Dominic. The same symbol is on the seal of the Holy Office in Portugal, denoting that it was conducted by the Dominicans.

The dog also accompanies other saints. The saint in pilgrim's garb with staff, wallet, and cockleshell, pointing to a plague sore on his leg, is probably St. Roch, the fourteenth-century patron saint of prisoners and those stricken with the plague. Anna Jameson describes numerous paintings of the life of this popular saint, including two by Rubens and Tintoretto, and observes that "in general he is accompanied by his dog." The dog which sits at the feet of a thirteenth-century woman saint in checkered habit or tugs at her hem belongs to St. Margaret of Cortona. She took the veil after a handsome youth with whom she had lived for nine years was murdered. The dog discovered the body.

There was even a dog-headed saint. St. Christopher, according to the gnostic Acts of Bartholomew, was a terrible, man-eating ogre with a dog's face. When he became a Christian and tried to tell the Roman governor about the new religion, he literally found himself in the hot seat. He was roasted in an iron chair over a slow fire and basted with boiling oil. But he survived, even when the chair melted under him, and he emerged with a face "beautiful as a new rose." Finally he was beheaded.

Some two hundred years later there was a special cult with dog-headed icons of the saint, and in medieval times representations of the dog-headed saint were made in Russia, Greece, Rumania, Germany, and elsewhere. The saint's task was to protect the faithful from sudden death, but in many of the legends he performs tasks similar to Anubis, Thoth, or Hermes. A point of confusion appears to have been reached in an early fifteenth-century drawing at Dresden, where a fashionably clad young man sports wings and the head of a hunting hound.

The dog in the figurative stag hunt requires special mention. The hart represented Christ, as in the legends of St. Eustachius and St. Hubert, or the unfortunate youth Actaeon, who was metamorphosed by Diana as a penalty for seeing her naked, or it might simply stand for the necessary object of a feast or for virtue itself. The dogs represented evil when they attacked, and virtue when they pursued. Renaissance emblem writers, however, and illustrators of the subject in tapestry and sculpture often saw the quarry as a man hunted and destroyed by his own passions. The emblem writer Whitney showed hounds attacking a stag while a huntsman looked on, with the caption *voluptas aerumnosa* (sorrowful pleasure). The stag represented Actaeon, who was killed by his own hounds:

> By which is ment, that those whoe do pursue
> Their fancies fonde, and thinges unlawful crave

64

Like brutish beastes appeare unto the viewe
And shall at lengthe, Actaeons guerdon have:
And as his houndes, soe theire affections base,
Shall them devowre, and all their deedes deface.

Translated into psychological terms, the Actaeon myth is explicit enough. Traditionally, the hunter and his dogs represent the male genitals. Actaeon's fate, when confronted with sex, is impotence. The metaphor of the hunter and his two dogs also turns up in several English and French seventeenth-century poems, the dogs waiting patiently by the side of the symbolic pond into which their master has plunged.

Other symbolic applications of the dog illustrated even further the variety of the conceptions concerning it. Horapollo regarded the animal as a judge; Valeriano, as symbol of friendship and of melancholy under Saturn. Ripa associated the dog with both fidelity and the sense of smell, and the dog appeared as an attribute of the five senses in illustrations of the Dutch and Flemish school.

More than any other animal the dog has given its name to terms not subsequently associated with the animal. Dog days, the hottest weeks in summer, are so named because of the ancient belief that the dog star, Sirius (from the Greek "hot" and "scorching"), rising with the sun, added to its heat. The dog-rose, from the Greek κυνόροδον was so called because it was supposed to cure the bite of a mad dog. Brewer and Leach cite many other terms not now in general use, including *dog's nose*, referred to by Dickens as a mixture of gin and beer.

As a derogatory epithet from ancient times, *dog* might be applied to any enemy, particularly heathen, and one cannot determine to what extent it has ceased to be used as a term of abuse or contempt. "She's a dog" to denote an ugly or unappealing woman was still current immediately after World War II, and "to have a dog in the third race" still means that one has backed a loser. On the other hand, *cur* as an opprobrious term and "a handsome dog" as a description of a good-looking philanderer are now to be found only in Victorian melodrama. Nor is the word *bitch* necessarily pejorative. Although "to bitch" means "to complain," among American college students "a bitchin' time" is a good time, and "a bitchin' dress" is an attractive one. "A bitch" no longer denotes a spiteful or promiscuous woman, but "a tease" or "someone who does not put out" in her relations with a young man. Nevertheless, an old lecher may still be called "an old dog," and in this phrase we see an ironic modification of medieval symbolism. In manuscript illustrations of the thirteenth to the fifteenth centuries, which depict a young squire courting a reluctant young lady, a dog is often present. The dog is not included as part of the domestic scene; it performs a definite function: it is either pursuing or avidly regarding a rabbit or hare. The little scene, which is often illustrated with charming vigor and realism, is symbolic of the main action: it is intended to represent the eternal pursuit by the male of the female.

Alciatus, cliv; *Ancrene Riwle* (ed. Morton), p. 288; Bartholomaeus Ang., xviii, "De aliis proprietatibus canum"; Beza, xxii; Brewer, pp. 365–68; Burchard, *PL*, cxl, col. 959; Burriss, pp. 32–42; Camerarius, lxiii; Crooke, pp. 215, 328–29; Hesiod, *Theogony*, v.312; Horapollo, i.xl; *Jacob's Well*, p. 263, xlii; Jameson, ii.38–40; Leach, *passim*; Loomis, p. 18; Lydgate, ii.814; Pliny, viii.40.61; Ripa, pp. 152–54, s.v. "Fedeltà," "Sentimenti," "Odorato"; Ryan, p. 282; Sambucus, p. 118; Tervarent, col. 95; Topsell, pp. 142–43; Valeriano, v, s.v. "Amicitia," "Saturnus"; Whitney, pp. 15, 39, 213.

Dragon

The first definition of *dragon* in the *New English Dictionary* is "a huge serpent or snake; a python." There is a difference, however: the snake existed; the dragon did not. Nevertheless the dragon aroused and awed the imagination for thousands of years, and so real did that symbol become that even Gesner, in his great *History of Animals* in 1564, put the dragon among the known fauna.

The word derives from the Greek δράκων (a snake), and many of its symbolic qualities are therefore identical with those of the snake. It was the beneficent, life-giving power, controlling storms, seas, and rivers; it was the malign force of evil and chaos. The word is connected with δέρκομαι (to see), and the dragon or snake was often credited with sharp eyesight and a watchful nature. As such it symbolized the guardian of treasure, the possessor of wisdom, and oracular vision.

In China the dragon was a symbol of power, of royalty, and of water. There were four supernatural, divinely constituted prophetic beasts called Ling: the unicorn, the phoenix, the tortoise, and the dragon, and of these the dragon was the chief. As a blue dragon, it symbolized the vital spirit of water; as a yellow dragon, the essence of divine, manifesting power; as a black dragon, it turned darkness (*yin*) into light (*yang*). It was also the symbol of the spirit of change, and as such was adopted by the Taoists, who regarded Tao as the spirit of cosmic change, the eternal growth which returned upon itself to produce new forms.

As a symbol of imperial sovereignty, the descending dragon belched forth a ball. This ball had various significances: it was thunder, a pearl, a sacred gem typifying divine essence, the force which controlled the tides, or, particularly when it appeared between two dragons, it symbolized the moon. The ancients thought of an eclipse as a dragon rising from the bowels of the earth to swallow the source of light and life.

This creature seems to bear little resemblance to Pliny's dragon, which was undoubtedly the Indian python. It appears to be based mainly on a description by Wang Fu, a philosopher of the Han Dynasty (206 B.C.–A.D. 220), who gave the dragon elephant's tusks, the head of a camel, horns of a deer, a crocodilean body with the feet of a tiger, and the claws of an eagle. But this and other conceptions of the dragon probably arose not only from a belief that such a powerful creature must be composed of the dominant parts of many animals, but also from the sight of the fossils of gigantic saurians.

The dragon was painted as a symbol of royalty on the upper garment of the Chinese emperor as far back as 2700 B.C., and in Japan it was the symbol of the mikado. Sometimes the dragon and the tiger were depicted together, the one typifying spring, heaven, and sky; the other, autumn and earth; and together they symbolized power.

Its protective qualities and also the terror which the idea of the creature inspired made it an ensign of war. In Trajan's time the dragon became the standard of the Roman cohorts, and under the later Roman emperors the purple dragon ensign was the imperial ceremonial standard. The Norsemen painted the dragon on their shields and carved its head on the prows of their ships; the dragon was one of the royal ensigns of war in Britain even before the Conquest. From Uther Pendragon, whose

The dragon being routed here is "the old serpent, called the Devil, which deceiveth the whole world" (Revelation xii.9).

67

vision of the flaming dragon in the sky betokened that he was to win a kingdom, the heraldic dragon passed to the Anglo-Saxon kings. According to the ninth-century historian Nennius and to Geoffrey of Monmouth later, the red dragon, representing the Britons, fought with the white dragon, representing the Saxons. After William the Conqueror came two more dragons, William II of England and Robert II of Normandy. The dragon was Richard I's ensign when he crusaded overseas in 1191 and was Henry III's battle standard against the Welsh in 1245. The Tudors bore the dragon as their badge, a winged, four-legged monster with a tail that ended like a blunt arrow, and of similar origin was the monster in the arms of Drake, blazoned by Tudor heralds as a wyvern. The dragon was finally restored to the ancient Britons in the twentieth century when it was incorporated in the armorial bearings of the Prince of Wales.

As an ecclesiastical symbol the dragon remained consistent. It was the Evil Spirit and his works. Included among the reptiles in the bestiaries, it had the characteristics of both a python and a crocodile. In its most frightful form it was described by St. John in Revelation xii.3:

> Behold a great red dragon, with seven heads and ten horns, and seven diadems upon his heads. His tail swept down a third of the stars from heaven, and cast them down to the earth.

Its identity was revealed when it was defeated:

> and the great dragon was thrown down, that ancient serpent, who is called the Devil and Satan, the deceiver of the whole world . . . .

The bestiaries describe how the dragon Draco killed even elephants by coiling itself around their bodies and lashing with its tail. This dragon was the Devil, whose power was not in his teeth but in his tail. Like the dragon, he drew men to him by deceit and strangled them.

What of the panther and dragon juxtaposed? At Alne Church, Yorkshire, a panther faces the head and wings of a dragon. At Newton Church, also in Yorkshire, a panther with open mouth confronts a terrible winged dragon, which has a forked tongue and a second head and tongue in its tail. In some of the illustrations in the bestiaries, the panther stands open-mouthed, charming all animals except the dragon, which either flees or cringes in fear. Here the panther signifies Christ and the dragon the Devil. The panther was believed to be able to attract all animals except the Devil by its aromatic breath. It behooved those whose souls were renewed in baptism to follow the sweetness of Christ's commands.

As more general representations of evil, two dragons appear in a sculpture of the late twelfth century at the church of Saint Pierre sous Vézelay. Avarice has a full purse slung around his neck, and two dragons eat his ears, indicating that he is deaf to the laments of the poor. By the works of the Devil is meant heresy, and Rabanus Maurus and others stress that the dragon signifies not only the Devil and his ministers but all those wicked men who persecute the church. In 1418, three years after John Huss was burned at the stake, the Emperor Sigismund instituted the knightly order of the vanquished dragon to celebrate the extermination of heresy.

Simeon Stylites cured a dragon of blindness, but most dragons were not amenable to either physical or spiritual enlightenment. Combats with dragons which were part of ancient folklore were taken over by the saints. At first, such combats symbolized the destruction of paganism; then they were incorporated into the archetypal legend in which a hero, such as St. George, delivered an entire populace from a devouring dragon.

Wretched pagan monsters tended to reappear in times of disaster. In 857, when some people took refuge in St. Peter's during a terrible storm at Cologne, a fiery dragon in the shape of a thunderbolt split the building asunder. In 1221, in England on St. Luke's day, when a great northeast wind blew down houses, trees, and church steeples, fiery dragons and evil spirits soared through the air. The custom of lighting bonfires on Midsummer Eve, according to Henry Bourne, a Newcastle curate writing in 1725, derived from ancient times when "Dragons, being incited to lust through the Heat of the Season, did frequently, as they flew through the Air, Spermatize in the Wells and Fountains."

Early Christian artists rendered the scriptural phrase "the jaws of hell" literally and showed a toothy open jaw of a dragon belching forth smoke and fire. They also believed in the ability of St. Michael to achieve the ultimate victory over evil and frequently represented him in full armor, as captain of the heavenly host, standing with his foot on the half-human, half-dragon form of Satan, whom he is about to destroy (Revelation xii.7–9).

Artists show many saints adumbrating St. Michael's achievement. Pope St. Sylvester (A.D. 335) is usually depicted with only a small dragon reassuringly chained or bound about the mouth with thread, but St. Germanus of Auxerre's dragon a century later has seven heads. St. George and St. Theodore, the early fourth-century saints, both wear armor as a defense. The first, the patron saint of England, Germany, and Venice and of soldiers and armorers, has the dragon at his feet and flourishes a standard, lance, and palm. Woman saints are also accompanied by dragons, and the bound dragon, the asperges, and the pot of holy water belong to St. Martha of Bethany, patron saint of cooks and housewives. The saint who achieves the greatest variety of postures with the dragon is St. Margaret of Antioch, who not only bursts out of a dragon but pierces, chains, and tramples on it. In a woodcut in Caxton's *Golden Legend*, St.

Margaret stands in a kind of tub scooped out on the dragon's back. The dragon lashes furiously with its tail while the saint, her face pious and serene, jabs her crucifix into its jaw.

Bourne, *see* Brand, pp. 272, 281; Loomis, p. 65; Morgan, p. 7; McCulloch, pp. 112–13; Pliny, VIII.11.11–13; Rabanus Maurus, *PL*, CXI, cols. 229–30; Réau, II.715; Whittick, pp. 176–78.

Elephant

In India from time immemorial the elephant was the symbol of divine wisdom. The gods wore its head as an emblem of intelligence. Rajahs assumed the title of "the elephant" or "lord of the elephants," and the premier prince of Hindustan or a sovereign added the further distinction, "the white elephant," or "the lord of the white elephant."

The qualities—patience, endurance, self-restraint, longevity, and strength—assigned to it prevailed throughout the Orient. The elephant was sacred to the sun, and Buddha himself was likened to a well-trained elephant.

The West learned of the elephant when Alexander the Great conquered King Porus and his tower-carrying elephants. These noble beasts, carrying on their backs castles filled with armed soldiers, captured the imagination. Alexander adopted the practices of the Indians. He dedicated to the sun the bravest of Porus' beasts, whom he called Ajax, and regarded the animal as the symbol of might and the embodiment of virtue. Minerva, goddess of wisdom, began to be represented with an elephant's skin on her head instead of the helmet, and on Seleucian coins she appeared with elephants drawing her chariot.

Because the elephant was used for triumphs, it soon became a symbol of the conqueror, and the Romans quickly learned the value of elephants in battle. Caesar even took an elephant to Britain, probably not so much for its martial as for its psychological value, surmising that its mere presence would terrify the enemy. Pliny wrote a long account of the elephant in the eighth book of his *Historia naturalis*. The crowning exploit of a gladiator's career in the days of Claudius and Nero was to be victorious against an elephant in single-handed combat. The elephant was, as it had been to the Hindus, a royal beast.

It continued as a secular symbol of triumph and power throughout the Middle Ages. The Malatesta family, the tyrants of Rimini, adopted the beast as their emblem. For generations this family committed every conceivable crime in its struggle for power, using the elephant as a symbol of force. The symbol was also appropriate in that the founder of the family, Malatesta de Verruchio, born

70

in 1212, lived to be one hundred years old. Sigismondo Malatesta had black marble elephants to support the temple of St. Francis, which he completed in 1450, and in one of its chapels, while his wife was still alive, he built a magnificent tomb for Isotta, one of his mistresses, with two elephants supporting the urn of the sarcophagus. At Cesena, the motto with two elephants over the entrance to the Biblioteca Malatestiana has reference to the oft-repeated story found in Pliny and others that the elephant destroys insects on its back by wrinkling its skin and crushing them to death: *elephas indus culices non timet* (the Indian elephant is not afraid of insects). Sometimes this device was abbreviated to *elephas non timet* (the elephant does not fear). In the same sense, the elephant was later adopted by François Regnault and his widow, Madeleine Boursette, with the motto *Sto sicut elephas* (I stand like the elephant).

The symbol persisted in practical use. Frederick II in 1237 entered Cremona in triumph followed by a chariot captured from the defeated Milanese. The chariot was drawn by Frederick's elephant and carried a wooden citadel, trumpeters, and imperial banners. A similar triumph with the same elephant was used by Richard of Cornwall for his entry into Cremona in 1241, this time with a band of musicians in the tower.

Other burdens appeared on the elephant's back and acquired additional symbolic value because of their association with the animal. Heckscher draws attention to an eleventh-century team of elephants supporting the Bishop's throne at Canosa. In a fifteenth-century manuscript of the Passion of St. Maurice, an elephant carries on its back the Doge's Palace at Venice and a pond with swans and ducks. In 1667, on the Piazza della Minerva in Rome, Bernini erected a monument for Pope Alexander VII, the meaning of which has been splendidly interpreted by Heckscher. This monument was an almost life-size marble elephant, and on its back was the symbol of divine wisdom, a small Egyptian obelisk, crowned by the insignia of the pope with the cross of Christ on top.

In the medieval church the elephant was a popular but varying symbol. In the figure of the elephant and castle, the war turret was the indestructible church supported by Mary, the elephant. A passage in "The Seven Joys of the Blessed Virgin Mary" quoted by Heckscher used the figure and described the Virgin's mystical victories over numerous animals. The same figure occurred again in a spectacle given at a banquet for Philip of Burgundy at Lille in 1473. A mechanical elephant was used, and its rider, dressed as a nun, in the name of the Holy Church, eloquently declaimed against the Turkish infidels who were threatening to destroy it.

The ancient story of the elephant's water nativity came in for a variety of interpretations. According to Pliny and others, the elephant delivered its child in an isolated

The elephant is so powerful that it can carry an army on its back.

watery spot for fear of snakes. Pseudo-Hugo St. Victor saw the baby elephant as a type of Christ, the Virgin being the elephant mother. Neckam, on the other hand, regarded the elephant as the sinner, pursued by the Devil, seeking the waters of grace.

The elephant and the snake gave rise to special symbolism. According to the ancient fable, the snake fatally stung its opponent, but the dying elephant fell on the snake and squashed it to death. In 1 Maccabees vi.43–46, Eleazar of Judah, fighting King Antiochus V on a war elephant, was crushed by the animal when he split open its belly. Here Eleazar was regarded by some exegetes as the spiritual victor, and his death was said to prefigure Christ's.

The elephant in the bestiaries could symbolize fallen humanity, the ideal Christian spouse, or Christ. According to some versions, when elephants are about to pair they go to the East, to Paradise, where man was first placed, and there the female elephant takes the fruit of the mandragora tree, renowned for its aphrodisiacal properties, and gives it to the male in order to awaken his sexual desires. In this story the elephants usually symbolize Adam and Eve eating the fruit of the Forbidden Tree. But since the elephant evidently required considerable incentive to intercourse, the fable was also used to illustrate the continent Christian who cohabited only for the purpose of begetting children.

72

The symbolism of the elephant as Christ developed from the fable of the jointless elephant, a fable which, though refuted by Aristotle, was related by Diodorus Siculus, Strabo, and others as a fact of natural history. The elephant could not bend its knees and therefore slept (as indeed it often does) in an upright position, leaning against a tree. If a hunter wished to capture it, he partly sawed through the tree; the elephant, trying to rest against the tree, crashed to the ground, and was unable to get up. According to the bestiarists, a big elephant—Hebrew Law—tried unsuccessfully to lift the fallen animal. Twelve others—the band of prophets—also tried and failed. Then came a small or insignificant elephant—Christ himself—who alone could save man from the Devil's trap. Some versions omit the happy ending: man the sinner, in the grip of pride, leans heavily on terrestrial things and is captured by the Devil. Rabanus Maurus was probably affected by this concept: he regarded the elephant as a grotesque, as a sinner debased by evil deeds.

A further example of the elephant as Christ occurs in a curious story in the popular medieval story book *Gesta Romanorum*. In order to capture an elephant, an emperor sends two beautiful virgins to sing in the forest. One carries a basin; the other, a sword. The elephant, attracted to the sound, fondles the maidens and then falls asleep in the lap of one of them. The other takes her sword and kills him. The first maiden fills her bowl with the blood. According to the signification, the emperor is God, the elephant Christ, and the two virgins are Mary and Eve.

The elephant continued to be an aristocratic symbol of prudence, intelligence, continence, and benignity in secular interpretations. In an engraving shown by Hollstein, the elephant is the mount of Pudicia, and she fights Libido who, appropriately enough, is mounted on a boar. Christian II, king of Denmark, the lover of a pretty Dutch girl called Dyveke who died under suspicious circumstances in 1517, chose the elephant as the symbol of chastity when he founded a chivalric order. In a fifteenth-century illustration of Scorpio, described by Heckscher, a man riding an elephant is said to be strong and stable. A proverbial expression did, indeed, already exist in England to the effect that virtue makes a man as strong as an elephant.

Virtue and strength were also linked with the elephant by Horapollo, whose work was widely admired in the early Renaissance. The elephant, said Horapollo, was supposed to flee from both the ram and the hog. The Egyptians therefore depicted the elephant with one or the other of these animals to symbolize a king avoiding intemperance or folly. Since the elephant's trunk was supposed to make the animal very discerning, an elephant standing by itself symbolized a powerful and perceptive man. Zoographers were delighted to confirm such traits in the examination of actual animals. Girolamo Cardano, for example, was able to observe an elephant brought from Spain to Vienna by Mary of Bohemia in 1552, and he concluded that except for its inability to speak the elephant did not appear to fall short of man.

The fable of the jointless elephant was taken by Renaissance writers such as Sambucus and Whitney to show the downfall of the great. Under the emblem *nusquam tuta fides* (trust is never sure), they showed an elephant leaning against a tree and a man with an axe:

> The Olephant so huge, and stronge to see
> No Perill fear'd: but thought a sleepe to gaine,
> But foes before had undermin'de the tree,
> And downe he falles, and so by them was slaine.

Thus, declared Whitney, may a state or a secure person fall because of fawning foes, feigned friends, pickthanks, blabs, and traitors.

The fable of the elephant and the snake was secularized by Whitney with the motto *victoria cruenta* (bloody victory), and he remarked that good captains are those who win with the least bloodshed.

The elephant today is merely an obvious symbol of clumsiness. The term *white elephant*, still used to designate something which is valuable but useless or unprofitable, requires explanation. In the East a white elephant was costly and required considerable upkeep. According to Brewer, the king of Siam made a present of a white elephant to such of his courtiers as he wished to ruin. This idea was presumably in Mark Twain's mind when he wrote the amusing short story called "The White Elephant."

Aelian, XIII.viii, XVI.xx; Aristotle, *Hist. animal.*, II.i (498a); Brewer, p. 1296; Diodorus Siculus, III.27; Druce, "The Elephant," pp. 33ff.; *Gesta Rom.* (ed. Oesterley), cxv; Heckscher, *passim*; Horapollo, II.lxxxiv, lxxxv, lxxxvi, lxxxviii; Neckam, II.225–26; Oppian, XI.xxv; Owst, p. 198; *Physiologus* (attr. to Epiphanius), pp. 13–17; Picinelli, p. 199; Pliny, VIII, 6.6–12; Pseudo-Hugo St. Victor, *PL*, CLXXVII, col. 72; Rabanus Maurus, *PL*, CIX, col. 1174; Ripa, p. 171, s.v. "Forza"; Sambucus, p. 173; Sillar and Meyler, *Elephants*, *passim*; Strabo, XVI.iv.10; Valeriano, II, s.v. "Suis viribus pollens"; Whitney, pp. 150, 195; Willet, lxxxix.

Ermine

The ermine, or white weasel, is a symbol of purity. Its meaning appears to derive from the folk belief that if the ermine is encircled with mud, it would prefer to be captured rather than to sully itself while trying to escape.

The emblem writers such as Valeriano, Camerarius, and Ripa use it as a symbol or attribute of chastity, and a similar symbolism occurs in paintings, engravings, sculpture, and tapestry.

In heraldry, Ferdinand I, king of Naples (1423–1494), took the motto *Malo mori quam foedari* (better to die than to be sullied), and showed an ermine in a circle of mud. Ann of Brittany, who married Charles VIII and Louis XII, took the ermine as her device, and so did her daughter Claude, wife of Francis I. In the seventeenth century the poet Marvell selected it as a suitable emblem for sovereignty—"whose honor, ermine-like, can never suffer / Spot or black, soil." The ermine which for centuries has decorated robes of state carries a moral implication reflecting the wearer's personal integrity.

The ermine or white weasel is, of course, a creature of the north and was not seen in ancient Greece or Rome. In the Renaissance, however, when Minerva was used to represent virtue, she was given the ermine as her attribute.

Camerarius, lxxxi; Réau, 1.104–105; Ripa, p. 90, s.v. "Continenza" and p. 420, s.v. "Pudicitia"; Tervarent, cols. 212–14; Valeriano, xiii, s.v. "De mure. Intaminata munditia"; Van Marle, ii.458.

Faun

Faunus was one of the oldest Roman deities and was worshipped as the protecting god of agriculture. When the worship of the Greek Pan was established in Italy, Faunus became identified with him and was associated with the generative principle. Horace's ode describes the popular belief about him:

> O faunus, when you catch the flying Nymphs, go kindly over my borders and sunny plains and take nothing from the young herds in my pastures. Do I not sacrifice to you every year at your appointed time, and well fill the beaker with wine for you, O companion of the goddess of love?

As the god manifested himself in various ways, the idea of a plurality of fauns arose, harmless enough in classical times, but, like satyrs, identified with demons by the Christian Church. "There are certain men of the woods [*silvestres homines*] spoken of," observes Jerome in his commentary on Isaiah xiii.22, "whom some men call a race of *Faunos ficarios*." Druce prefers to take the reading *Faunos vicarios*, "quasi-fauns," rather than "fig-tree fauns," but the associations of the fig tree make its application here most appropriate. Jerome includes fauns among the lascivious demons, the hairy creatures who are to dance in ruined Babylon.

In Chaucer's *Troilus and Criseyde* (i.465), when the young knight, Troilus, falls in love with the beautiful widow whom he has seen in the temple, we are told that desire bred no other "fownes" in him but arguments to the effect that the lady would have compassion on him. Robinson translates the word as fawns and adds, "i.e. young desires." Something of the same idea appeared to be expressed by John Galsworthy in a phrase of which he was fond. Even Soames Forsyte, when out for a walk, spotted a country girl whose attraction momentarily "roused the fawn in him." (I am indebted to Professor F. L. Utley for pointing out to me that, despite the curious spelling, the reference appears to be to *faun*, rather than to *fawn*.)

The reputation of the faun as a satyr, or even as a kind of incubus, continued, and while the disposition to regard the gods as forerunners of civilization caused Jacopo da Bergamo to include Faunus under *viri doctrina excellentes* (men eminent in learning), the emblem writers did not regard the faun with favor. Frequently it is used, as by Ripa, as the symbol of lust.

Druce, "Some Abnormal . . . ," p. 148, n. 2; Horace, iii. xviii; Ripa, p. 295, s.v. "Libidine, ò Lussuria"; F. N. Robinson, ed., *Chaucer*, p. 816; Seznec, pp. 22, 101.

Fox

An "old fox" today means what it did in the fourteenth century. When Chaucer's heroine Criseyde says to her uncle, who has arranged for her seduction: "Fox that ye ben [are]," she indicates that he has been crafty and dissimulating. In Biblical times it had the same meaning. "Go ye and tell that fox," says Christ, alluding to Herod Antipas, "Behold, I cast out devils" (Luke xiii.32).

Although the fox still retains the quality anciently attributed to it, it was always regarded as pejorative. In China the fox was a shape-shifter as well as a symbol of craftiness. It might possess the soul of a deceased mortal and was, therefore, the emblem of longevity.

In the Middle Ages the fox's symbolic role was extensive. Of all the animal figures it was the one most frequently used in art and architecture. We can still see that symbolic fox in ecclesiastical sculpture and carvings, on tiles, croziers, embroidery, and in illustrations in Gothic manuscripts.

Its popularity was due to the early importance of the fox in fable and in beast epic. Appearing in the fables of Aesop, a compiler who, according to Herodotus, lived in the sixth century before Christ, in the tales of the *Panchatantra* and other collections, the fox came to play the role of the trickster-hero similar to the coyote, the great hare, and the master rabbit in American Indian folktales. By the late twelfth century, a cycle of stories with Reynard as the hero was widely disseminated in western Europe. Like all trickster-heroes, he symbolized anarchy against order, individualism against collectivism. In France, where the beast epic was the most fully developed to satirize feudal society, the name given to the hero even ousted *goupil*, the common French word for "fox." Reynard represented the most intelligent and resourceful of the common folk pitting his wits against the barons, as represented by Ysengrim, the wolf. His victories were the triumph of astuteness over brute force.

As early as the twelfth century Jacques de Vitry, abbot of Oignes, speaking of confession without true repentance, indicated a colloquial use of the Reynard stories: "*Haec est confessio vulpis, quae solet in Francia appelari confessio Renardi*" (this is the confession of the fox which it is customary to call Reynard's confession in France). Illustrations of that confession can still be seen in many churches. Reynard, in the role of a penitent, makes his confession while carrying a fat chicken or duck in a sack on his back.

Even more common is the depiction of the fox as a preacher. In the garb of bishop with miter and crozier, of monk or friar, he is represented as preaching to gullible ducks or chickens while the unfortunate bird which will be his next meal peeps sadly over his shoulder. Some

77

The fox feigns death in order to catch birds.

representations show the fox reading to a congregation of hens and surreptitiously strangling their cock at the same time. There are also instances of two foxes: one, with poultry already in his cowl, is preaching to some birds while his cowled vulpine confederate lies in wait behind the confessional box. Similar satires on the clergy appear in the lyrics where the false fox shrives the hens and gives them absolution. That the figure was common in popular speech is suggested by its appearance in the *Towneley Mysteries*: Cain, tired of the pious warnings of his brother Abel, calls him a preaching fox.

More specific in reference and indicating currency of one of the oldest tales about the fox is the illustration of the fox lying on its back, apparently dead, while fowls peck at it. What might seem to be a reversal of fortunes is, in fact, only a ruse to trap the birds. This fox feigning death is the Devil, and it is depicted on a misericord at Chester, over the church doorway at Alne, Yorkshire, and elsewhere. The engraving in the *Physiologus* of Epiphanius shows four guineafowl flying to the attack while three other fowl peck at the hairy, prostrate form, one inspecting his open mouth, another his stomach, and the third his rear. The accompanying text points the moral:

Nec aliter diabolus cum illaqueare hominem vult, tentat ipsum, ut quam negligenter se in oratione gerat: sicque facillime irretitur.

(Just as the Devil, wishing to entrap man, tempts him so that he is careless in his speech and is thus more easily caught.)

The *Physiologus* also stated that in the Scriptures foxes symbolize heretics. Dante used the same symbolism in the *Purgatorio* to indicate the heresies which threatened the early church. Similarly, the fourteenth-century preacher John of Sheppey in his tale of the foxes and the sheep observed that the foxes were *falsi religiosi*. The foxes in Matthew viii.20, who were regarded as fortunate in having holes, were heretics according to Rabanus Maurus; more recently, the foxes running out of their holes on a misericord at Worcester Cathedral have been interpreted by Evans as types of the Devil: "Opposite this populous kennel is John the Evangelist. . . . The beholder is called upon to choose between the wily adversary and the herald of divine truth." A similar Scriptural interpretation was given in Pseudo-Hugo St. Victor's *De Bestiis*. "Stinking vixen" was also a classic epithet for heresy. Dante made use of it as a symbol for political heresy in a Latin letter to Henry VII of Luxemburg in which he castigated Florence.

The fox's outstretched tail appears to have symbolized fraud itself. A Latin commentary on a twelfth-century Spanish Apocalypse has an illustration of a fox, its tail extended, running off with a cock in its mouth. The theme is the same as Chaucer's *Nun's Priest's Tale*. According to the text: *Dum gallus canit viribus, vulpis capit fraudibus & Fraudis causa tendit cauda* (while the cock eloquently sings, the fox takes it through guile and its tail stretches out because of guile). Later, when a foxtail becomes one of the badges of the motley, the secular meaning is different: in Rabelais to fasten a foxtail on someone is to make a mockery of him.

The Renaissance emblem writers made use of various fables. Popular was Aesop's story of the fox who, unable to reach some grapes, remarked that he did not want them anyway because they were probably sour. Freitag, for example, provided the motto: *ficta eius quod habere nequit recusatio* (feigned is the refusal of that which cannot be had).

Whitney has two emblems in which the fox appears to illustrate foresight rather than traditional craftiness. In one, a boar whets his tusks on a tree while a fox watches. The moral is: be prepared for the enemy—*in pace de bello* (in peace for war). In another, a fox looks at a lion and gradually grows less afraid of him—*dura usu molliora* (hard things become softer with use). A further emblem indicates that the fox's wiles do not defend it from mischance and shows a fox caught on a floe by the breakup of ice—*nullus dolus contra casum* (no strategy against bad luck). Camerarius, however, retains the idea of foresight: he shows a fox on the river bank testing the ice, with the motto: *fide, et diffide* (trust and distrust). His moral, that caution is necessary before undertaking any enterprise, is repeated by Aldrovandi and others. Under the caption *intrepida securitas* (undaunted safety),

Camerarius also makes curious use of the belief that a pregnant fox is scarcely ever captured by dogs. Here the fox is a symbol of the man who is wise and circumspect in anticipating trouble.

Until the eighteenth century, fox-hunting was not an exclusive sport of the aristocracy, nor did the hunting treatises such as *The Master of Game* rate the fox highly as a beast of the chase. Foxes in the Middle Ages were vermin to be put down in any season not so much with dogs but with clubs, traps, or any other weapon to hand. Today, few of us have seen a fox except in a zoo, and we hear little of the pursuit by the unspeakable of the uneatable except when animal lovers in England demonstrate against the barbarity of the sport. Perhaps the last most distinctive literary use of its symbolism is in D. H. Lawrence's "The Fox." Here, to the two girls trying to run an impoverished farm, the fox preying on their fowls is untamed, predatory nature, hostile to their way of living. The young soldier who intrudes on the girls' lives is identified with the fox, and his killings are inevitable, even ritualistic. He is the embodiment of what the fox stands for: the essential ruthlessness of life.

Since the fox is no longer a common animal, it has tended to disappear in proverbial phrase. Samuel Pepys, after a convivial evening, could remark: "I drank so much wine that I was almost foxed." The expression stemmed from the earlier phrase "to flay or prick a fox," current also in France as *écorcher, piquer un renard*. It presumably referred to the fox's habit of running in circles rather than in a straight line, a characteristic which made Isidore of Seville, the Spanish encyclopedist (circa 560–636), deduce that *vulpis* (fox) came from *volupes* (twisty-foot). The fox does remain in proverbial phrase as an illustration of craftiness, but when we use the common expression "sour grapes," we no longer even think of the fox nor of the Aesopian fable in which it originated.

Aldrovandi, p. 208; Anderson, *Med. Carv.*, pp. 114, 130; Camerarius, lv, lvi; Dante, *Epist.*, VII.135–38; *Purg.*, XXXII. 118–23; Evans, p. 210; Flinn, *passim*; Freitag, p. 127; Isidore, XII.ii.29; John of Sheppey, IV.424–25; *Master of Game*, p. 213; Morgan, p. 65; Pepys' *Diary*, 23 April 1661; *Physiologus* (attr. to Epiphanius), pp. 78–79, 81; Pseudo-Hugo St. Victor, *PL*, CLXXVII, col. 59; Rabanus Maurus, *PL*, CXII, col. 1084; Rabelais, *Garg.*, 11.16; Rowland, *Blind Beasts*, pp. 53–56; *Towneley Plays*, p. 12, l. 84; Varty, *Reynard the Fox, passim*, "Reynard . . . ," pp. 347–54; de Vitry, *Serm. ad pueros et adolescentes*; Whitney, pp. 22, 153–54, 156.

Goat

"There is no beast that is more prone and given to lust than is a goate," said the Elizabethan zoologist Topsell.

That which is most strange and horrible among other beastes is ordinary among these . . . . Herodotus declares that in his time a Goat of Mendesia in Egypt, had carnal copulation with a woman in the open sight of men, and afterward was led about to be seene.

From earliest times the goat has been a symbol of libido and procreation and as such has had an important role in myth and ritual. The famous act at the Egyptian town of Mendes was, in fact, a religious rite, centering on the worship of the goat.

An attempt even seems to have been made to introduce similar devotions into Italy. When Juno's oracle was consulted regarding the prolonged barrenness of Roman wives, it answered: *Iliadas matres caper hircus inito* (let the rough goat have intercourse with the Trojan matrons). The Romans, however, interpreted the oracle to mean that a goat should be sacrificed and the skin, cut in thongs, be applied to the bare backs of the women. Fortunately, this less drastic method proved effective. *Virque pater subito, nuptaque mater erat* (men suddenly became fathers and wives mothers), Ovid recorded. This flagellation occurred at the celebrated festival of Lupercalia, and some consider that the name itself derives from *luere per caprum* (to purify by means of the goat). According to Festus, the women were purified when the priests covered them with goatskins. One of the important tasks at this festival was the caprifying of the fig, itself an emblem of the phallus, whereby the wild male fig tree was used to fertilize the cultivated female fig tree.

It was at this celebration in 44 B.C. that Mark Antony, naked and, according to Cicero, drunk, came running into the forum to offer Caesar the fatal diadem twined with laurel. Comparable caprification ceremonies in Greece and her colonies involved human sacrifice. Two scapegoats, usually a man and a woman, were selected to bear the sins of all the people. Wearing strings of figs around their necks, they were paraded at the festival and then stoned to death.

Better known is the association of the goat with the celebrations of Dionysus. Here again, along with the goat, the fig was a common symbol and was carried with the phallus in processions. The animal was sacrificed, and the choral odes sung in honor of the god were called *tragodiai*, or "goat songs." Dionysus was identified with the goat, and, as Frazer observes, "when his worshippers rent in pieces a live goat and devoured it raw, they must have believed that they were eating the body and blood of the god." Such festivals provided an escape from inhibitions. They were a group expression of repressed desires, both in the killing of the father-god and in the atonement, the release from all guilt.

The goat was at the center of these celebrations because the participants were worshipping the activity which it represented. The goat has always had a reputation for lasciviousness, one buck allegedly being sufficient for one hundred and fifty females. It is, therefore, not surprising that the goat or the goat-god with the face and legs of a goat should be taken from earliest times as a symbol of the active male principle, nor that, since one of the functions of a god was to bestow his fecundity on his worshippers, he should be represented as doing so, either directly, as at Mendes, or by means of an attribute.

In Egypt the goat was worshipped both in its caprine form and in the form of a phallus, as a symbol of the abstract generative principle for which it was commonly associated with Priapus in Greece. Diodorus Siculus remarks: "they have deified the goat . . . because of the generative member: for this animal has a great propensity for copulation." He adds that Pan and satyrs were worshipped for the same reason: "and this is why most people set up in their sacred places statues of them showing the phallus erect and resembling a goat's in nature." But despite the Mendesian rite and the delineation of the god in the form of Pan in Egypt, it is mainly in Greek, Roman, and Etruscan art that we find illustrations of the personification of the generative attribute—the male and female satyr. In medieval times these half-goat, half-human attendants of the god were to serve as a terrible warning of what a man would become if he surrendered himself to carnal desire.

The goat-god was a kind of accessory attribute to other deities, the purpose of whose existence was generation. For this reason its horns are included in the winged globe, the Egyptian symbol par excellence commemorating the victory won by Horus, representing light and virtue, over Seth, representing darkness and evil. Two uraeus snakes twist symmetrically around the disk with their heads erect on either side and sometimes wearing a crown. Behind the uraei are the outstretched wings of the sparrow hawk, and on top the undulating buck horns. The headdress of Noum, in her capacity as the humid principle, included the buck's horns, and so did Ammon's, representing, as Horapollo observed, generative force and fecundity. For the same reason the horns were also given to Phtha-Socharis, who had the head of a hawk, the symbol of domination. The member of a prolific man, Horapollo concluded, was symbolized by the goat. The term *old goat* is an ancient metaphor. Topsell quoted its use in a comedy of Plautus with reference to lecherous old men and implied that a pungent odor strengthened the analogy.

Cosmologically the goat was associated with storm clouds from which came rain and lightning; hence among the Hindus, Agni, in his celestial form, was mounted on a buck, and among the Scandinavians two bucks drew Thor's chariot across the sky. Both Zeus and Minerva bore the thunderbolt, the emblem of fecundation and nutrition as well as of destruction; the infant Zeus was suckled by a white goat, and Minerva used the goat's skin both as her buckler and her aegis.

The goat's horn, in general a symbol of generation, became the horn of plenty in its association with Amalthea, the sacred goat which suckled Zeus. When Amalthea broke this horn Zeus filled it with fruit, flowers, and grain, making it a symbol of spiritual and material wealth which the gods give men. It was particularly associated with agricultural wealth because the goat herself was a symbol of the crop-producing rain storms. For a similar reason Neptune was often represented carrying the same horn. Payne Knight, in *The Worship of Priapus*, shows a medal struck in honor of Augustus in which the goat terminates in the tail of a fish; under the animal's feet is the terrestrial globe and on its back the cornucopia, the horn of plenty. Knight interprets the figure to represent generative power fusing with the moist principle; the earth is fertilized by this union, and the horn shows the results of it.

The goat continued to be associated with phallic worship when the Romans conquered Gaul. At Nîmes in the south of France, where symbols of this worship appeared on the walls of its amphitheaters and other buildings, many small phallic amulets have been discovered. Called *fascinum*, "the male organ" (from which the word *fasci-nate* is derived), such amulets were suspended round the neck and were supposed to have supernatural qualities. These amulets, as Knight shows, were often furnished with the legs of a goat, particularly in the case of the triple phallus, where one phallus served as the body, the second occupied the usual place of the organ, and a third appeared as a tail, signifying a multiplication of the productive faculty.

With the introduction of Christianity such practices were modified. In the south of France—Provence, Languedoc, and the Lyonnais—Priapus was worshipped under the name of St. Foutin. A large wooden phallus attributed to him was set up in numerous churches. Women scraped its surface and steeped the shavings in water to make a potion against barrenness. Or they poured wine over it, left the liquid until it became sour, and then employed this *sainte vinaigre* for similar purposes. Such practices continued until the seventeenth century, with the phallus gradually being replaced by some more equivocal object such as a chair or a pillar. The church of Orcival in Auvergne contained one of these famous relics. Dulaure related that one day a country woman entered the church. Finding a burly canon there, she anxiously asked him: "Where is the pillar which makes women fruitful?" "I, ma'am," replied the canon, "am the pillar."

In Britain, priapic attributes appear to have accrued to Robin Goodfellow and to the half-man and half-goat hobgoblins of English folklore, but there are also many evidences of more formal rites of worship. In 1282 at Inverkeithing, a parish priest named John made the young girls of the town dance round a figure of the god; he himself danced before them, carrying aloft a wooden image of the male members of generation and urging them to licentious actions.

Perhaps it was demonstrations such as these which encouraged throughout Christendom the identification of the Devil with Pan and gave him the caprine horns, rough beard, cloven feet, and tail. Certainly, in the Middle Ages, the *Bock*, or "billy goat," was the Devil's favorite disguise. Heretics were accused of worshipping him in this form. A Waldensian, William Edeline, was said to have adored the Devil *non in humana effigie, sed in vilissimi hirci forma* (not in human form but in that of a most vile goat). According to an investigation at Toulouse in 1335, various women gave themselves to the Devil in the form of a gigantic goat. In the seventeenth century Sir Thomas Browne explained the symbolism:

> A conceit there is, that the devil commonly appeareth with a cloven hoof; wherein although it seem excessively ridiculous, there may be somewhat of truth; and the ground thereof at first might be his frequent ap-

pearing in the shape of a Goat, which answers to that description. This was the opinion of ancient Christians concerning the apparition of Panites, Fauns and Satyrs . . . the same is also confirmed from expositions of holy Scripture. . . .

Browne observed that the Devil, according to the confessions of witches, appeared in that shape to them in later times "and thereof a Goat is not improperly made the Hieroglyphick of the devil . . . so it might be the Emblem of sin, as it was in the sin-offering; and so likewise of wicked and sinful men." When Christ separated the sheep from the goats, concluded Browne, it meant He would separate the sons of the Lamb from the sons of the Devil.

One of the authorities whom Browne cited was Jean Bodin, a French philosopher who, though liberal-minded in some ways, denounced all who dared to disbelieve in witchcraft. In his work *Demonomanie des sorciers* he observed that the he-goat was the Devil's favorite metamorphosis because it was the symbol of lasciviousness: *Mais c'est bien chose estrange, que Satan . . . prend la figure d'un Bouc, si ce n'est pour estre une beste puante et salace.*

Since the Jews were regarded as the Devil's own, the goat was a symbol of Judaism and the Jewish God.

When Ikey came a-riding
On a billygoat
He had the Jews believing
It was their precious God,

runs a piece of doggerel which, according to Trachtenburg, arose in the late Middle Ages and was widely current. Jews were mounted on goats, often nose to tail, a posture reserved for criminals. They wore a goat's beard. They were said to stink like a goat. They even took over his horns: in 1267, the Vienna Council ordered the Jews to wear a "horned hat," and Philip III compelled the Jews of France to attach a horn-shaped figure to the usual Jewish badge.

The Biblical concept of the scapegoat supported the pejorative symbolism. Basically, the scapegoat was simply the means by which all the accumulated ills of the past year were publicly expelled. Annual expulsions of embodied ills occurred in many countries, and the vehicle might be a cow, llama, monkey, or even a human being. Among the Babylonians the scapegoat was a goat because the animal was sacred to Marduk, the Babylonian sun god. The Hebrew Jehovah, who appeared to Moses like a devouring fire on the mountaintop and included goat hair and skin among the sacred appurtenances of the temple, decreed that two goats should be chosen for the rites of the Great Atonement: one to bear away the sins of the people, the other to be consecrated. Despite the implications of this distinction, however, the goat came to be regarded entirely as a creature of ill repute rather than as a holy animal.

In ancient times Aphrodite, the goddess of love, had young bucks sacrificed to her, and she was represented by Skopas as mounted on a buck. In the Middle Ages her appurtenances became the property of Luxuria, the incarnation of lust. In a drawing by Pisanello in the Albertina in Vienna, Luxuria in the form of a slim young woman with a Medusa-like headdress reclines on a goatskin. On a misericord at Coventry Cathedral she had the goat as her mount. In the porch of the cathedral at Freiburg, among the group of vices, Voluptas, the symbol of sensual pleasure, is clad in a goatskin. A similar idea is expressed in a woodcut "imprinted by John Day dwelling over Aldergate 1569," where a woman rides on a goat and is guided by an old woman who walks with a goat's beard in one hand and a serpent-headed staff in the other. Here the goat is said to symbolize lechery; the old woman, a bawd; and the younger woman, whoredom.

The medieval encyclopedists repeated the earlier defamatory opinions of the goat. It was so lecherous, they said, that its blood was hot enough to dissolve a diamond. Its very eyes, slanting and narrow, were an indication of its lust. Moralists such as Berchorius, the bestiarists, and

The keen-sighted wild goat, pasturing in the valleys, is a symbol of Christ.

the homilists underlined the symbolism: the goat signified the incontinent.

The bestiarists made a distinction between the lascivious he-goat (*hircus*) and the mountain goat (*caper*, *caprea, dorcas*). The latter, which was reputed to be keen-sighted and to like mountains, was a symbol of Christ himself. "Behold my cousin cometh like a he-goat leaping on the mountain, crossing the little hills, and like a goat he is pastured in the valleys." The acute vision of the goat signified God's omniscience and his perception of the Devil's deceits. The wild goat (*caprea*) was said to be very selective in its feeding, moving higher and higher as it pastured, and if wounded it cured itself with a plant called dittany (*dittanus*). In this way it symbolized the good preacher who selected good thoughts from bad and who, when afflicted by sin, sought out Christ. The healing herb might be called dogma or, to use a pun, Christ himself—"*bene-ditantius.*"

It was presumably for this reason that the Count of Soriano bore the device of a wild goat with the motto: *hinc vulnus, salus et umbra* (whereby the wound, safety and protection). Such a colorful device might have been expected to appeal to his enemy Francis I, king of France, who had been brought up on the Arthurian romances and loved tournaments, masquerades, and tennis. Nevertheless, the count was felled by the royal hand at Pavia.

The national emblem of Wales is the goat, and there is an ancient Welsh folktale of a prince who followed a white goat which turned into a beautiful maiden. Such fairy tales in which one partner appears at first in the guise of an animal occur in many countries, and the animal is, of course, the indirect representation of sexual wishes. The transformation of the animal into a human represents the overcoming of resistance to sexuality: the breaking of the spell is a release from guilt feeling. In the lives of the saints a kind of reversal of the Welsh folktale occurs: Mochulleius changed a certain proud woman who lived bestially into a goat.

The emblem writers made little use of the goat. Whitney showed a goat suckling a wolf cub simply to demonstrate the folly of a man who prepared disaster for himself by nurturing in his house an enemy who would ultimately kill him. Alciatus and Valeriano, however, regarded the goat as a symbol of lechery. This symbol survives today not only in the expression "old goat," but in superstition as well; in rural parts of Austria and Bavaria the beard of a goat is still sometimes worn on the watch chain or placed in the cradle of a male infant to increase its procreative power.

Aelian, vii.xix; Alciatus, lxxii; Browne, v.xxii; Diodorus Siculus, i.88; Dulaure, ii.286, n. 1; Frazer, p. 391; Herodotus, ii.xlvi; Horapollo, i.xlviii; Isidore, xii.i.14; Katzenellenbogen, p. 61; Knight, *Priapus*, pl. vii, figs. 3, 4 and pl. x, fig. 3; McCulloch, pp. 119–20; Ovid, *Fasti*, ii; Topsell, pp. 231, 233, 243; Trachtenberg, *Devil*, pp. 44–47; Valeriano, x, s.v. "De capra. Libido"; Whitney, p. 49; Wright, *Generative Powers*, pp. 28, 32.

Griffin

The griffin is a mythical beast with a lion's body and the wings and head of an eagle. It is thus composed of the most royal of beasts and birds, who are in themselves the symbols of both dominion and destruction.

It is an ambivalent symbol. Dante, inspired perhaps by the frequent comparisons of Christ to the lion and the eagle, made the griffin the symbol of Christ and described a procession in which the griffin drew a burnished two-wheel chariot, the symbol of the church. In medieval sculpture the griffin frequently symbolized the Devil, probably on account of its fabled ability to carry off animals and people at one swoop of its talons.

The griffin was made the emblem of Scientia or Knowledge in the medieval cycle of the virtues and vices as the result of an allegorical interpretation of the statement found in Aelian and other early natural historians. The griffin, so these writers declared, had a passion for discovering and guarding gold. The same trait brought it into disrepute in the Renaissance. Batman, translating a twelfth-century encyclopedia, commented on the griffin as a symbol of the usurer, and Thomas Lodge made a similar analogy in *Catharos* in 1591.

In the next century, however, Sir Thomas Browne, after noting that the griffin was "a mixt and dubious ani-

The griffin either tears a man to pieces or carries him to its nest.

mal" and "a symbolical phansie," concluded that it was the symbol of a guardian:

> the ears implying attention, the wings, celerity of execution, the Lion-like shape, courage and audacity, the

hooked bill, reservance and tenacity. It is also an Emblem of valour and magnanimity, as being compounded of the Eagle and Lion, the noblest Animals in their kinds; and so it is appliable unto Princes, Presidents, Generals and all heroick Commanders; and so is it also borne in the Coat-Arms of many noble Families of Europe.

Aelian, IV.xxvii; *Batman uppon Bartholome*, fol. 363; Browne, III.xi; Dante, *Purg.*, XXIX.106–14; Lodge, *Works* (Hunterian Club), II.ii.38–39.

Hare

In an early fifteenth-century tapestry called "Conversation galante dans la verdure," shown by van Marle, a young lady is sitting on a bench in a meadow. She has a dog with her and she is listening to a young gentleman, who is addressing her with some ardor. Around the couple are a number of plump hares. How is the young man making out? The attitudes of the animals provide the answer. The young lady allows the dog to put its front paws on her knees and bury its snout in her lap. Nearby, a hare, although appearing to be running away, turns its face toward the dog with an amiable expression. Since the dog is the pursuing male and the hare is the symbol of woman, our conclusion is that the young man's advances are being welcomed by the lady. Although the hare has various symbolic qualities and might stand, among other things, for timidity, swiftness, blindness, madness, ill-luck, supernatural evil, treachery, and uncleanliness, its value in this illustration is unequivocal.

An old Scots song by Robert Burns indicates more frankly what the hare stands for:

> Madgie cam to my bed-stock
> To see gif I was waukin;
> I pat my han' atweesh her feet,
> An' fand her wee bit maukin [hare].
> Fal, lal, etc.

The girl with the swansdown seat who was the joy of the young bloods (including Winston) in the London West-End clubs of the last century and her modern trans-Atlantic counterpart, the callipygian bunny-girl, have the same symbolism. But it would probably surprise members of the Playboy Club to learn that the insignia which they sport on their cuff-links, garters, ties, and shirts should derive from anything as "square" as ancient mythology.

In ancient times the hare was a divine animal, worshipped almost universally for its fertility and mystically connected with the female cycle and therefore with the moon which governed it. In China, where it is often depicted on porcelain as the emblem of longevity, the hare compounded the elixir of life in the moon and was the attribute of the moon goddess Gwallen. In Egypt it was associated with Osiris in his aspect as moon god, and as the hieroglyph meaning "to be" the animal was linked with many deities. In India, Buddha took the form of a hare and voluntarily sacrificed himself; in Africa it was part of the creation myth.

The hare's values are clearly stated in the spring rituals enacted in many countries, particularly in ancient Greece and Rome. As an animal which mated openly and indiscriminately every month during the whole summer, it was libido and therefore sacred to Aphrodite. It was also *fecundatrix*, popularly believed to conceive even while still pregnant, and as such it was sacred to Diana in her aspect as Lucina, the moon goddess who presided at childbirth. In illustrations of the great spring festival the hare often accompanied the Bacchic panther, and on Roman tombs it ate the grapes of these orgies, the symbol of the male fruit, signifying the promise of rebirth.

Totemistic rituals always involved the sacrificing and eating of the animal at the major festivals so that its strength might pass into the celebrants. The strength of the hare became characterized as an aphrodisiac. Pliny refers to the vulgar superstition that the eater of a hare acquires sexual attractiveness for nine days. From such rituals came the observances associated with the Easter

The hare is a swift and timid beast.

myth, with Christ as a surrogate for the hare, and with the hare still being eaten both as a Eucharist and as a confection. The hare is, indeed, particularly suitable as a symbol of voluntary sacrifice: the death wish is often attributed to it, and even today farmers declare that the animal remains on its form in a burning field until its fur blazes.

The Easter symbols of fecundity, of life itself, the hare and the egg, are strikingly illustrated in a work published at Antwerp early in the seventeenth century by Richard Verstegan, *A Restitution of Decayed Intelligence: in Antiquities*. Here in chapter three, headed "Of the ancient manner of lyving of our Saxon ancestors: of the Idolles they adored whyle they were pagans," the hare appears in the vestigial deified form as a Saxon hare-goddess, wearing a headdress representing the form and shoulders of a hare. She clasps a circle to her belly, a circle which is the moon by which life is made fertile and which suggests the egg, the fruit itself. This goddess, whose worship among the ancient Britons was often deplored by early Christians, is none other than Diana and her hare, the same who became the goddess of witches and was denounced in the collection of decrees made by Abbot Regino of Prüm.

In addition to the hare's lunar association, the peculiarities of its vision enhanced its reputation as a magic animal. On the one hand, the hare was supposed to have poor sight, and it did, in fact, give its name to a pathological eye condition called λἄγωφθαλμἱα, *lagophthalmia*; on the other hand, the hare was believed to sleep like the moon, ever on the watch, with its eyes open. This latter belief Horapollo even attributed to the Egyptians, remarking that the animal symbolized an opening (ἄνοιξις) because of it. That the hare was regarded as intuitive and occult was probably the result of such beliefs. Certainly the animal was widely used for purposes of divination and was credited with a dramatic role in an incident in early British history. According to Dio in his *Roman History*, Boadicea, the British warrior queen, let a hare escape from the folds of her dress after she had addressed her warriors, and "since the animal ran on what people regarded to be an auspicious side, the whole multitude roared with delight."

A Greek coin dating from about 410 B.C. in the British Museum shows two eagles feeding upon a hare. Here we have two kinds of prophetic animals, and the scene is that which is described by the chorus in Aeschylus' *Agamemnon*, where it was taken as an omen. Calchas, the soothsayer, interpreted the two eagles as signifying the Greek princes Agamemnon and Menelaus. They were represented as destroying not only the living Trojans but, because the hare was said to be pregnant, the Trojan generations yet unborn. That the hare was also a symbol of desire, the ostensible reason for the conflict, gives the portent a further dimension.

As a prophetic animal, the hare presaged misfortune, for its association with the moon caused it to be identified with change, with fickleness, with the mischief exemplified in its role as a great trickster god in Africa and North America. It was a bewitched animal and therefore the incarnation of a witch. For this reason hare-witches were burned during the May Day rites; to meet a hare was thought to be unlucky, and the doughty fishermen of Fifeshire are said to quail even at the sight of a dead one. "Summe bestes," declared a fourteenth-century travel book, *Mandeville's Travels*, "han gode meetynge, that is to seye for to meete with him first at morwe, and summe bestes wykkyde meetynge." The hare was in the last category: among the reliefs in the south porch of the cathedral of Chartres is one of a warrior dropping his sword and fleeing from a hare in terror.

Even in this respect its evil reputation was probably partly due to its sexual characteristics, for the hare was thought to be abnormal. "At one time he is male, at another female," remarked the huntsman Twici, early in the fourteenth century, and he was merely voicing a superstition which, though not found in Aristotle, was given currency by Pliny and Aelian, Bartholomaeus Anglicus, and others, as well as by writers of hunting treatises who might have been expected to know better. Sir Thomas Browne in the seventeenth century refuted the fallacy and, in speculating on the reason for it, concluded that

> men observing both sexes to urine backwards . . .
> might conceive there was a foeminine part in both;
> wherein they are deceived by the ignorance of the just
> and proper site of the Pizzel, or part designed unto the
> Excretion of urine; which in the Hare holds not the
> common position, but is aversly seated, and in its dis-
> tention enclines unto the Coccix or Scut. Now from
> the nature of this position, there ensueth a necessity of
> Retrocopulation, which also promoteth the conceit: for
> some observing them to couple without ascension, have
> not been able to judge of male or female, or to de-
> termine the proper sex in either.

But whatever the reason, the hare was commonly regarded as a kind of hermaphrodite, and in Wales during the eleventh century the Gwentian code declared it to be incapable of legal evaluation because of its sexual variations.

The animal was also held to be able to conceive without a male and, according to some medieval encyclopedists, was even able to give birth without losing virginity. As such it was, of course, a fitting symbol for chastity and for the Virgin birth—and was sometimes so used by medieval carvers. One might note that the Virgin Queen, Elizabeth I, was called a hare—usually, however, by her enemies.

The symbolism of the hare, whether religious or secular, was almost always pejorative. Exegetical writers declared the hare signifies incontinence; it belonged to the lascivious hunt of Venus, the hunt of lust, rather than to the virtuous hunt. In a vigorous Romanesque sculpture at the twelfth-century Collegiate Church in Königslutter, Lower Saxony, two hares with wide, glaring eyes and gaping mouths prance over a prostrate man whose feet are bound. Like the demons' heads on the apse below them, they appear to symbolize evil. To the bestiarist the double sex of the creature—*aliquando masculus sit, aliquando femina* (sometimes it may be masculine, sometimes feminine)—made the hare a type of the double-minded man. The hare which had once attended Aphrodite on Greek vases, or had been exchanged as a love gage by Greek youths, or had watched the sexual encounters of Poseidon and Amymone, of Nessos and Deianeira, or had merely stood between the legs of the phallic horse, became the attribute of Lust. In the Albertina at Vienna, Vitorre Pisano's young woman has a startling muscular emaciation, high breasts, long limbs, and a fashionable, snake-like wig. But the hare crouching at her feet reveals that, close as she might come to the standards of a model for *Vogue*, she is simply Luxuria, the symbol of sensual delight. According to popular legend, Aristotle, the venerable Greek savant, became so besotted with an attractive woman that he agreed to become her palfrey and let her ride him. A bas-relief underneath a console on the façade of the cathedral church of Saint-Jeans at Lyons dating from the fifteenth century depicts the philosopher in his humiliating position. Behind him lurks the hare, the symbol of libidinousness.

Jamieson's *Scottish Dictionary* states that the hare in Roxburgh and Aberdeen has the meaning of *bawd*, a word which in medieval times could mean "harlot" as well as "procurer" or "rogue." The hare's sexual significance was, in fact, enhanced by the opportunities which the word offered for verbal play, for the Middle English word for harlot was *hore*. The Monk in Chaucer's *Prologue* to *The Canterbury Tales* seems unsuited for life in the cloister. He is a rebel, a *bon viveur*, with a passion for hunting. The terms whereby Chaucer describes the Monk's interests suggest that he enjoyed two kinds of

venerie and that, with a reckless disregard of the cost, he hunted not only the first beast of the forest but the animal sacred to Venus:

> Grehoundes he hadde as swift as fowel in flight.
> Of prikyng and of huntyng for the hare
> Was al his lust, for no cost wolde he spare.
> (191–92)

By this time, too, the rabbit, as well as the hare, was being used for a similar significance, again with etymological assistance. The Latin *cunnus*, "the pudenda," developed into the old French *con* which, with the addition of the diminutive, became *conon*, while the Latin word for rabbit, *cunniculus*, became *conil* or *connil*, then *conin*. The English *cony* or *coney* evolved from the French. Rabbits were, however, unknown in classical lands before the first century B.C. and were not introduced into Britain until the thirteenth century. In the Middle Ages sharp distinctions were made between the rabbit and the hare, not only in hunting treatises and cookery books but also in art, where the rabbit was usually drawn smaller and with a burrow. The hare was, of course, the first beast of the chase while the rabbit was merely vermin to be taken with nets or ferrets or shot at with a bow. The hare and the rabbit shared, however, the same sexual symbolism.

But it is the hare which remained synonymous with

evil: a thirteenth-century poem on the *Names of a Hare* draws on a long popular tradition to give seventy-seven deprecatory terms for a hare, and most of these are to be found elsewhere. It was a symbol of cowardice; a satirical poem speaks scoffingly of those who were lions in the hall but hares in the fields. The emblem writers used the same figure of the hare and the lion when they depicted Achilles and his companions desecrating the dead body of Hector. The accompanying engraving usually shows hares biting a dead lion, and Claude Mignault, in his note to Alciatus, quoted an epigram which Hector was supposed to have uttered: "Now after my death ye pierce my body; the very hares are bold to insult a dead lion." Alciatus, Whitney, and others pointed out a contemporary moral: the sin of speaking ill of the dead; the motto was *Cum laruis non luctandum* (we must not struggle with phantoms).

The hare was also a symbol of filth, an idea which probably derived from the popular view of the hare's excretory habits which, according to the hunting treatises *The Master of Game* and *The Book of St. Albans*, were excessive and distinctive. The Middle English poem on the *Names of a Hare* calls the hare *soillart*, "a filthy beast"; a comparable Welsh poem, "Ysgyfarnog," terms it *budrog*.

The idea of the hare's poor sight is still retained today in the Welsh *ygibddall* (the purblind one), but in earlier times this physical defect appears to have found compen-

sation in the animal's ability to hear the slightest sound. Plutarch declared that the hare's use as an Egyptian hieroglyph symbolized its acute hearing, and the same implication is made in proverbial expressions "as a blind man starts a hare" and "as a cripple starts a hare," the last of which is illustrated in an initial on the first folio of the Bury Bible. The idea that a peculiar and unwitting noise would set off a hare presumably accounts for a remark of unusual levity in the *Paston Letters*, the correspondence of a prosperous Norfolk family dourly concerned with property and status: "Raff Blaundrehasset wer a name to styrt an hare."

As we have already observed, the most popular symbolism associated with both the hare and the rabbit is now reserved for the latter. Nevertheless, the peculiar zeal associated with the hare's uninhibited mating is still reflected in the expression "as mad as a March hare."

Aelian, XIII.xii; Alciatus, cliii; Bartholomaeus Ang., XVIII, "de lepore"; Browne, III.xvii; Burns, *Merry Muses*, p. 191; Busch and Lohse, pl. 49; Dio, *Rom. Hist.*, LXII.6; Hassell, pp. 81–84; Horapollo, I.xxvi; Layard, *passim*; *Mandeville's Travels*, p. 110; van Marle, 1.462, fig. 458; *Master of Game*, p. 14; Mignault, *see* Green, p. 304; Owen, 1.735; *Paston Letters*, III, no. 721; Petti, pp. 79, 84; Pliny, VIII.55. 81; Ross, *passim*; Twici, pp. 44, 47, 51–53; Verstegan, pp. 45, 69–70, 155, 158; Whitney, p. 127.

Hart

In Christian art and architecture the hart is one of the earliest and most frequent animal symbols. In Hildegard of Bingen's *Liber Scivias*, circa 1175, the allegorized virtue Constantia has two windows in her breast to signify the mirror of faith, while above them a leaping stag symbolizes heavenly longing. The same symbolism, but with the animal in a different position, occurs in decorations of fourth-century baptisteries where, for the sake of symmetry, stags often appear in pairs to drink from the waters of Paradise. In a ninth-century mosaic of the Church of St. Praxede in Rome, four stags, possibly representing the four apostles, surround a lamb which is standing on a hill. A popular decoration for the eucharistic chalice was the cross or tree of life flanked by two harts panting to quench their thirst in the waters of life. In a thirteenth-century mosaic of the Church of St. Giovanni Laterano in Rome, the four rivers of Paradise flow from a mountain on which the cross stands, and stags and sheep, emblems of faithful Christians, drink from them.

Sometimes, instead of being an allegory of longing in the good sense, the deer simply implies lack of restraint. In the macaronic poem "Holy mother, mother mild, mater salutaris," the poet says that his thoughts were wild, "like any roe." A similar idea of undisciplined vigor occurs in the simile which Wordsworth used as he looked back at his earlier appreciation of nature in the Wye country. In "Lines Composed above Tintern Abbey," he wrote:

> . . . like a roe
> I bounded o'er the mountains, by the sides
> Of the deep rivers, and the lonely streams,
> Wherever nature led.
>
> (67–70)

The ancient belief, recorded by Pliny and Aelian, that the deer sniffed snakes from their holes after spurting water on them became a motif to denote Christ or the Christian fighting evil. According to one version of the fable, the deer subsequently trampled the snake to death, thereby symbolizing Christ trampling on the Devil. Another version maintained that the deer was affected by the poison of the snakes and had to run to water to quench its raging thirst. "Men, too, are deceived by the wiles of the serpent," declared Theobaldus, "and we run to Christ, our living water." The fable also included the idea that the stag was able to renew its youth—and was so cited in one of Martial's epigrams.

The cry of the Psalmist, "As the hart panteth after the waterbrooks, so panteth my soul after thee, O God" (xlii.1), reinforces the equation of the hart to the contrite man seeking the waters of baptism. The symbolism is explicitly stated not only in some of the bestiaries but in the hunting treatise *Livres du roy Modus et de la royne Ratio*, in which the hart's horns are said to be the commandments whereby he is equipped to withstand the World, the Flesh, and the Devil. The symbolism, as Picot has shown, was popular in the Middle Ages and the Renaissance in tapestries and miniatures, in which the stag hunt was portrayed as an allegory of human life. This symbolism continued to exist side by side with another, expressed by Bede and also by the bestiaries, which equated the hart with Christ.

In Elizabethan times the Biblical symbolism was used to support the fable as a fact of natural history. According to Topsell:

> Pliny saith, that when the Hart is olde, and perceiveth that his strength decayeth, his haire change, and his horns drye above custome, that then for the reneweing of his strength, he first devoureth a Serpent, and afterward runneth to some Fountaine of water and there drinketh, which causeth an alteration in the whole body: both changing haire and horne: and the Writer of the Glosse upon the 42. Psalme, which beginneth, Like the Hart desireth the Water springes so longeth my soule after God: confirmeth this opinion.

More recently, however, the symbolism has been associated with the Greek mysteries. Lanoe-Villène has suggested that the fable of the hart and the snake derived

The stag is the enemy of the snake.

from rivalry between ancient Greek cults and that the deaths of Actaeon and Pentheus were both ritualistic murders associated with the Dionysian and Delphic mysteries; the stag was a symbol of the anchorite or the celibate and was therefore an enemy of the Python, the phallic symbol of the Delphic rites; Actaeon, a Delphic priest, discovered the mysteries of Diana, took refuge among the Dionysian Anchorites (changed into a stag), but was detected and killed; Pentheus was slain in revenge for trying to discover the Dionysian mysteries.

95

As a symbol of the supernatural or the marvelous, the hart has a long history. The prophetic powers of the hind are mentioned by Pliny in connection with Quintus Sertorius, who shortly before the Christian era conquered and ruled the Spanish tribes with the aid of a hind. Plutarch has a more sceptical account. He tells how a countryman presented Quintus with the hind:

> He received this present like the rest, and at first took no extraordinary notice of it. But in time it became so tractable and fond of him, that it would come when he called, follow him wherever he went, and learned to bear the hurry and tumult of the camp. Little by little he brought the people to believe that there was something sacred and mysterious in the affair; giving it out that the fawn was a gift from Diana, and that it discovered to him many important secrets. For he knew that natural power of superstition over the minds of barbarians. In the pursuance of his scheme, when the enemy was making a private irruption into the country under his command, or persuading some city to revolt, he pretended the fawn had appeared to him in a dream, and warned him to have his forces ready. And if he had intelligence of some victory gained by his officers, he used to conceal the messenger, and produce the fawn crowned with flowers for its good tidings, bidding the people rejoice and sacrifice to the gods, on account of some news they would soon hear.

The Druids used the white hart in their mysteries as a symbol of the anchorite and of prophecy. Sertorius' hind was also white. Both hart and hind persisted in popular tradition as magical symbols. In Celtic legend the hart might be a visitor from the fairy world and if the hunter slew him he fell under an "illusion." Generally speaking, the slaying of a deer was the way to secure a vision or some magical happening. The famous dream of Paris in the medievalized story of Troy occurs under such circumstances; in the fifteenth-century poem "The Weddynge of Sir Gawen and Dame Ragnell," when King Arthur shoots a great hart with his bow, a strange knight suddenly appears and swears to have his life. A vision might also occur prior to the meeting with the deer. St. Berachus was told in a vision that he should load his baggage upon a deer and follow it. He did so, and at a site divinely predetermined the creature stopped and the saint built his church. Many saints survived the rigors of forest life because of help given by deer. When St. Giles was living as a hermit in a forest cave in France, he was fed by a hind who gave him her milk. One day the king of the Goths went hunting in the same forest; he pursued the hind and followed it to the hermit's cave, where she sought refuge. When the king discovered St. Giles, he treated him with great reverence, built a monastery on the spot, and made the saint the first abbot.

Other saints were miraculously converted in the middle of a hart hunt. Such was the experience of St. Hubert; hunting in the forest of Ardennes during Holy Week, he encountered a milk-white stag bearing a crucifix between his horns. This stag with the crucifix was, said Anna Jameson, one of the ancient symbols to express piety or religious aspiration in a general sense or "the conversion of some reckless lover of the chase, who, like the Wild Huntsman of the ballad, had pursued his sport in defiance of the sacred ordinances and the claims of humanity." The hart might turn out to be a perplexing quarry, initiating a difficult quest. In Malory's *Morte d'Arthur*, the pursuit of the hart marked the beginning of the mysteries associated with the quest of the Holy Grail. According to Malory, King Arthur was hunting in the forest when he saw a great hart:

> This hart will I chase, said King Arthur, and so spurred the horse and rode after long, and so by fine force he was like to have smitten the hart; whereas the King had chased the hart so long, that his horse lost his breath, and fell down dead; then a yeoman fetched the King another horse. So the King saw the hart embushed, and his horse dead: he set him down by a fountain, and there he fell in great thoughts . . . .

In ballads, the white hind often symbolizes the soul of a dead or an other-world mistress. In *Leesome Brand*,

The hart keeps its young hidden in a dense wood and is always watchful.

an eleven-year-old girl is brought to the "grief and pain of child-bearing" in a forest. She makes a strange request to her lover:

> "Ye'll take your arrow and your bow,
> And ye will hunt the deer and roe.

"Be sure ye touch not the white hynde,
For she is o' the woman kind."

A similar request is made to the brother-lover in *Sheath and Knife*, and the outcome is the same as in *Leesome Brand*. After losing himself in the pleasures of the hunt, the lover finally hastens to the greenwood tree only to find his young mistress and her infant son lying there, dead.

In the Breton song *Le Seigneur Nann et la Fee*, an analogue of *Clerk Colvill*, a fairy in the shape of a "fair white doe" insists that a young man marry her or suffer dire consequences. In *The Three Ravens* a fallow doe is the metamorphosed mistress: while the ravens wait to breakfast on a slain knight,

> Downe there comes a fallow doe,
> As great with yong as she might goe.
>
> She lift up his bloudy hed,
> And kist his wounds that were so red.
>
> She got him up upon her backe,
> And carried him to earthen lake.
>
> She buried him before the prime,
> She was dead herselfe ere even-song time.

As a symbol of grief or solitary death, the stricken deer came in for special treatment long before the unhappy poet Cowper used it autobiographically in *The Task*. The image is based on natural history: the wounded stag, implacably pursued by the hunter, tries every artifice, according to Oliver Goldsmith:

> Sometimes he will send forth some little deer in his stead, in the meantime lying close himself that the hounds may overshoot him. He will break into one thicket after another, to find deer, rousing them, gathering them together, and endeavouring to put them upon the tracks he has made. His old companions, however, with a true spirit of ingratitude, now all forsake and shun him with the most watchful industry, leaving the unhappy creature to take his fate by himself.

Usually the stricken deer denoted unhappy love. An early example occurs in the ninth century, in a song cited by Curtius, in which a Veronese clerk laments for a boy whom a rival has taken from him. "I for my fawn, like a stricken deer, sorrow." In Gabriel Symeoni and Paradin the wounded stag appears with a branch of dittany in its mouth. The herb is supposed to cure all injuries, but, say the emblem writers, there is no remedy for the wounds of love.

In heraldry and political allegory, it is the white hart or hind that is conspicuous. The white hart was the favorite badge of Richard II. The king is supposed to have inherited it from his mother Joan, "the fair maid of Kent." For this reason it appears conspicuously in the molding under the windows in Westminster Hall. According to Boutell, the hart lodged (in repose) occurs eighty-three times in Westminster Hall, and no representation is the exact counterpart of any other. In 1397, when he was preparing to meet a difficult Parliament, Richard II summoned all his lords, squires, and knights to ride with him to Westminster wearing the livery of the hart.

In *Richard the Redeles*, the fable of the hart and the viper is used to criticize Richard II and his followers. It is natural, says the poet, for the hart to attack the adder but not the colt, the horse, the swan, or the bear—the symbols for Thomas Fitz-Alan, the earl of Arundel, the duke of Gloucester, and the earl of Warwick. In Dryden's poem "The Hind and the Panther," the milk-white hind symbolizes the Roman Catholic Church—white because infallible:

> A Milk white *Hind*, immortal and unchang'd,
> Fed on the lawns and in the forest rang'd;
> Without unspotted, innocent within,
> She fear'd no danger, for she knew no sin.
> (1–4)

The panther, full of spots of error, is the Church of England.

The emblem writers tended to find a harsh lesson in the deer. According to Thynne, in 1600 a stag "with grynding teeth feedes on the ground," not hearing dogs or hunters. In the same way a man "full fraught with worldlie toyes" is unable to hear "the gladsome voice of heavens delight" (Emblem 55). To medieval theologians, the hunt of Diana, accompanied by hounds and deer, had represented the virtuous hunt, the pursuit of heavenly virtue. In Renaissance tapestries and miniatures the quarry frequently symbolized Everyman pursued by all the experiences of life. When secularized by Thynne, the same hunt became virtuous industry (Emblem 6). His idea was the same as that which prompted cold baths and cross-country runs in the English Public School: exercise, said Thynne, quenches lechery.

The myth of Actaeon, already briefly referred to, evoked even grimmer reflections. Actaeon was the Greek youth who peeked between the bushes and caught sight of Diana bathing naked in a pool. The irate goddess punished him for the sacrilege by turning him into a stag. His own dogs, failing to recognize him, tore him to pieces. "Indulge in hunting and sports and you pay," said Sambucus and Whitney. Pleasure is purchased by anguish. An engraving of a man with the head of a stag and with dogs attacking him illustrated the moral. Other emblemists sometimes included a tiny drawing of Diana and her nymphs busy with their toilet. Alciatus concentrated on the dogs, seeing them as murderers of the innocent: "You think yourself hospitable but you are harboring assassins and will be a new Actaeon." Aneau regarded the dogs as parasites: the wretched master who fed them became a slave bearing horns—a new Actaeon. In D'Urfey's seventeenth-century collection, a poem called "The Wife-Hater," which deals with the miseries of matrimony, uses Actaeon as a symbol of the cuckold:

> And rather than her Pride give o'er
> She'll turn perhaps an honour'd Whore,
> And thou'lt Actaeon'd be:
> Whilst like Actaeon, thou may'st weep,
> To think thou forced art to keep,
> All such as devour thee.

Modern psychology has given the Actaeon myth a further meaning: it depicts a youth, confronted with sex for the first time, shocked into impotence.

Two fables were cited by Horapollo as having a pejorative symbolism and may have affected Renaissance concepts. One, a curious inversion of another fable already mentioned, asserted that the stag fled at the sight of a viper, and for this reason the stag symbolized to the Egyptians a man who was quick but imprudent. The other, stemming from Aristotle and other natural historians, maintained that the stag was so entranced by the music of the pipes that it remained transfixed and could easily be captured by hunters. This stag, said Horapollo, symbolized a man deceived by flattery. Similarly Ripa, the Renaissance emblem writer, made use of the music-loving stag. In *Adulatione*, he pictured a woman playing the flute, with a hart sleeping at her feet. A beehive is also attributed to Adulatione, because bees are an emblem of flattery, carrying honey in their mouths and a secret sting.

Because it annually renewed its horns, the stag could renew its youth, according to ancient belief. In Japan, Djiou-Ro-Djin, who presided over longevity, was for this reason also sometimes represented by a hart, and in the Western world the hart was taken as the symbol of a long life. Often quoted was Pliny's story that Alexander put gold necklaces on some stags; some one hundred years later the necklaces were still there, covered up by the hide in great folds of fat. In the seventeenth century, however, Sir Thomas Browne in *Vulgar Errors* denied that the animal lived to extreme age: longevity was impossible because of the animal's "immoderate salacity, and almost unparallel'd excess of venery, which every September may be observed in this animal." Coition, declared the Norwich physician, was the enemy of long life:

> For though we consent not with that Philosopher who
> thinks that a spermatical emission unto the weight
> of one drachm, is aequivalent unto the effusion of sixty
> ounces of bloud; yet considering the exolution and
> languor ensuing that act in some, the extenuation and

marcour in others, and the visible acceleration it maketh of age in most: we cannot but think it much abridgeth our days . . . they live longest in life that exercise it not at all.

Sir Thomas Browne also refuted the popular opinion that "the males thereof do yearly lose their pizzel . . . . Experience will contradict us: for Deer which either die or are killed at that time, or any other are always found to have that part entire."

The alleged licentiousness of the stag presumably accounts for its symbolism in the strange Devonshire custom known as "skimiting riding," which took place as late as 1822. To show their disapproval of sexual license of someone in the community, villagers would gather to take part in a ritual act. After selecting one of themselves to play the part of the hunted stag, they set off on horseback in hunting garb to track him down. They would "kill" the quarry close to the house of the offending person. The same custom was once observed in India, but the quarry in this instance was the offender, and when he was caught he was mutilated.

We have seen that for the cenobite Dionysian priests in ancient Greece and for the Druids the hart was the symbol of the holy man who withdrew from normal society. Today a vestige of the idea may linger in that the word *stag* is applied to an exclusively male gathering. On the other hand, in French argot, *cerf*—because of its horns —denotes a cuckold.

Aelian, xi.9; Alciatus, lii; Aneau, fol. 41; Audsley, p. 128; Bede, *PL*, xcii, cols. 702–703; Browne, iii.ix; Boutell, p. 81; Curtius, p. 114; Drake, 217–18; Goldsmith, 1.325; Hildegard, *see* Katzenellenbogen, p. 44, n. 1; Horapollo, ii.xxi, lxxvii, xci; Hulme, p. 176; Jameson, ii.363–65; Krappe, "Guiding Animals," p. 238; Lanoe-Villène, iii.72–75; *Livres du roy*, 1.140–41; Loomis, p. 61; Martial, xii; Paradin, *see* Green, p. 399; Philippe de Thaon, *Best.*, p. 86; Picot, pp. 57–67; Pliny, viii.32.50; Plutarch, *Lives*, Sertorius, xi; Ripa, pp. 6–7, s.v. "Adulatione"; *Roman de Troie*, i, ll. 3860–76; Sambucus, p. 118; Symeoni, *see* Green, p. 398; Thynne, pp. 8–9, 42; Theobaldus, pp. 201–209; Topsell, p. 127; "Wald. Phys.," p. 409; Whitney, p. 15; Wimberly, pp. 51–54; Woodruff, p. 250.

Hedgehog

Those amusing medieval illustrations of little creatures bowling along with apples or grapes stuck to their quills are intended to instruct us. According to Pliny and other early natural historians, hedgehogs fixed apples and other fallen fruit to their spines by rolling on them so that they

The hedgehog carries fruit to its young.

could carry such items away to hollow trees and store them. The Christian fathers drew a moral to the tale. The hedgehog, says the accompanying text in the medieval bestiaries, is the Devil: man should care for his vineyard and for his spiritual fruits lest the Devil carry them off.

Although the hedgehog's ability to impale fruit has been discounted, Maurice Burton, the natural historian, states that he has seen a hedgehog stick apples on its spines and carry them off. In the Renaissance the hedge-hog's reputed skill made it a symbol either of avarice or of foresight and providence. It was also an attribute of a sense of touch, representing roughness in contrast to the softness of ermine.

Aelian, III.x; Burton, pp. 92–97; Guillim, p. 152; McCulloch, pp. 124–25; Philippe de Thaon, *Best.*, p. 105; Pliny, VIII.37.56; Tervarent, cols. 211–12.

Hippopotamus

The Egyptians represented the evil god Typhon by a hippopotamus, and the animal was also regarded as a symbol of impudence and impiety. Like Oedipus, it was supposed to kill its father and mate with its mother. The two claws of a hippopotamus turned downward, declared Horapollo, symbolized an unjust and ungrateful man.

Horapollo's statements on the Egyptians and their symbols were repeated in the Renaissance, and the hippopotamus acquired additional pejorative significance. The hippopotamus, says Aldrovandi, is ferocious to its own kind but less bold to men; similarly, the Devil is powerless against the righteous. The animal is also a symbol of greedy men who despoil the poor but do not dare to touch the powerful and rich.

Aldrovandi, p. 191; Horapollo, 1.lvi; Knight, *Symbolical Lang.*, p. 74; Plutarch, *De Iside* 50; Tervarent, col. 214.

Horse

Until recently, Norwegian peasants would preserve a horse's penis as a specially treasured heirloom. Surprising as it may seem, they were simply paying tribute to the aspect of the horse which has captivated human imagination in all ages, and it is this aspect which accounts for the horse's dominant role in myth, legend, superstition, and in anxiety dreams. For the horse is a symbol of virility. In ancient times, with its glistening body, swift movement, and tossing mane, it was a god or the fiery steed of the god of sun or sea or wind. Today it retains its significance as a phallic symbol.

The ancient mother goddess of the Britons was a horse goddess—Epona, or mare-headed Demeter. Her cult was widely diffused in northwest Europe in Iron Age times and spread even wider under the Roman empire. Juvenal in his eighth satire referred to her altars, and Giraldus Cambrensis showed that relics of the cult survived in Ireland until the twelfth century. Hengist and Horsa, the famous twin heroes of the Anglo-Saxon migration, bore names meaning "horse" as indications of their god-like status. Even in sixteenth-century England the fact that the horse had been widely worshipped was still known, and Topsell in his *Historie of Foure-Footed Beasts* described equine rites associated with Celts, Romans, Persians, Indians, and others. Soho restauranteurs in wartime London were, therefore, flouting a centuries-old taboo when they surreptitiously served up horseflesh in the guise of beef steak. No one was ever allowed to eat a sacred animal as an ordinary item of diet. The church, naturally antagonistic to pagan sacrificial feasts, enforced the taboo, and witches were burned for not observing it. But if desperate wartime cooks managed to overcome the exigencies of meat rationing, they usually knew better than to disclose their sacrilege and arouse prejudices that might have been the unconscious survival of ancient beliefs.

The phallicism of the horse has endowed various parts of the animal with typical supernatural qualities. The leg and foot symbolize in folklore the male generative organ, and the curved shoe the female organ. The hoof was therefore well suited to symbolize the reproductive powers of both male and female, and it appeared in numerous legends and folktales as a life-creating symbol. Striking infertile ground, the foot caused luxurious streams to gush forth; on other occasions ambrosia (semen) burst forth from the foot itself. Hippocrene (the Horse's Well), the famous sacred spring of the Muses on Mount Helicon in Boeotia, was horseshoe shaped; it was created when it was

103

Pegasus, symbol of the art of poetry, whose hoof produced the inspiring fountain Hippocrene, soars over the nine Muses on Mt. Helicon.

struck by the hoof of the horse Pegasus, whose name means "springs of water." In a pejorative sense, the life-giving foot became the property of the medieval Devil and of all those evil creatures whose natures were predominantly libidinous—of heretical witches, of incubi and succubi who visited men and women at night in their beds and forced them to have intercourse.

The head with its glorious mane and upstanding ears was the quintessence of the phallic animal. Its significance can be seen in the hobbyhorse, the horse's head on a pole which replaced Odin, the horse-god, in religious processions, and which has figured importantly for centuries in folklore. The root *hob* is a variant of *Rob*, from the French *Robin*. In Cornwall the word still means "phallus," and both Robin Hood and Robin Goodfellow were ithyphallic gods. The Victorian child would ride a hobbyhorse while reciting:

> Ride a cock horse to Banbury Cross
> See a white lady on a white horse
> Rings on her fingers . . . .

The white lady might be none other than the sacred mother, the horse-goddess herself. The same symbol is said to have been carried as an ensign by the followers of Widukind in their fight against Charlemagne.

The importance of the horse's head as a symbol of virility is also evident in innumerable folktales having to do with the headless rider. In such tales the horse and horseman are one unit and are interchangeable. The headless horseman has been castrated. He is—like Samson —deprived of his manhood. A similar idea occurs in the bestiaries which state that the horse loses its virility when its mane is cut.

In Shakespeare's time, *hobbyhorse* could mean a lustful person, a loose woman, or a prostitute, and is so used by Shakespeare, Jonson, and Beaumont and Fletcher. "Cals't thou my love Hobbihorse?" Don Adriano de Armado asks his page in *Love's Labour's Lost.* Today, of course, a hobbyhorse is a topic or idea in which one has an obsessive interest. But the verbs associated with the horse such as *ride* and *prick* have retained their sexual significance.

The body of the horse is the repository of sex and as such is often equated with woman. Proverbial expressions in many countries compare courting a woman to buying a horse, or urge a man to keep a tight rein on both his wife and his horse, or declare that well-traveled women, like well-traveled horses, are never good. From medieval times writers of treatises on husbandry repeated equine properties of woman, declaring she should be "merry of chere, brod-buttokyd, and esey to lep [leap] on, good at long-rynnyng and steryng under a man." Sebastian Brant in his *Narrenschiff* made the equation explicit when he wrote on the importance of guarding wives (*Von Frowen Huetten*):

A pretty wife on folly's course
Is like unto an earless horse
The man who plows with such a nag
His furrows oft diverge and sag.
(tr. Zeydel)

Token symbols are often substituted for the whole animal. The bridle, whip, harness, collar, or saddlegirth have all been applied to woman in her relations with man. In cases of wife-selling, recorded as late as in the last century, the unfortunate woman always wore a halter. From the sixteenth to the nineteenth century, a nagging woman might be punished by having the scold's bridle, an iron noose, slipped over her head. The bit held down her tongue, and the noose often had a chain and ring attached so that the woman could be led about like a horse. One such contraption, preserved in Walton Church and said to be dated 1633, bore the inscription: "Chester presents Walton with a bridle / To curb women's tongues that talk too idle." The symbolism persists today in the marriage ceremony, in which the ring is the halter used by the groom to harness his bride.

In such instances the man is the rider, and in every language *riding* is a commonplace term for coitus. In Germany a feeble lover is called a *Sonntagsreiter* (a Sunday rider), or *Bauerreiter* (a peasant rider), and the honeymoon can be termed *Stutenwocke* (mare week).

Treading, trampling, spurring are all equivalents. The punishment of Swanhild in the *Volsunga Saga* for having sexual intercourse with her bridegroom's son is one made to fit the crime: she is trampled to death by horses.

The French word for nightmare, *cauchemar*, derives from *calcar* (a spur) and *mara* (the crusher or incubus), and points directly to the sexual origin of the experience. The helpless dreamer's repressed impulses and fears become a terrifying and uncontrollable fantasy, so real that he actually feels he is being ridden upon. The horses and riders seem to be psychopomps bearing him away to castration or death.

The superstitions of ghostly night riders such as Odin, Herne the Hunter, and John Peel are the external manifestations of the same anxieties of the dreamer of the nightmare. From many parts of Europe come stories of sinister huntsmen with hounds baying at their heels who ride over the moors on stormy nights or when the moon is full. The chief huntsman might be a legendary figure or he might be the Devil himself on a black horse, but the purpose of the Wild Hunt or Furious Host never varied. The riders were hunting souls. To meet any of them, so the legend runs, was to find death.

Sometimes the position of the sexes is reversed, and it is the woman who is the rider and the man the horse. Misogynist clerics in the Middle Ages often depicted women as riding their unhappy husbands like beasts of burden. Chaucer realized the implications of the figure well enough when he described the sexually aggressive Wife of Bath as riding astride instead of sidesaddle and as sporting a pair of sharp spurs. Since primitive times female night-fiends have ridden on horses, become horses, and acquired masculine characteristics. Petronius, in the time of Nero, believed in them, and throughout the early Christian era they were the subject of innumerable clerical denunciations. Witches, flying to the Black Sabbath to have intercourse with the Devil, were said to mount a broomstick, a token form of the horse, or the Devil himself in the form of either a horse or a he-goat. They were called *Scobaces*, riders of the *scoba* (broom), and riding verbs, *chevaucher* and *equitare*, were used to describe their flight.

Occasionally the figure was a subject for jest. A popular medieval joke concerned the venerable Greek philosopher Aristotle. He was supposed to have become so infatuated with the queen of Greece that he permitted her to ride him like a horse. His ignominious position was celebrated in poetry, in sculpture, and wood carving. A somewhat similar idea found expression in a medieval phallic emblem shown by Thomas Wright in *The Worship of the Generative Powers*. Here, in the form of a brooch, a woman rode a giant phallus which she held by the bridle. Recently, a popular magazine carried an advertisement for bridles to be used on "sugar-daddies."

Equally ancient is the equation of the horse and rider to body and soul. Plato used the image in *Phaedrus*, and Plutarch referred to it when he described Antony's passion for Cleopatra:

> The unruly steed, to which Plato compares certain passions, once more broke loose, and despite honour, interest and prudence, Antony sent Fonteius Capito to escort Cleopatra into Syria.

The figure became a popular one with expository writers. Philo Judaeus, for example, writing in Hellenic Alexandria in the first century of the Christian era, made the image serve as a graphic commentary on Exodus, x.1: "I will sing to the Lord, for he has triumphed gloriously: the horse and his rider he has thrown into the sea." The horseman, he explained, was the mind (νοῦς), the mount was appetite and passion (ἐπιθυμία καὶ θυμός). When the rider lost control, that is, failed to subdue his passions, he was thrown headlong.

The image was still popular with the Renaissance emblem writers. Whitney used it twice. In an emblem addressed to Sir Philip Sidney, he has an illustration of a plumed horseman on a prancing war-horse with the motto *non locus virum, sed vir locum ornat* (not place the man but man the place adorns). The man of grave judgment and other fine qualities owes his position to his virtues; the fool, like an incompetent rider, is thrown

Horses are called equi *in Latin because when they are teamed in four, as they are here, they are made equal, matched in shape and pace.*

107

out of office. The emblem for *temeritas* ends with direct moralizing. The man possessed of foul and untamed affections comes to grief. "Bridle Will," urged Whitney, "and Reason make thy guide, / So maiste thow stande, when others doune doe slide." The accompanying engraving shows a waggoner brandishing a single thonged whip at two recalcitrant, prancing horses. Less typical is the emblem of Ripa, which makes the horse a symbol of Europe's military might.

In the eyes of the church, woman was, of course, the evil receptacle of sex. The female horse was thoroughly despised. Aelian recorded that it was extremely lustful and that for various reasons no person of quality ever rode on one. The biographer of Thomas à Becket, describing the saint's evangelizing in Normandy, lamented bitterly that the only mount he could find was a mare. It was the very symbol of ignominy. Criminals in the same era rode to the gallows strapped in a reverse position on the back of a mare. When the hero in the Middle English romance *Havelok* dispatched a traitor to be burnt at the stake, he "keste him on a scabbed mere, / Hise nese went unto the crice" (2448–49). Priests' concubines were supposed to turn into black mares at death and have carnal intercourse with the Devil.

Further uncomplimentary equine terms applied to woman were *jade* and *stot*. *Jade*, from the Old Norse *jalda*, meant a mare too old to foal. It occurs in the early English proverb:

> He that lets his horse drink at every lake
> And his wife go to every wake
> Shall never be without a whore or a jade.

Applied figuratively, it was subsequently used to denote either stubbornness or worthlessness occasioned by licentious living. *Stot* also occurs early and means "adulteress." In a pageant in the medieval mystery cycle, usually called the *Ludus Coventriae*, the Scribes address the woman taken in adultery as "thou stotte . . . thou hore . . . thou stynkynge bych-clowte," and it is interesting to note that the equine term here is coupled with a popular term for nightmare (*bicheclowte*). A more favorable concept is to be found in Tom Pearce's old grey mare who is a female ghost. There is also an instance of the mare symbolizing the Virgin Mary: using the ancient fable that mares could conceive merely by turning their hindquarters to the wind, Lactantius, the late third-century church father, saw the mother of Christ as a mare impregnated by the Holy Spirit.

In medieval times the horse was widely used to represent the sinner or the sensual appetite, which must be controlled if man is to find salvation. The unknown writer of "A Tretyse of Gostly Batayle" stated that "like as one horse welle-taught beryth hys mastere over many perylls and saveth hym fro perysshyng, so the body well-rewled bereth the soule over many peryllys off thys wrecched worlde." Uncontrollable steeds, on the other hand, were used to illustrate the vigorous conflict between the virtues and vices in Prudentius' *Psychomachia*, the early fifth-century epic which was one of the most popular didactic works of the Middle Ages. Here the steeds were mounted by Pride and Lust, and they threw their riders headlong. In addition to the traditions previously mentioned, the figure doubtless owes much to such passages as Jeremiah v.7–8:

> How can I pardon you?
> Your children have forsaken me,
> and have sworn by those who are no gods.
> When I fed them to the full,
> they committed adultery
> and trooped to the houses of harlots.
> They were well-fed lusty stallions,
> each neighing for his neighbor's wife.

The horse's neigh or snort had, in itself, sexual implications, and it was used by Darius in order to make him king of Persia. According to Herodotus, there were six contestants to the throne. They agreed to ride out together to the outskirts of the city; the one whose steed neighed first after the sun was up should have the king-dom. Darius' sharp-witted groom, Oebares, coupled his master's stallion with a favorite mare at a strategic spot on the previous evening, and when the stallion reached the same place the next morning it neighed. This account assumed that the heavens cooperated in the strategy. Another version given by Herodotus left less to chance:

> They say that in the morning Oebares stroked the
> mare with his hand, which he then hid in his trousers
> until the sun rose . . . . Then he suddenly drew his hand
> forth and put it to the nostrils of his master's horse,
> which immediately snorted and neighed.

The significance of neighing did not escape Chaucer: he made his Miller who, by tradition, was a figure of lechery, snort like a horse as he lay snoring in his bed.

While the stallion was a symbol of lust to the Hebrews, it was also a symbol of retribution and of war. Jeremiah drew upon the familiar image of the god whirling across the sky in his chariot to describe the might of Jehovah:

> Behold, he comes up like clouds,
>   his chariots are like the whirlwind;
> his horses are swifter than eagles—
>   woe to us, for we are ruined!

The horse and chariot were much dreaded by the foot soldier, and religious writers often used them to represent divine power.

The pale horse of the Apocalypse as a symbol of death is too well known to require discussion here. The white horse was a prophetic horse used for divination by Teutons and Orientals. In some parts of Europe white horses were bred at public expense in sacred groves, and their neighings and snortings were carefully observed as auguries. The white horses still gleaming on the downs of Berkshire and Kent are vestiges of this ancient practice. The Persian Magi are said to have practiced similar methods of divination, and in the East in particular the white horse symbolized unblemished intellect and reason. T. S. Eliot's "old white horse" in *The Journey of the Magi* is thus richly symbolic. World saviors such as Christ and Vishnu were envisioned as appearing on white horses, and when Buddha decided to become an ascetic, he chose a white horse as his mount. Durandus, a medieval writer on church symbolism, saw white horses as symbolizing just men or prelates. Topsell, in Elizabethan England, rationalized the poetic use of white and black horses thus:

> Homer saith, that the names of the day-horsses are *Lampus* & *Phaethon*, to the moon they ascribe two horsses, one blacke and another white, the reason of these inventions, for the day and night is, to signifie their speedy course or revolution by the swiftnes of horsses, and the darkenes of the night by the blacke horsses, and the light of the day by the white, and the Moone which for the most part is hidde and covered with earth, both encreasing and decreasing, they had the same reason to signifie her shadowed part by a black horse, and her bright part by a white one.

The golden or brass horse or the horse with the golden mane which appears in many folktales is the descendant of the sun horse, of the sun god who, in a Vedic hymn for example, is addressed as a horse. The sun with its warmth, generative power, and diurnal rise and decline is in itself a comparable phallic symbol; the sun's streaming rays which parallel the flowing mane of the horse are, of course, symbols both of the phallus and of semen, and gold itself is the most typical unconscious symbol of feces.

The wooden horse of Troy was magical. In some accounts of the siege of Troy, the Trojans did not bring the horse through the city gates: it breached or flew over the walls; it broke the protective magic circle and rendered the citizens helpless. In Elizabethan times Topsell tried to rationalize the event. He said that the traitor Sinon persuaded the Trojans to pull down the walls because the horse was too large to enter by the gates. He also suggested that the horse was a fiction, that it either signified a mountain near Troy called *Equus*, "by advantage thereof Troy was taken," or an engine of war "like unto that which is called *Aries*."

The green horse belongs to the vegetation myths. Frazer remarks that the horse or mare is sometimes regarded as the corn spirit. In the case of the green horse, it and its rider symbolize the year which must die; the green color stands for the holly bush which flourishes at Yuletide. According to some scholars, the Green Knight in the story of *Gawain and the Green Knight* represents the Old King and the Old Year and is beheaded at the New Year by the New King in the person of Cuchulain or Gawain. *Holly* means "holy," and in the "Holly Tree Carol" various properties of the Holly Knight's or Green Knight's role are taken over by Christ.

The horse is the attribute of various saints. The bishop standing at a forge holding a severed horse's leg or hoof is probably St. Eloy or St. Eligius, the seventh-century bishop of Noyon. As a young man he was a farrier. When he had a turbulent horse to shoe, he cut off its hoof and miraculously joined it on again later. Sometimes he holds a pair of pincers; these are to twist the nose of the Devil, who tempts him in the guise of a beautiful woman. The Irish saints Fechin and Segni restored dead horses to life, and at least a dozen other saints are depicted with horses. Some illustrations show the horse beside the saint, as in the case of the martyred saints Irene (April 5) and Severus (February 1); others portray a less harmonious relationship: a not uncommon mode of martyrdom involved being dragged at the tail of a wild horse.

Lighthearted, promiscuous sexual experience and a down-to-earth folk culture have, it seems, been features of Presbyterian Scotland for centuries. According to James Barke, in a prefatory essay to *The Merry Muses* which he edited with S. G. Smith, the tradition of bawdiness was extremely vigorous and if it smelled, it was like the not unpleasant smell of horse droppings, reeking "of the stable rather than the urinal." However, accustomed as Scotswomen were to viewing the sexual mating of animals in their season, they were under no circumstances permitted to see a stallion making love to a mare:

> I have been assured, on unimpeachable testimony, the effect on certain otherwise staid and respectable women (married and spinsters) of witnessing the mating of mare and stallion was to induce an almost instantaneous fainting away (orgasm) and an inability to resist the sexual advances of any male who might be on the spot, regardless of age or social condition.

But if the Scots realize the power of the horse as a phallic animal, the English, whose young females or "fillies," as they call them, are renowned for their devotion to horses, do not. Recently an English actress in Hollywood broadcast her views on teenagers and sex. "They develop too early," she lamented in a prim, high-pitched voice which had a shade of bewilderment in it. "You send them away to the country to be with horses and things but it makes no difference. Every little girl in England is crazy about horses—it is a tremendous passion with them. But suddenly, from not being able to stand boys, they become crazy about them instead and forget all about horses."

Aelian, IV.xi; Barke, p. 29; Beckett, *see South English Legendary*, II.1179–80; Brant, pp. 80–81; Browne, v.xx; Dent and Goodall, *passim*; Durandus, pp. 135–36; Frazer, p. 459; Giraldus, *Wales*, II.xii; Herodotus, III.lxxxvi; Jewett, "Scolds," pp. 65–78; "Additional Examples," pp. 193–94; Juvenal, *Sat.*, VIII.157; "Lai d'Aristote," v.cxxxvii; Lanoe-Villène, III.186; *Ludus Covent.*, p. 205, ll. 145–48; Philo Judaeus, *De agricul.*, ll. 15–16; Plato, *Phaed.*, pp. 247, 248, 253–56; Plutarch, *Lives*, Antony, xxxvi; Prudentius, fols. IIv, 12, 13, 15v, 16, 18, 18v; Ripa, pp. 332–34, s.v. "Europa"; Rowland, *Blind Beasts*, pp. 129–40; Topsell, pp. 334–39; "Tretyse of Gostly Batayle," *Yorkshire Writers*, II.421; Utley, pp. 418–20; Vogel, *passim*; Whitney, pp. 6, 38, 227; Wright, *Generative Powers*, p. 63; Zeydel, no. 32; Zirkle, pp. 95–104.

Hyena

The hyena was usually represented in medieval art and sculpture as a dog-like creature gnawing at the limbs of a corpse which it had just dug out of a tomb. Such feeding habits contributed not only to the detestation with which the animal was universally regarded but also to its symbolism. The hyena symbolized either vice feeding on corruption or the Jew who had a knowledge of the true and living God but preferred to subsist on dry bones and dead things. In Elizabethan times the poet Spenser made the hyena an epitome of lust feeding on women's flesh or saw the creature as corrupted flesh and a sign of sin, concupiscence, and a fallen nature.

Spenser's evaluation may owe something to another widely popularized trait. Although Aristotle refuted the notion that the hyena had two pudenda, one male and one female, and accounted for the error by correctly remarking on the extreme similarity of the genitals of both sexes, for centuries natural historians declared that the hyena, like the hare, changed its sex. This supposed characteristic meant that the hyena could typify sexual perversion or any kind of unnatural behavior, and also gave rise to other symbols. The hyena could stand for the Israelites, who were neither faithful nor pagan—who first served gods and then adored idols; it could symbolize the double-minded or untrustworthy man or, according to Horapollo, someone who was unsettled (ἄστατον), sometimes strong and sometimes weak. Even in the sixteenth century John Ferne in his book *The Blazon of Gentrie*, written "for the instruction of all gentleman bearers of armes," still repeated the idea that the hyena symbolized an inconstant man.

Further symbolism was occasioned by the fact that the hyena was regarded as a magic animal. If it walked round any animal three times, that animal could not move; a dog crossing its path lost its voice; it imitated the human voice and lured people out of their homes in order to devour them; it had a jewel in its eye which enabled persons to foresee the future; its gall cured blindness or, at least, "helpyth moost ayenst dymnesse of eyen." Such lore is significant in that in the East the animal was regarded as a metamorphosis of a sorcerer. Arabian folktales, in particular, have many terrifying accounts of wizards and witches who assumed its form for diabolical purposes.

Other magical characteristics assigned to the hyena account for a further symbolism attributed by Horapollo to the Egyptians. The man who overcame his private enemy was symbolized by a hyena turning to the right; the man who was himself overcome was symbolized by a hyena turning to the left. The man who passed fearlessly through the evils which assailed him even unto death was symbolized by the skin of a hyena because this skin itself afforded magical protection. In later commentaries it was the spotted hyena, the largest species, which was most frequently censured, for the exegetical writers and natural historians commonly interpreted spotted

The hyena feeds on corpses until its stomach is blown up like a drum.

beasts as figures of guile and enticements to destruction.

Aristotle, vi.579b; Evans, pp. 139–42; Ferne, ii.40–41; Horapollo, ii.lxix; Isidore, xvi.xv.25; McCulloch, pp. 130–32; Pliny, viii.30.44, 46; Spenser, *FQ*, iii.vii.22.

The lamb always knows its own mother.

Lamb

The lamb was a symbol of purity, and even its Latin name *agnus* was thought to come from the Greek ἄγνος, meaning "chaste."

In the Bible the lamb was a symbol of Christ and as such appeared as early as the fourth century. There were three main kinds of illustration: the Lamb of the Crucifixion, bearing the cross and usually depicted as having blood flowing from its breast into a chalice; the Lamb of the Resurrection, carrying a triumphant cross-emblazoned banner; the Apocalyptic Lamb, usually characterized by the Book Sealed with the Seven Seals, symbolic of Christ as the judge at the end of the world.

There are also bas-reliefs in the catacombs where Christ is represented in the form of the Lamb, performing miracles such as the raising of Lazarus and the feeding of the five thousand. The lamb with a nimbus sometimes stands on a hill (Revelation xiv.1) from which four rivers flowed. Here the hill symbolizes the church and the waters, the four gospels or the four rivers of Paradise.

When a synod at Trullo in 692 forbade the use of the lamb as a symbol of Christ, the symbolism became more varied. At the cathedral at Chartres, St. John the Baptist was depicted with the cross-bearing Lamb in his hands,

114

the textual basis being John i.29: "The next day John seeth Jesus coming unto him and sayeth 'Behold the Lamb of God.'" But in some later paintings the lamb was naturalistic and was probably simply an attribute. The formalized *Agnus Dei* continued to appear, however, on numerous tapestries and sculpture. Even many centuries later Van Eyck in his *Adoration of the Lamb* showed the actual lamb standing on the altar.

From medieval times the lamb also appeared in sculpture and engraving as the attribute of St. Agnes and as an attribute of patience, sweetness, innocence, mercy, and humility. It had not lost its traditional qualities when Blake wrote his famous poem beginning "Little Lamb, who made thee?" in his *Songs of Innocence* (1789). But today the lamb connotes mildness and helplessness in a slightly pejorative sense.

Appleton and Bridges, pp. 55–56; Chew, pp. 75, 119, 123, 125, 162, 201, 225; Isidore, XII.i.12; Twining, pp. 19–20.

Lamia

This creature owes her notoriety to the fact that, in some versions of Isaiah xiii.22, she was to haunt the city of Babylon, laid waste by Jehovah, along with dancing satyrs and other evil creatures.

Originally she was the unfortunate common-law wife of Jupiter. When her own children were destroyed through the jealousy of Juno, she roamed about in distraction, killing the children of others. Pitying her, Jupiter gave her the power to take whatever shape she chose, and henceforth she was a shape-shifter, a child-killer with some vampiric traits, and a seducer of young men.

There was soon more than one lamia, but none so famous as the one in the story of Philostratus. A young man became infatuated with a beautiful woman whom he met near Corinth. He planned marriage but was stopped just in time by a philosopher friend who denounced the woman as a phantom creature who would utterly destroy him. This is the incident which Keats used. In his poem, Lamia is a tragic figure and symbolizes the life of the imagination and of the senses, a life which Keats felt to be incompatible with a life of serious thought—"Do not all charms fly at the mere touch of cold philosophy?"

The Elizabethan naturalist Edward Topsell devoted several pages to determining what a lamia was. He regarded the various stories, including that by Philostratus, as "beautiful allegories of beautifull Harlottes who, after they have had their lust by men, doth many times devour and make them away, as we read of *Diomedes* daughters, and for this cause also Harlots are called *Lupae*, shee-Wolves, and *Lepores*, Hares." He concluded that such beasts lived in some parts of Libya and appeared in the Bible under various names.

Philostratus, *Vita Appollonii*, iv; Topsell, p. 454.

Leopard

There may be a chance of the leopard's outclassing mink as a status fur, but the Madison Avenue copywriter who urges the public to be more aspiring and "think mink" would hardly regard the leopard as having a similarly irresistible appeal. For most people the leopard symbolizes either swift ruthlessness or an immutability undesirable in itself. Both these traits have ancient antecedents.

Keats in his *Ode to a Nightingale* preferred to be carried on the "viewless wings of Poesy" rather than be "charioted by Bacchus and his pards." His remark shows that he was familiar with the art of ancient Greece and Rome. Leopards were frequently depicted with the god of wine, in some instances either devouring grapes or drinking wine. A year earlier than Keats's ode, the controversial Richard Payne Knight published his interpretation of the symbolism:

On a very ancient coin of Acanthus, too, the leopard is represented instead of the lion, destroying the bull; wherefore we have to doubt that in the Bacchic processions, it means the destroyer accompanying the generator, and contributing, by different means, to the same end. In some instances his chariot is drawn by two leopards, and in others by a leopard and a goat coupled together, which are all different means of signifying different versions and combinations of the same idea.

The conception of the leopard as the destroyer and as a thoroughly evil beast received support from the natural historians. The leopard was the result of an adulterous and unnatural union—it was a cross between a lion (λέων) or lioness and a pard (πάρδυς).

In exegetical and homiletic literature the leopard symbolized the sinner. Garnerus, taking Isaiah xi.6 for his text, *Pardus haedo accubabit* (the leopard shall lie down with the kid), said that the prophet was speaking of converted sinners and added that the leopard himself was any man bespattered with crimes—*quid enim per pardum, nisi peccatis variis aspersum.*

In a hymn by Alexander Neckam the conversion of Mary Magdalene is symbolized as the changing of the leopard's variegated coat into one color. The miracle is achieved by the skill of the Greatest Physician:

Arte summi medici
Fit solocis unici
Pellis pardi varia.
(By the art of the Greatest Physician the variegated skin
of the leopard becomes a single coat.)

This motif is associated with several Biblical references such as *Si mutare potest Aethiops pellem suam aut pardus varietates suas?* (Can the Ethiopian change his skin or the leopard his spots? Jeremiah xiii.23) and *Et bestia quam vidi, similis erat pardo* (And the beast that I saw was like a leopard; Revelation xiii.2). Rabanus Maurus united these texts and found that the leopard was the Antichrist. St. Ambrose felt that the pard's variegated hue signified the various impulses of the soul. St. Jerome interpreted the *pardus* of Jeremiah v.6 as referring to Alexander's conquests, and gave a similar significance to the leopard in the vision of Daniel vii.6.

The pejorative symbolism of the leopard continued throughout the Middle Ages. At the beginning of *The Inferno* it was one of the three beasts of worldliness that blocked Dante's path to the Mount of Joy. The leopard's coat was a symbol of unchangeability to Wycliffe and of "diverse subtleties and guiles of the Devil" to other moralists. In heraldry, however, the leopard assumed the same shape and qualities as the lion, but was drawn to show the full face.

The leopard's spots are indicative of its evil nature.

St. Ambrose, *PL*, xiv, col. 262; Garnerus, *PL*, cxciii, col. 114; St. Jerome, *PL*, xxiv, col. 742 and xxv, col. 530; Knight, *Symbolical Lang.*, p. 90; Neckam, *see Anal. Hymn.*, xlviii.287; Rabanus Maurus, *PL*, cxi, col. 220; Topsell, p. 584.

117

The lion, when he sleeps, seems to keep his eyes open.

Lion

Majestic heads of lions which are supposed to pour water from their jaws fetch high prices in the junk shops of Toronto and New York. The heads are usually re-castings of eighteenth-century neoclassic lions, but they derive from Greek and Roman fountains and, before that, from Egypt, where they symbolized the overflowing of the Nile. The motif may have arisen because the sun is in Leo when the river floods occur. It probably also reflects the lion's connection with the sun, symbolizing the way in which the sun separates water from the salt of the sea and distributes it over the earth by exhalation.

The lion, always emblematic of invincible power, was frequently associated with the sun. To illustrate the power of modifying solar heat, the Chaldeans, Hindus, Greeks, and others depicted one or two lions contending with the sun god. The prophet Daniel had seven lions in his den, but he is usually represented as fighting with only two. His stance, with arms outstretched between two rampant lions, is that of a solar hero.

The lion was also the symbol of watchfulness. It was reputed never to sleep, and, according to Aelian, the Egyptians assigned the lion to the sun because "the sun is the most hard-working (φιλοπονώτατον) of the gods." Guardian lions stood at the entrance of Shinto and Buddhist shrines or faced each other at the gates of cities. Among the Assyrians these lions were winged; among the Egyptians they were given human heads to typify the union of strength and intellect.

In Christian times the same symbolism persisted. The lions which appeared most frequently in Romanic and early Gothic architecture were symbols of vigilance: they stood on either side of main doorways, on pillars or porticoes; they became ornamental door knockers.

Biblical winged lions probably owed much to the fabulous creatures of the ancient world, such as might be seen on the sculptured walls of Nineveh, but their symbolism was different. The winged lion in Daniel's tetramorph symbolized Babylon; the winged lion which appeared in the tetramorph of the vision of Ezekiel i.5–11, and stood with the man, the eagle, and the ox around the throne of the Lamb in Revelation iv.7 was variously interpreted: Jewish scholars saw the winged lion as one of the four archangels, one of the four prophets, or as royalty. St. Gregory regarded the tetramorph as Christ incarnate: a man at birth, an ox at death, a lion at the resurrection, and an eagle in his ascension. St. Jerome took the four beasts as the writers of the Gospels, the man standing for St. Matthew, the lion for St. Mark, the ox for St. Luke, and the eagle for St. John. This last interpretation was widely accepted by the second century, and some three centuries later these symbols appeared in art and sculpture.

In terms of medieval theology, the lion was Christ, the scion of the tribe of Judah, of which the lion was the symbol (Genesis xlix.9). A curious allegory based on pseudo-natural history was used to amplify the symbolism. According to the bestiaries, the King of Beasts was said to have three dominant characteristics: inhabiting high mountains, it erased its tracks with its tail; it slept with open eyes; it revived its dead whelps three days after birth. So likewise, Christ concealed all traces of His God-head when He became man. He never closed His eyes to mercy; He was raised up on the third day from the dead. The lion's whelp as well as the lion thus came to denote the risen Christ, and in illustrations of Christ's infancy, a sleeping lion was often brought into tropological relationship with Jesus. In manuscript illustrations, and on misericords at Lincoln, Chester, Carlyle, and other places, Christ is represented as a lion. Sometimes the lion fights the dragon; on stained glass windows at Freiburg in the Breisgau and St. Etienne at Bourges, the lion breathes upon his whelps and is accompanied by another symbol of Christ's crucifixion—the pelican feeding its young with its own blood. Sometimes the lion cowers at the sight of a white cock. According to Philippe de Thaon, "the white cock signifies men of holy life who, before God died, announced his fate, which he feared very much according as he was man." Later the lion came to be engraved on helmets with an inscription such as *Domine vivifica me, secundum verbum tuum* (Lord, restore me to life, according to Thy word), expressing the hope that the warrior, if killed in battle, might be raised up on the last day.

Since the medieval mind was accustomed to antithetical

symbols, the lion could represent utterly opposing principles. In the most extreme form, Christ, the Lion of Judah,
was set against the great adversary, the Devil, which "as
a roaring lion walketh about, seeking whom he may
devour" (1 Peter v.8). Who would not rush into the jaws
of that lion, asked St. Augustine, if the Lion of Judah
should not prevail? Thus Daniel's seven lions symbolized
the Seven Deadly Sins, and Samson's lion might signify
death or the Devil, since Samson's victory prefigured that
of Christ. Some carvers even depicted the lion's jaws, instead of the whale's or dragon's maw, as the mouth of
hell, showing the contorted faces of dead sinners within.

What of the amiable lion so frequently depicted in
sculpture? This is usually the grateful, fawning lion such
as Androcles or St. Jerome encountered. St. Jerome, indeed, often appeared with such a lion. It limped into his
monastery at Bethlehem with a thorn in its foot. The
saint was lecturing in the schoolroom at the time, and his
pupils fled in terror. The saint bravely removed the thorn,
and in gratitude the lion remained with him as his
servant.

The lion's high reputation for magnanimity derives
also from Pliny, who said that the lion spared any crea-

(top) *The sick lion cures himself by eating a monkey;*
(center) *The noble lion spares his prostrate enemies;*
(bottom) *The lion is afraid of a white cock.*

120

ture that prostrated itself to him. For this reason, the lion is found at the feet of medieval knights in effigy: it signifies that they died for their magnanimity. "Loo, the gentile kynde of the lyoun!" remarks Chaucer in his Prologue to *The Legend of Good Women*. "For whan a flye offendeth him or biteth, / He with his tayl awey the flye smyteth / Al esely" (F391–94). When the Duke of Anjou arrived at Antwerp in 1581, the citizens put a representation of a lion holding a sword on the platform prepared for him in the marketplace. Their act indicated both acceptance of the duke's magisterial authority and the hope that he would be merciful.

In Elizabethan England, however, it was commonly believed that the lion spared only royalty. In the first part of *Henry IV*, Falstaff tells Prince Hal, "Why, thou knowest I am as valiant as Hercules, but beware instincts; the lion will not touch the true prince. Instinct is a great matter; I was a coward on instinct" (II.iv).

Nor was antithesis lacking even here: in contrast to the merciful lion, there is the lion of retributive justice which derives from a story told by Aelian. A lion, bear, and dog lived happily together until the bear killed the dog for teasing it. The lion then killed the bear out of righteous indignation. Thus to Chaucer the lion could also be the symbol of "a lord that wol have no mercy," and the lion's fierceness and cruelty became proverbial.

Polarities of symbolism are even more evident in the

The lion's cubs are born dead and are brought to life by their parents.

Renaissance. The lion is an attribute of endurance, prudence, clemency, but also of pride and wrath. It is the mount of Wrath in the first book of the *Faerie Queene* (IV.xxxiii); in the third book, in the *Mask of Cupid*, it becomes visual evidence of the remarkable power of love. Young Eros in Lucan's *Dialogue of the Gods* declares that he is not afraid to climb upon the backs of lions and make them do his bidding; the emblem writers and mythographers use the passage to illustrate *amor vincit omnia*

121

(love conquers all things). Spenser's idea is similar:

> . . . the winged God Himselfe
> Came riding on a lion ravenous,
> Taught to obay the menage of that Elfe.
> (XII.xxii)

Also ambivalent in their symbolism are Whitney's emblems. *Desiderum spe vacuum* (desire devoid of hope) shows a dog watching a lion eating and symbolizes the greedy heir waiting for the death of an aged sire. To illustrate *Ex damno alterius, alterius utilitas* (from misfortune of one advance of the other), a lion fights a boar. A vulture watches, pleased because from the fighting of mighty men he will derive the profit. *Vigilitantia et custodia* (watchfulness and guardianship), an emblem dedicated to the bishop of Chester, shows a cock as the weathervane of a church and a lion at the gates. This emblem modifies the tradition that the lion is afraid of the cock. Here the cock is the preacher, and the lion symbolizes his behavior:

> The Lion shewes, they [the pastors]
> should of courage bee,
> And able to defende their flocke from foes:
> If ravening wolfes, to lie in waite they see.

In heraldry, the lion was the first animal. Henry I is said to have hung a shield decorated with six little gold lions around the neck of his son-in-law, Geoffrey Plantagenet of Anjou, at his marriage in 1129. An enamel plate over Geoffrey's tomb shows him bearing a long shield of azure with six golden lioncels. Such lioncels, or young lions, symbolized knightly virility even in medieval fiction. In the romance of *Merlin*, an emperor has a dream of a sow embracing twelve "lionsewes." To his dismay he found that it signified his nymphomaniac wife and his court. One of the oldest armorial shields, that of Philip of Alsace (1164), bore the rampant lion of Flanders, and in England five years later the seal of Richard I showed his shield charged with a lion ramping on the sinister side.

From that time the lion appeared on the armorial insignia of British royalty as well as on that of powerful barons such as the Bohuns, Fitz-Alans, Lacies, Percies, Mowbrays, and others. It had various postures, including *rampant* (erect, one hind paw on the ground, other paws raised, the animal looking forward and having his tail elevated), *passant* (walking, three paws on the ground), *dexter* (forepaw raised, tail displayed over back), and *couchant* (asleep, with head resting on his forepaws). The leopard, believed to be the result of the lioness' adulterous association with a pard, appeared heraldically as a lion at all points but was commonly *passant*, looking sidelong showing the whole face, whereas the lion in its most common posture looked forward.

The English kings' beasts were leopards in blazon,

chronicle, and ballad until far into the fifteenth century and were recognized as such in battle—even Napoleon's gazettes spoke of the English leopards. Nevertheless, the animal facing the unicorn on the arms of the United Kingdom is usually termed a lion *rampant* and *gardant*. A rhyme commemorating the decisive victory of the English over the Scotch in 1651, when Cromwell met Prince Charles at Worcester, makes use of the unicorn to represent Scotland and the lion, England:

> The Lion and the Unicorn
> Were fighting for the Crown;
> The Lion beat the Unicorn
> All around the town.

As a British national emblem, the lion was particularly popular in the age of imperialism, and all the qualities it might symbolize, such as sagacity, ferocity, and magnanimity, were brought into play. When treaties were signed, the British lion "kissed the feet of peace"; it "roared" when treaties were broken, and in victory it could spare the "fallen foe."

Aelian, iv.xlv; d'Alviella, pp. 87–88; Anderson, *Miser.*, p. 9, and *Drama and Imagery*, p. 140; St. Augustine, *PL*, xxxviii, col. 1210; Ditchfield, p. 49; Graves, "Mother Goose," pp. 591–92; St. Gregory, *see* Réau, ii.688–89; Horapollo, i.xxi; St. Jerome, *PL*, xxvi, col. 19; *Merlin*, p. 430; Petti, pp. 71, 79; Philippe de Thaon, *Best.*, p. 78; *Physiologus* (attr. to Epiphanius), pp. 1–7; Pliny, viii.16. 19; Whitney, pp. 44, 119, 120; Whittick, p. 212.

Lioness

Since the natural historians, including Pliny, believed that the leopard was the offspring of a lioness and a pard, the lioness had a reputation for infidelity. The fourteenth-century translator of the encyclopedia of Bartholomaeus Anglicus wrote that "the lyennesse . . . is a righte lecherous beest and lovyth alwaye the dede of lechery." Noble the Lion's queen, in the Reynard cycle, exhibited traditional traits. The lioness in the *Gesta Romanorum*, a popular storybook of the Middle Ages, became the subject of allegory when her adultery was detected and punished by the lion, her husband. Here the lion symbolized Christ and the lioness, the erring soul.

To the medieval prelate Berchorius, the lioness was *luxuriosa* and signified the adulterous woman. The longevity of the symbolism can be gauged from the account given by the Elizabethan Edward Topsell, in his *Historie of Foure-Footed Beasts*, concerning the Greek courtesan Lais, who preferred to die rather than betray a confidence:

There was a noble Harlot called *Leena*, which was acquainted with the tiranies of *Harmodius* and *Aristogiton*; for which cause, she was apprehended, and put to greivous tormentes, to the intent she should disc[l]ose them, but she endured all unto death, never bewraying any part of their counsell. After her death, the Athenians devising how to honor that vertue, and because shee was a Harlot or common curtizan, they were not willing to make a statue for her in the likenesse of a woman, but as her name was *Leena*, that signifieth a lyonesse, so they erected for her the picture of a lionesse, and that they might express the vertue of her secrecy, they caused it to be framed without a toong. Upon the grave of *Layis* there was a covering containing the picture of a lyon, holding a Ram in his forefeet by the buttockes, with an inscription, that as the lyon held the Ram, so do Harlots hold their lovers.

The same symbolism was applied to another Lais, famous for her greed and cruelty, by Thynne in his *Emblemes and Epigrames*:

> . . . Uppon whose curious tombe, engraven by skill,
> Did stand a feirce and cruelle Lyonesse
> Which did the simple Ram, even at her will,
> Hould by the Loynes with clawes of bludinesse;
> Which unto us this morrall did expresse,
> That by the Loynes she still did hould and keepe
> Her fonde lovers, as Lyonesse doth Sheepe.

Aldrovandi, p. 4; Bartholomaeus Ang., XVII, "de Leena"; Berchorius, fol. 134v; *Gesta Rom.* (ed. Oesterley), CLXXXI; Pliny, VIII.16.17; Thynne, p. 42; Topsell, p. 484.

Lynx

Although its vision is unremarkable, the lynx has been a symbol of acute sight from early times. Pausanias—apparently misunderstanding a passage in Pindar—thought Lynceus, the Argonaut, possessed such keen sight that he could look through the trunk of an oak tree. Lynceus' extraordinary powers of vision passed to the animal. Medieval writers such as Brunetto Latini declared that a lynx could see through a wall or even a mountain. Because of the piercing quality of its vision, the lynx was a symbol of the omniscience and vigilance of Christ.

In the Renaissance the emblem writers used the animal as the symbol of a man who saw clearly in the metaphorical sense. Because of this symbolism, Francis of Gonzague, the powerful prelate, chose it as his emblem.

According to Aldrovandi, however, the lynx not only demonstrated keen-sightedness but forgetfulness and avarice, and could symbolize these qualities. Its reputation for avarice stemmed from what it did to its urine. According to Pliny and other early natural historians, the

The lynx's urine turns into carbuncles in seven days.
The man is angry because, as usual, the animal was mean
enough to cover up its urine with sand before
any transformation could occur.

lynx's urine had a curious property: it hardened into precious stones. But the ungenerous beast buried it in the
earth so that no one could get his hands on the treasure.

Aldrovandi, pp. 99–100; Brunetto Latini, *Tresor*, p. 167
(*luberne*); Chew, p. 109, n. 3; Pausanias, *Desc. Gr.*, iv.ii.7;
Pliny, viii.38.57; *Pricke of C.*, 576–77; Réau, 1.94; Tervarent, cols. 255–56; Valeriano, xi, s.v. "de lynce."

Manticore

"This beast or rather monster," observed Topsell in the

The manticore in the Middle Ages is a symbol of the Devil.

sixteenth century:

is bred among the Indians, having a treble row of teeth
beneath and above, whose greatness, roughness, and
feet are like a Lyons, his face and ears like unto a mans,

125

his eyes gray, and color red, his tail like the tail of a Scorpion, of the earth, armed with a sting, casting forth sharp pointed quils; his voyce like the voyce of a small Trumpet or Pipe, being in course as swift as a Hart; his wildness such as can never be tamed, and his appetite is especially to the flesh of man. His body is like the body of a Lyon, being very apt both to leap and to run, so as no distance or space doth hinder him.

The word *manticore* derives from an old Persian word meaning *man-eater* and may simply refer to a man-eating tiger. A similar description to that of Topsell's is given by Brunetto Latini and other medieval writers, as well as by the early natural historians, who name Ctesias' *Indica* as their source. In terms of medieval Christian symbolism, the manticore was the Devil.

Félicie d'Ayzac, pp. 28–29; Brunetto Latini, *Trésor*, p. 168; McCulloch, p. 142; Topsell, p. 343 (1658 ed.).

The mole lives in darkness.

Mole

Although Sir Thomas Browne knew otherwise, the ancients thought that the mole neither heard nor saw. Among the Egyptians it was a symbol of a blind man.

Proverbially the mole is still associated with blindness, but its symbolism has varied. In an early thirteenth-century bestiary of Pierre de Beauvais, it was the symbol of earth, one of the four elements; in a Spanish hymn in which animals symbolized events in the life of St. Marina, the mole represented the saint before her conversion; in a medieval Latin sermon cited by Owst, it symbolized the avaricious. In exegetical writings, its habitat and blindness made it a natural symbol for those engrossed with earthly cares and vain delights or for the heretic blind to the true faith. In Elizabethan times, Topsell reminded his readers that the mole had once been regarded as a magic animal, able to foretell events—"because if a man eat the heart of a Mole newly taken out of her belly and panting, he shall be able to devine and fortell infalliable events," but he warned against such beliefs.

Aldrovandi, p. 423; Browne, iii.xviii; Chew, pp. 106–107, n. 7; Horapollo, ii.lxiii; Owst, *Lit. and Pulpit*, p. 201, n. 1; Pierre de Beauvais, iii.274; Pliny, xi.37.52; Szövérffy, p. 79; Topsell, p. 502.

Mouse

According to Pliny, the mouse was the most prolific of all animals, and even a lick between lovers could result in pregnancy. One hundred and twenty mice were said to have been born to one female, and mice were even found pregnant in their mother's womb. Since fertility was equated with salacity, the mouse soon became a symbol of lechery and, in particular, of female sexuality, with *mouse-trap* and *mouse* signifying the pudendum. Aelian cited a passage from a Greek chorus:

> The accursed go-between fooled me completely,
> swearing . . . that the wench was a heifer, a virgin,
> an untamed filly—and all the time she was an
> absolute mousehole.

He explicated, "By calling her an 'absolute mousehole' (μυωνίαν ὅλην) he wished to say that she was excessively lecherous."

This symbolism has persisted through the centuries. The most extraordinary instance of its use occurred in a story of Albertus Magnus, a learned theologian and encyclopedist of the thirteenth century, a story which was subsequently repeated by Aldrovandi and others. Albertus said that he knew a mouse in upper Germany which, on a sign from its master, acted as a candlestick for him

by holding a candle in its mouth when he was at supper. This improbable feat has meaning only when interpreted symbolically. The idea of coition as supper is still current, but candle and candlestick have lost their significance as sexual symbols now that they are no longer in daily household use. Their metaphorical value, however, can be traced through Rabelais, through English and French farce, and popular verse in the fifteenth and sixteenth centuries; that value even survives in the nursery rhyme "Wall flower, wall flower," in the last line, telling of the accomplishments of the chosen child—"She can hop, she can skip, she can turn the candlestick." The compliant Teutonic mouse was, in fact, a symbolic one, and the implication must have been obvious to anyone who was familiar with the argot of the streets.

The mouse is "a verie ravenour or greedigut" according to John Maplet (1567). Here it seems to be nibbling the sacred host.

"As good a mayde as a mouse" is an ironic expression recorded by Topsell as being current in ancient times to describe a "lustfull woman." He also cited Politianus, a Roman writer, who called a woman a mouse's hole— "signifieng that her virginnity was lost, and that she suffered any lovers as a Mouse-hole doth any Mice."

In a medieval lyric a generous young woman uses related imagery to describe her amorous relationship with her master:

> Ser Iohn ys taken In my mouse-trappe.
> Ffayn wold I have hem both nyght and day.

In *Romeo and Juliet*, when Lady Capulet accuses her husband of having been a woman-chaser, she says: "Ay, you have been a mouse-hunt in your time" (iv.iv).

Similar symbolism, long forgotten, probably lies behind a nursery rhyme recorded in the writer's infancy in Scotland. The rhyme was accompanied by gesture: the speaker tickled the hand of the child and finally circled up to the "housie" (the armpit):

> Round a bit, round a bit,
> Catch a wee mousie,
> Up a bit, up a bit,
> In a wee housie.

Like the snake, another chthonic animal, the mouse was associated with death as well as with fertility. Apollo Smintheus, Apollo the Mouse Slayer, was probably a mouse god worshipped by people of Thraco-Phrygian speech who lived in the eastern part of central Europe during the second millennium of the pre-Christian era. According to Krappe, this worship of the great chthonic deity in mouse shape was very widespread. The association with death was strengthened by the realization that the mouse was connected with the bubonic plague. The Philistines were advised to make gold images of mice in order to rid themselves of the plague (1 Samuel vi.4, 5).

As a death symbol, the mouse came to symbolize the souls of the departed. Common in ancient Europe and India was the story which Gregory of Tours told of the Frankish King Guntchram. The king was having a nap in the open air, and a soldier guarding him saw a mouse slip out of his mouth and run toward a narrow ditch. The soldier placed his sword across the ditch, and the mouse passed over it and entered a mound on the other side. After a while the mouse came back, crossed in the same way, and returned to the king's mouth. The king woke up and told the soldier that he had dreamed he was going over a steel bridge into a treasure house. The soldier related what he had witnessed, and when the mound was opened treasure was found inside. There was a widespread belief that the mice infesting the fields were the souls of stillborn children and of children deceased in early infancy who were condemned to wander the earth. The mice who ate up the cruel archbishop of Mainz in the ancient German legend were simply the souls of the poor whom he had burned alive. Souls of the departed were believed to spend their first night with St. Gertrude. She performed duties peculiar to mouse gods: she not only averted plagues of mice but punished sinners by sending mice to devastate their fields. Her center was at Nivelles, where a cult of a Teutonic goddess of death flourished in pre-Christian times, and she is still depicted with mice on her distaff and mice swarming around her feet.

The greed of the mouse was proverbial. Rabanus Maurus stated: *Mystice autem mures significant homines cupiditate terrena inhiantes et praedam de aliena substantia surripientes* (Mystically mice signify men who in their breathless eagerness for earthly gains filch their booty from another's store). Whitney depicted a mouse investigating an oyster and being caught by its shell. The moral was that in this way gluttons come to grief. The extreme thirstiness of the mouse, evinced in such phrases as "drunk as a mouse," may account for Topsell's curious recipe for enuresis:

> Sodden mice are exceeding good to restraine and hold in the urine of infants or children being too abundant, if they be given in some pleasant or delightsome drinke.

Aelian, xii.x; Albertus Magnus, *see* Aldrovandi, p. 418; Drake, p. 192; Krappe, "Ἀπόλλων Σμινθεύς," pp. 136–39; Pliny, x.64.85; Rabanus Maurus, *PL*, cxi, col. 226; Robbins, *Lyrics*, p. 20; Rowland, "Forgotten Metaphor," p. 19; Topsell, pp. 506–507, 515; Whitney, p. 128.

Otter

The otter in medieval times was taken as a type of Christ and of the Devil. It was sometimes identified with the hydrus, in which case it killed the crocodile by entering the mouth and devouring the bowels before reappearing. This fable was an obvious allegory of Christ's descent into hell and was widely used as such by the church fathers.

But the otter was also confounded with the hydra, an animal whose numerous heads sprouted again as soon as they were cut off; the hydra was said to symbolize the prolific and indestructible nature of Original Sin. Hence, in the Waldensian *Physiologus* the otter symbolized the Devil, who insinuated himself into the heart of man in order to bring about his destruction.

The voracity of the otter was sometimes used pejoratively in the Renaissance period. Camerarius took the otter as a symbol of the bloody tyrant by showing it pursuing a fish into the sea. The motto was *saevit in omnes* (he is fierce in all things).

Aldrovandi, p. 297; Camerarius, xcv; Druce, "Crocodile," p. 322; Evans, pp. 131–33; McCulloch, p. 129, n. 82; "Wald. Phys.," p. 416.

Ox

Industry, patience, and strength are the qualities which this animal has traditionally stood for. Even more anciently, however, it was the principal medium of trade, the symbol of wealth.

In the writings of the early Christian fathers it was a symbol of Christ, the true sacrifice. The ox was also the symbol of prophets and saints slain for their faith and of all those who patiently bore the yoke and labored silently for the benefit of others.

In illustrations of the nativity scene, the ox's symbolism varied. As I have already observèd, the ox was introduced together with the ass in accordance with the prophecy "the ox knows his owner, and the ass his master's crib" (Isaiah i.3). In some instances the ox symbolized the Jews and the ass the Gentiles; the ox was likened to the Jews because it bore the yoke, whereas the ass represented the Gentiles because it carried Christ willingly when he rode into Jerusalem. In a fifteenth-century Book of Hours, cited by Franc, however, the ass represented the Old Law of unenlightened Israel, menacing the Child with its teeth. The ox was a symbol of sacrifice and of the New Testament, seeking to protect the Child with its horns.

The ox was assigned to St. Luke because it was an animal of sacrifice. Durandus explained the symbolism of the four evangelists:

> Matthew is signified by a man, because his gospel is principally occupied concerning the humanity of Christ: whence his history beginneth from his human pedigree. St. Mark by a lion which roareth in the desert, for he chiefly describeth the Resurrection; whence his gospel is read on Easter Day. The lion is said to rouse his whelps on the third day after their birth. His gospel beginneth, "The voice of one crying in the wilderness." St. Luke by the ox, an animal fit for sacrifice: because he dwelleth on the Passion of Christ. St. John by the eagle, because he soareth to the Divinity of Christ, while the others walk with their Lord on earth.

In its traditional secular meaning, the ox appears as the badge of the Whitney family. An ox's head decorates the frontispiece of Geoffrey Whitney's *A Choice of Emblemes* with the words *victoria ex labore, honesta, et utilis* (victory, achieved by labor, honorable and useful).

The *black* ox of the proverb "the black ox has not trod on his foot" had a specialized meaning in the Renaissance which has now lost its significance. Death riding on a black ox was a well-established tradition in late medieval iconography, and the black ox of the proverb originally alluded to death itself. Then the black ox came to represent the cares of life in general. As used by Robert Greene and others, the phrase meant that the individual in question had not yet experienced unhappiness.

Durandus, p. 46, n. 37; Franc, p. 45; Greene (ed. Grosart), XII.158, 270–71; Taylor, pp. 266–78; Whitney, p. iv; Whittick, p. 232.

Panther

The most distinctive quality of the panther was the sweet smell of its breath. Its exhalations were said to be capable of stunning into acquiescence all other animals, however fierce. According to Pliny and other early natural historians, the panther used its gift to lure other animals to their destruction. Christian tradition, however, effected a change in the symbolism.

The panther was said to derive its name from πανθήρα because it was a friend of "all animals" except the dragon. In illustrations in bestiaries, in carvings and sculptures, the panther may be seen breathing upon smiling, transfixed animals. At Alney Church and Newton Church in

The ox, accustomed to draw the plough, looks around for his companion.

Yorkshire, the panther, open-mouthed, confronts a terrible winged dragon. This panther symbolized Christ overcoming the Devil (in the form of a dragon) and drawing all men unto him. Sometimes its breath was likened to the virtue which went out of Christ and healed the woman who touched the hem of his garment.

131

The breath of the panther is so sweet that it attracts all animals except the dragon.

As in the case of the leopard, the panther's variegated coat had from earliest times caused it to be charged with deceit. It allured only to destroy. The ancient Egyptians, according to Horapollo, used the animal to symbolize a man who concealed an evil disposition.

Although Christian symbolism saw the panther's coat as signifying the many attributes of Christ, the interpretation in the Renaissance was mainly pejorative. Both its coat and its breath were said to represent guile. *Allicit ut perimat* (it attracts in order to destroy) was an emblem repeated by Aldrovandi and others. Reusner's motto *abstine Venere et Baccho* (avoid Venus and Bacchus) hinted at the panther as a sexual symbol and also made use of a traditional notion that the panther was easily overcome by strong drink.

The Elizabethan clergyman Topsell considered that the panther was the animal which most closely resembled woman, "for it is a fraudulent though beautiful beast"; Topsell used the fable of the panther's sweet breath to enforce the analogy:

> for as the Panthers by their sweet smels drawe the beastes unto them and then destroy them, so also doe harlots decke and adorne themselves with all the alluring provocations, as it were with inchaunted odors, to drawe men unto them, of whom they make spoyle and rapine.

132

Aldrovandi, p. 81; Evans, p. 135; Horapollo, ii.xc; Mc-Culloch, pp. 148–51; Philippe de Thaon, *Best.* pp. 82–83; Reusner, ii.xx; Topsell, pp. 578–82.

Porcupine

The porcupine's quills gave it a curious fighting power, according to early natural historians such as Pliny: *Ora urguentium figit canum et paulo longius iaculatur* (it pierces the mouths of the dogs when they close with it, and shoots at them when further off).

This kind of individual archery made it a fine heraldic animal. Charles the Bold took the device of the porcupine with the legend *qui s'y frotte, s'y pique* (who provokes, gets stung); the Duke of Orleans in 1397 instituted the Order of the Porcupine with the motto *cominus et eminus* (from far and near), meaning that he would attack his enemy John, Duke of Burgundy, both at a distance and near at hand. The knights of the Order wore a ring engraved with the porcupine and a necklace with a gold porcupine as a pendant. The Duke of Orleans' grandson abolished the Order but retained the porcupine as a hereditary badge.

Aldrovandi, p. 477; Camerarius, lxxxiv; Pliny, viii.35.53; P. S. Robinson, p. 161; Tervarent, col. 315.

Rabbit

The fecundity of the rabbit, like that of the hare, has made it a symbol of generative power from early times. Today's bunny-girl testifies to the strength of that symbolism. *Bunny* is a diminutive of *bun*, a northern word meaning "rabbit's tail," and this word, as we shall see later, had a special meaning in the argot of the streets. Essentially, the bunny-girl is callipygian: her most provocative feature is a bobbing movement of the buttocks —a reminder of the rabbit's distinctive scut.

The rabbit is a comparatively recent import to England. In ancient Rome it was the hare (*lepus*) which was highly valued, not only as the animal of Venus, goddess of love, but as a medical remedy for sexual deficiencies and as a beast of the chase. Pliny, writing his *Historia naturalis* in the first century of our era, told of the rabbit (*cuniculus*) in Spain and of its damage to crops on the Balearic Islands. But the rabbit probably did not become established in England until the thirteenth century. Even in the fourteenth century its price was high, suggesting that the rabbit was by no means common.

The rabbit quickly assumed the symbolism of the hare. A play on words enforced the meaning. The Latin words *cunnus* (the pudendum) and *cuniculus* (rabbit) devel-

ant que trop ont la este
di sa coupe en a dame
len a molt gabe
nt por le mengier haster
cillies si fist leue donner
tuit assis au disner

Comment alixandre troue
grant nombre pour comb
Omara a non
ou se vont he
Il su midis p
quant il dure

A soldier shoots at two cowering rabbits; in medieval times a timid soldier was called a rabbit.

oped into *conin*. Thus, an animal prized for its fertility became the perfect symbol for woman as a whole and for a specific part of her anatomy. One of the most obvious references to this kind of word-play dates from the middle of the fifteenth century, according to the *Glossarium* of Du Cange, but even earlier instances of the symbolism occur in the *Roman de la rose*, in poems of Eustache Deschamps, and others. In English the metaphor carries similar meanings: Skelton's repulsive Elinour Rumming is called by her husband "his nobbes and his coney, / His sweeting and his honey" for the good ale which she brews. "A pox on your Christian cockatrices!" exclaims a gentleman in *The Virgin Martyr* by Massinger and Dekker. "They cry, like poulterers' wives, No money, no coney" (II.i). The expression *larder le connin* in early French farce was probably a colloquially current term for seduction, and a similar meaning still attaches to the act of chasing rabbits—*faire la chasse aux conins*.

In England *coney* and *bunny* have had the meaning of *pudendum* up to the present day. *Cunny-warren*, according to Partridge, may have meant "brothel" in the latter half of the eighteenth and the first half of the nineteenth century. The use of *bun* for "prostitute" was recorded in Glasgow in 1934.

An entirely different meaning comes from Robert Greene's entertaining pamphlets of life in the London underworld in the last decade of the sixteenth century.

134

Here *coney* means "dupe," and *coney-catching*, "swindling." In the early part of the seventeenth century a collective society of sharpers was called a *warren* and their victims *rabbit-suckers*, according to Dekker's *English Villainies*.

Today, apart from having a sexual significance, the rabbit is a symbol of timidity. Even this symbolism is longstanding: in the Middle Ages the rabbit denoted a soldier who burrowed underground or someone who fled from his pursuers.

Deschamps (ed. Raynaud), IV.281; Greene (ed. Grosart) x; Partridge, *Slang*, pp. 108, 110, 171, 197; Pliny, VIII.55.81; *Roman de la rose*, 15138–42; Veale, pp. 209–14.

Ram

When Shakespeare's heroine Desdemona runs off with a Moor, the words which Iago uses to describe the event to her father would be judged indelicate even today:

> Zounds, sir, you're robb'd; for shame, put-on
>   your gown;
> Your heart is burst, you have lost half your soul;
> Even now, now, very now, an old black ram
> Is tupping your white ewe.
>
> (*Othello*, I.i)

But the suggested act is one for which the black ram is symbolically renowned. As an ancient astronomical symbol, the ram is traditionally associated with virility and violence, and it is an attribute of Mars. Its aggressiveness is frequently demonstrated in illustrations in bestiaries and psalters, where two butting rams collide head on with their horns, and in heraldry where the ram is represented as *sautant*, the symbol *d'autorité, de puissance, d'amour brutal et fécondant.*

Because of its symbolism, the black ram was used in a primitive custom observed in certain parts of England for several centuries. In the manors of east and west Enbourne in Berkshire, in the manor of Torre in Devon, and in other areas of western England, the widow of a copyhold tenant was entitled to continue the tenancy provided she was chaste. Should she be otherwise, she could regain her rights in a certain manner: she had to ride into the court of the manor backward on a ram, holding its tail in her hand and reciting:

> Here I am riding upon a black ram,
> Like a whore as I am.
> And for my Crincum Crancum
> Have lost my Bincum Bancum,
> And for my tailes game
> Am brought to this worldly shame.
> Therefore, good Mr. Steward, let
> Me have my lands again.

Duchaussoy, pp. 88–89; Carroll, p. 63; Hazlitt, pp. 109, 149–50, 182; Rowland, *Blind Beasts*, pp. 147, 151–52.

Rat

The black or ship rat was not known to the ancient Greeks and Romans and was probably imported into Europe from the Levant by the Crusaders. The brown or common rat is even more recent; on its arrival this rat quickly assumed the current symbolism of the mouse

Rat with cat.

as a supernatural creature. Its nature gave it a reputation as a portent of evil, particularly in dreams, and incantatory charms were used to try to get rid of it—hence the expression "rhyming a rat to death."

The pejorative significance, which it still retains, is apparent in an early fifteenth-century political squib:

> The Rat, the Cat, and Lovell the Dog,
> Rule all England under the Hog,

referring to the triumvirate Ratcliff, Catesby, and Viscount Lovell (the king's "spaniel"), and to Richard III, whose crest was a boar. The symbolism was only too obvious and cost the writer his head.

Two rats had a special significance. In the mid-thirteenth-century *Golden Legend*, in the story of Barlaam and Josaphat, two rats gnawing at a tree trunk were said to symbolize the way life erodes, night and day. Subsequently, in religious art, in themes which illustrate the fleeting nature of time and earthly pleasures, a white rat and a black rat were used to symbolize night and day.

Whitney shows an emblem of rats playing around caged cats, with the caption *Impunitas Ferociae Parens* (Impunity, the parent of cruelty). Here the rat stood for the wicked man who rejoiced in imprisoning worthy men.

Krappe, *Folklore*, p. 253; Panofsky, *Studies*, pp. 80–81, and n. 42; Tervarent, cols. 321–22; Whitney, p. 222.

Satyr

The hairy nature god Pan was commonly represented both in Egypt and Greece under the symbolic form of a goat. Pan was half-humanized and possessed a phallus of disproportionate magnitude to signify his predominant attribute. Among Pan's companions were human-like creatures with the legs, horns, and tail of a goat. These creatures were usually called satyrs. *Satyr* was believed to derive from σαθή (*membrum virile*). The implication of lasciviousness probably accounts for Hamlet's finding it a suitable name for his uncle:

> So excellent a king; that was, to this,
> Hyperion to a satyr.
>
> (I.ii)

Shakespeare's contemporary Topsell regarded it as a kind of lustful ape, as indeed did some earlier writers.

At the beginning of the Christian era, Philostratus condemned the satyr as a creature addicted to wine and women, and in medieval times it was a symbol of vice. Its currency no doubt owed something to Isaiah's grim prophecy of the fall of Babylon, in which he pictured satyrs dancing in the ruins.

In medieval times also the satyr's goat-like body, cloven hoofs, and tail became the property of the demons of hell,

Satyrs are addicted to wine and women.

137

and Pan himself was transformed into the Prince of Incubi. The commentators were well aware of the significance of the caprine features: "Satyrs are depicted with horns of a goat," wrote a Vatican mythographer, "because they are never satisfied in lechery."

Bode, pp. 252–53; Druce, "Some Abnormal . . . ," p. 152; Evans, p. 317; Philostratus, *Imag.*, 1.22; Pliny, v.1.1, vi.30. 35; Réau, 1.118; Topsell, p. 12.

Sheep

The sheep still possesses the quality that it had in moral lessons in the Sacred Books: it symbolizes stupidity and blind submission. The animal is also associated with the concept of the innocent victim going helplessly to the slaughterhouse or into the jaws of the wolf—the symbol of cunning and rapacity.

In early Christian times, however, the symbolism of the sheep was elevated by association with the sacred Lamb, the symbol of Christ. In the mosaics of the early churches and on the sarcophagi of the catacombs, twelve sheep were often depicted standing in two rows on either side of a central sheep or lamb. Here they symbolized the twelve apostles. Sometimes the sheep were shown coming out of two cities—usually interpreted as being Jerusalem and Bethlehem—and going toward the holy mountain on which the Lamb of God stood.

To the theologians the sheep was a perfect symbol of kindliness and gentleness because it surrendered its most precious possessions, its wool and its milk. Since the sheep was a sacrificial animal, a gift to Jehovah on the part of the community, as well as a domesticated animal which fed and clothed humanity, it also became an attribute of charity in medieval times. It appears thus in the circle of virtues and vices decorating the plinths of the jambs on the central porch of the façade of Notre Dame. As in the case of the other virtues, Caritas holds up a circular disc, and the symbolic device of the sheep upon it helps us to establish her identity.

The term *black sheep* usually symbolizes someone who is a disgrace to his family. Its origin is not clear. The black sheep was apparently already proverbial in a derogatory sense in 1598. An English writer used it while commenting on the disastrous effect of the contemporary drive to produce more sheep at the expense of appropriating arable and common land:

> Sheepe have eate up our pastures, our
> meddowes, and our downes,
> Our Mountaines, our men, our villages
> and Townes;
> Till now I thought the common proverb
> did but jest,

138

> That states a blacke sheep is a biting
>   beaste.

The pejorative sense may derive from nothing more than the fact that a black sheep looks different from the rest of the flock. On the other hand, I consider that it may be a synonym for the French *une brebis galeuse* (an itchy, scabby sheep). For centuries sheep were subject to numerous cutaneous infections for which an application of tar from the shepherd's tar-box was the usual remedy. Both the tar and the bare patches of diseased skin might account for the term.

In ancient China, sheep were a symbol of the retired life; the lamb symbolized filial piety. In ancient Greece, as the effigy of Lais indicated, the sheep caught in the haunches of a lioness might have a popular significance more in keeping with that sometimes attached to a black sheep.

Hulme, pp. 120, 123, 168; Katzenellenbogen, p. 76, n. 1; Morgan, pp. 59–60; Topsell, p. 626; Twining, pp. 22, 26.

Siren

Sirens and mermaids were once antithetical in character. In Homer's *Odyssey* a mermaid, Ino of the Fair

Enchanted by the sirens' song, the sailors fall asleep.

The siren represents sensual pleasure; hence she is accompanied by an ape.

Ankles, saved the life of Ulysses; sirens, on the other hand, sought to lure him to destruction and would have done so had he not tied himself to the mast of his ship and stopped up the ears of his mariners with wax. Ino lived in the sea; Homer's sirens were not sea-creatures but inhabited an island and had the Earth as their mother.

Ino of the Fair Ankles was, of course, formerly mortal.

Nevertheless, mermaids may have originally been fertility or fish goddesses. Certainly early in the Christian era they came to possess one or even two fishtails, whereas sirens, once all voluptuous female, acquired bird-like characteristics, probably on account of their alluring voices.

Pliny did not believe in them; Ovid gave sirens feathers. In the Middle Ages the features of both mermaids and sirens became confused. They might be all woman, part fish, part fowl, or even part horse. A misericord at Carlisle shows a mixed transitional stage: a siren with feathers and claws, and a fishtail. Lord Byron's crest of the mermaid with comb and looking glass comes from this period.

There was never any doubt concerning their symbolic meaning: medieval theologians thought them "stout whores," serving as deterrent examples of sexual enticement. To support their belief, the theologians cited a pre-Vulgate translation of Isaiah xiii.22, which made sirens dance with satyrs and other evil creatures in Babylon.

To the mythographer, sirens represented corporeal pleasures: Ulysses was restrained by virtue from such enticements; the wax that stopped the ears of the sailors consisted of the precepts of salvation. Ulysses tied to the mast also became the figure of Christ on the cross; the ship in this instance was the church, the ear wax the Scriptures, and the sirens fleshly lust.

The sirens' music might be voice, flute, or stringed instrument, but the result was the same: their victims were lulled to sleep and destroyed. "Such are they," declared Hugh of St. Victor, "who love the delights of this world, its pomp and theatrical pleasures. Made dissolute by tragedies and comedies, as if overcome by a heavy sleep, they become the prey of the Devil." Honorius "of Auton" made even finer distinctions: the singing mermaid was avarice, the pipe-player was pride, and the siren who plucked the lyre was lechery. These were "the three delights which soften the human heart to vice and lead it to the sleep of death."

The siren that Dante dreamed of was a hideous, stuttering crone, squint-eyed, club-footed, with deformed hands and the dead white complexion so often attributed to prostitutes. In his eyes, however, she grew beautiful, and he could hardly resist her song until his guide, Virgil, callously ripped her bare—"all of her front, her loins and her foul belly." The stench which then arose was so overwhelming that Dante awoke in nausea. Here the siren symbolized excessive physical appetite to which man was constantly tempted.

The moral significance of the siren was still stressed in the Renaissance. Camerarius told of the sweet song of the siren with the motto *mortem dabit ipsa voluptas* (pleasure itself will give death). Whitney referred to the story of Ulysses and observed that the man who succumbed to the snare of sirens destroyed himself.

When she ceased to be a supposed fact of natural history, the siren-mermaid lost most of the baleful aspects of her nature except among psychologists who saw her as "none other than the beloved and incestuously desired mother . . . whose all but inconquerable lure brings death (castration) in its train." For the rest, she has continued to exist in the imagination because she represents all the bitter-sweetness of love and beauty that is sung of in ballad or dreamed of in long, lonely nights at sea. When Mallarmé looked at the glass of champagne in which he was to toast poetry and fellow poets, he saw the froth turn into the foam of magic seas in which there was a glimpse of the white flanks of the sirens. T. S. Eliot's poor old Prufrock, the humdrum product of a humdrum civilization, heard the sirens singing each to each but he knew they would not sing to him. Their song symbolized all the unattainable loveliness that man was capable of imagining.

Anderson, *Med. Carv.*, p. 100; Bunker, p. 429; Camerarius, *see* Green, p. 255n; Dante, *Purg.*, XIX.1–33; Homer, *Od.*, v.346, XII.166f.; Honorius, *PL*, CLXXII, cols. 855–57; Pseudo-Hugo St. Victor, *PL*, CLXXVII, col. 78; Mallarmé, *Salut*; Ovid, *Metam.*, v.552; Pliny, x.49.70; Whitney, p. 10.

Snake

The snake has been regarded as a phallic totem from earliest times. The snake may owe its predominant symbolism to the fact that, with its head reared up, ready to strike, it resembles an erect phallus. Some snakes even expand the head or neck just before the kill.

Its phallic meaning is most obvious in ancient Hebrew myth. The Tempter in the Garden of Eden was the serpent, and the first thing Adam and Eve did after the Fall was to cover their genitalia: their sin was sexual.

In most early civilizations, however, this symbolic phallic power, far from being pejorative, combined with the snake's genuine physical characteristics—its apparent tenacity for life which causes it to pulsate even in death, its longevity, its ability to cast off its skin—to make it a god. "Paint two snakes, my boys," dryly observed Persius in one of his satires, "and the place is then holy."

The reasons which made the serpent divine also made it the symbol of healing power. "They have set apart the serpent to Aesculapius," explained Phurnutus in his work on the nature of the gods, "because those who are engaged in this healing art make use of it as a symbol for becoming young, as it were, after sickness, and for putting off old age." The serpent coiled around the staff became not only the insignia of Aesculapius but that of Hippoc-

rates and of Hygeia, the goddess of healing. It was lifted up by Moses in the wilderness to cure the Israelites of snake bites, and, as in all serpent cults, it was worshipped and had to be destroyed—"and he [King Hezekiah] broke into pieces the bronze serpent that Moses had made, for until these days the people had burned incense to it" (II Kings xviii.4).

The caduceus or two copulating serpents between the scepter or spear of dominion, which remains the symbol of the medical profession to this day, was the adjunct of the man or god who had power over life. In ancient Greece and Rome the caduceus was therefore carried by heralds and, in mythology, by Hermes, whose function it was to proclaim war.

The entwined serpent pair, a motif seen in earliest Mesopotamian art, had a similar meaning. It was a symbol of the life-giver, and for that reason, in India, women desiring children set up stone slabs called *nagalkals*, decorated with these serpent forms, in temple courtyards and under holy trees.

The snake head of Medusa represents an inversion. At Corfu, Medusa belonged to the matriarchal stage of religious belief, and like many ancient deities she had snake characteristics simply as symbols of immortality and sacredness. She combined with the Gorgons only when the male superseded the female deity as leader of the Parthenon. The shift from maternal to paternal dominance gave her the fatal head. It was the pudendum, at once an attraction and symbol of castration to those who dreaded her power.

A similar symbolism is associated with the orgies of Dionysus. According to Plutarch, respectable Greek matrons ran screaming through the forest with live serpents entwined in their hair. In literal accounts, they tore living animals to pieces with their teeth; in myth, they killed Pentheus, king of Thebes, who tried to witness their rites, and Orpheus, who spurned their attentions. For a man to meet these women in their divine frenzy meant death.

This antithetical symbolism is not exceptional. Because it was chthonic, the snake frequently represented the destructive principle. Its malignant role is most strikingly depicted in conjunction with the eagle, the latter representing lightness or good overcoming darkness or evil. This motif is not only very early—it appears on a sacrificial goblet of King Gudea of the Sumerian period, circa 2600 B.C.—but also widely diffused. In Mexico the sun, the supreme deity, took the shape of an eagle. It killed the snake and the rabbit, symbols of the night sky and the moon; when the solar priests dispatched the sacrificial victims, they wore collars decorated with the snake. In India, Garuda, an eagle-like bird, was the champion of heaven and was addressed as *nagantaka, bhujagantaka* (he who kills nagas or serpents).

Similar symbolism in Greek mythology is the basis of a dramatic episode in Homer's *Iliad*: an eagle carrying in its talons a bleeding snake appeared above the Greek heroes who were besieging Troy. Calchas rightly interpreted the omen as denoting the ultimate success of the Greeks: the configuration symbolized the victory of the patriarchal principle over the female one of Troy, whose Asiatic goddess, Aphrodite, had induced Helen to break the bonds of her marriage under the masculine order of the Greeks and to select her own mate, Paris.

In medieval Christendom the various symbolic meanings were modified, although the polarities remained. The Evil Serpent was, of course, the Devil, and in the cosmic conflict between the eagle and the serpent, Christ replaced Zeus, for whom the eagle was the surrogate.

The Devil was the Old Serpent in more ways than one. If he had its reputed wisdom, that wisdom was now suspect: he was a lion on account of his ferocity, declared St. Augustine, and a serpent on account of his guile. According to his devotees, the Devil also had a snake-like sexual organ. It was hard and exceptionally large, and because it was forked like a serpent's tongue, he was able to perform coition and pederasty simultaneously. Since the church attributed pacts with the Devil to primarily sexual motives, throughout the Middle Ages he continued to be represented as a gigantic serpent or dragon with tail, penis, and even arms composed of snakes.

The serpent offers Eve an apple.

The malign female power anciently symbolized in the snake was curiously reflected in the myth of the Fall. As in the Hebraic tradition, Christian myth held that the serpent caused sin to enter the world. The symbolism is somewhat confused, as this serpent was also a woman. In the Talmud myth, Lilith, the former wife of Adam, became a serpent and gave Eve forbidden knowledge. In ecclesiastical art and architecture this myth was frequently superimposed on the Christian myth, and the serpent twining around the tree of knowledge was often given a woman's face. In the fifteenth-century manuscript of *Tres Riches heures of Jean de France*, the Eden serpent coils its reptilian rump around the trunk of an apple tree, and above, in the branches, a long-haired nymph with a thirty-eight-inch bosom coquettishly hands out an apple. The serpent in *Ortus sanitalis*, a Latin herbal first printed in 1491, lacks hands to proffer the apple. She twines round the trunk and hangs two seductive breasts over one of the lower branches. Father Petrus Comestor, quoting from a now lost statement by Bede, confirmed that the serpent in Eden had a maiden's face (*virgineum vultum*), and in the medieval Chester mystery plays the costume assigned to the Devil for his role in the Garden of Eden was called "adder . . . with a mayden's face." Artists such as Ercole di Giulio Grandi, Filipinno Lippo, and Pietro d'Orvieto all showed the tempter as a serpent woman.

144

Facts and fictions of natural history concerning the snake gave rise to an ambivalent symbolism in the bestiaries: the snake sloughing off his skin was used as a symbol of Man putting off the old Adam:

When the snake has grown old, its eyes become dim and are oppressed by sloth. So it abstains from food and fasts many days in order that its skin shall loosen, and it seeks out a narrow crack in a stone, enters therein and works itself through and thus casts off its old skin. Thus it behoves us to enter by the narrow gate through many sorrows and fastings, so that, when the burden of our years has been cast aside and our old age already, as it were, sloughed off, we may take on ourselves a new nature in that Jerusalem which is on high.

But the snake's reputed habit of exposing its whole body in order to shield its head from the blows of an assailant lent itself to an entirely different moralized explication. Here the snake was the good Christian enduring every affliction for the sake of Christ, who was his head.

The cross or scepter entwined by the serpent still symbolized renewal, especially spiritual. Moses' serpent became a symbol of Christ crucified, both in John iii.14 and in the apocryphal Epistle of Barnabas xii.7. Barnabas stressed that the serpent hung on "a wooden thing" and was a life-restorer. Some exegetical writers, on the other hand, declared that the cross was brass because brass was the most solid and durable of metals and could best express the divinity of Christ and the eternity of his reign. Jesus was the new serpent who had vanquished the old. "What is the serpent lifted up?" asked St. Augustine. "The death of the Lord on the cross. For as death came by the serpent, it was figured by the image of the serpent."

In the Renaissance ancient motifs reappeared with a variety of secular interpretations. The serpent with its tail in its mouth, forming a circle, which was the Egyptian symbol of eternity and immortality, was similarly used by the emblem writers. The colophon of Alciatus' *Emblematum libellus* (1534) shows a snake rising from the sea to bite its tail. Inside the circle is a fishtailed mermaid with the muscular arms and well-developed breasts of a powerful swimmer. The motto is *ex literarum studiis immortalitatem acquiri* (acquire immortality from the study of literature). Here the serpent is immortality and the mermaid and her song are literature.

Marsilio Ficino (1576) declared that, like the Egyptians, one could learn everything about time from the emblem. Samuel Richardson, a printer by trade, used the same emblem nearly two centuries later, placing it on the coffin of Clarissa in his novel of that name. While he intended the figure to have its traditional significance, in association with his inhibited, narcissistic heroine it appears to stand for ceaseless or self-consuming desire.

The snake in the bosom was a symbol of envy or ingratitude. In the medieval *Gesta Romanorum*, an emperor out hunting found a serpent frozen to a tree. He released the snake and warmed it in his bosom, only to be bitten for his pains. Here the serpent was the Devil in true medieval tradition, and the emperor was any good ecclesiastic. But Renaissance writers used the story allusively with a secular allegory: "Snakes in my heart blood warm'd, that sting my heart," exclaimed the king in *Richard II* (III.ii), on hearing that some of his nobles had made peace with Bolinbroke. Engravings in emblem books show the fabled emperor as a peasant, with the climactic scene taking place in a country cottage. A snake, too large to twine round any tree or to be accommodated in any bosom, rears up by a blazing fire, and the peasant lifts his axe to defend himself. With Freitag the motto was *maleficio beneficium compensatum* (a good deed recompensed by maliciousness). Whitney used the motto *in sinu alere serpentum* (to nourish a serpent in the bosom) and applied it to Antwerp which, because of internal dissensions, fell victim to a siege in 1585.

The snake twining decoratively around leaves, fruit, and flowers of strawberry plants in the engravings of the same writers had a similar significance. It was the snake in the grass, the epitome of dissimulation and malice. A medal struck to commemorate the discovery of the Gunpowder Plot in 1605 showed the word JEHOVAH set in solar rays on one side and a snake gliding through lilies and roses on the other.

The snake in the grip of the eagle was used as a personal device by ecclesiastics even in the Middle Ages. In the Renaissance, both Charles of Bourbon and Charles of Navarre had medals struck with the same device, with the motto *dimicandum* (we must fight), implying that the owner was a victorious fighter. Henry III of France used the eagle and the snake in 1588 to celebrate the murder of Henry of Guise; according to the motto, the king saw himself as a man of piety and courage overcoming the wicked. Printers such as Rouillé and Thomas Laisne used the eagle and the snake for their colophons as a symbol of victorious virtue. The eagle with its two feet on a snake with reared head was the emblem of Christianus II, king of Denmark, again with the motto *dimicandum*. At the end of the eighteenth century the device became a symbol of Napoleonic conquest.

The snake and the dove were traditionally associated with wisdom and gentleness—"Be ye wise as serpents and harmless as doves" (Matthew x.16). As such they were the attributes of the medieval virtue Prudence, who was herself the descendant of the goddess of wisdom, Minerva. The symbolism accounts for the device of Marguerite of France, daughter of Francis I. Here an olive branch is entwined with serpents, with the motto *rerum sapientia custos* (Wisdom, the guardian of affairs). Queen

Elizabeth I was given a "monument" at Norwich in 1578 which was engraved with a serpent and a dove, and in a poem to her on New Year's Day, 1600, intended to flatter her, she was said to have a serpent's head.

There are numerous examples of the serpent appearing alone as the symbol of prudence, and probably for this reason it was adopted as a device by many early printers. Sometimes the serpent of prudence is in the form of a circle. Gabriel Symeon made for Catherine de Medici a device of a star encircled by a ring in the form of a snake, with the legend *fato prudentia major* (wisdom greater than destiny). Catherine, with her taste for lavish parties at Fontainebleau and for sumptuous art, must have been delighted by its ornateness. But the repercussions of St. Bartholomew's Eve, 1582, when she caused the massacre of fifty thousand Huguenots, suggest she would have been wiser to have let destiny take its course.

Emily Dickinson's snake aroused a "chilling at the bone"; D. H. Lawrence threw a stick at his and then wished he had been more hospitable. Less inhibited people have no trouble in accepting the snake's symbolism: until a few years ago young Neapolitans bought for a few cents representations of the phallus entwined with a serpent as lucky charms; among the Australian aborigines, when boys of the Murngin tribe are about to be circumcised in puberty rites, they are told: "The Great Snake smells your foreskin; he is calling for it," and their moth-ers wail over them ceremonially to prevent the Great Snake from swallowing them; in the Western world permissive flappers of the 1920s sported feather boas as they danced the "shimmy," and young people now drape large plush, violent-colored snakes around their necks or on their beds.

Yet, while the snake retains its hold on the imagination as a phallic symbol, apparently not everyone is consciously aware of its significance. "If we teach sex education in the schools," said a Toronto clergyman recently, "we will stir up a nest of snakes."

St. Augustine, *PL*, xxxvi, col. 867 and xxxvii, col. 1578 and xxxviii, col. 1342; *Bestiary*, Camb. FitzWilliam MS. 254, fol. 40; Creuzer, ii.ii.445; Ficino, ii.1768; Freitag, pp. 176–77; *Gesta Rom.*, clxxiv; Homer, *Il.*, xii.201 ff.; Horapollo, i.lxiv; Persius, *Sat.*, i; Petrus Comestor, *PL*, cxcviii, col. 1072; Petti, p. 75; Phurnutus, *De nat. deor.*, xxxiii; *Physiologus* (attr. to Epiphanius), pp. 50–70; Plutarch, *Lives*, Alexander, ii; Reusner, ii.xxii; Whitney, pp. 24, 76, 78, 118, 166, 189, 212; Wittkower, *passim*; Zimmer, pp. 72 ff.

Sphinx

Representations of this animal, part human and part animal, appeared in Egypt, Asia Minor, and Greece.

With its human head and lion's body, the Great Sphinx of Giza, looking due eastward from the pyramid field over the Nile valley, represented vigilance. Assyria gave the sphinx wings; the Hittites altered its hairstyle, preferring curly hair to the corrugated wig lappets; Greek sphinxes, usually either female or androgynous, were winged. The most famous sphinx was that at Thebes. The muses taught her a riddle which she then posed to every passer-by. Whoever failed to guess the riddle was carried off and devoured. The riddle—"What goes on four feet, on two feet, and on three?"—was at last correctly answered by Oedipus, who replied that man as a child crawled, as an adult he walked upright, and as an old man he supported himself with a stick. The image of the sphinx as a devourer seems to have been widely diffused in both Egyptian and Greek art.

In the Renaissance the sphinx was variously regarded as a symbol of impenetrable mystery, of ignorance, or of evil. On one of the fifteenth-century compartments in the pavement of the cathedral at Sienna, the two sphinxes accompanying the fabled sage, Hermes Trismegistus, illustrate an enigmatic quality that is now proverbial. The Italian philosopher Pico ascribed to the Egyptian sphinx the same quality. In an engraving formerly attributed to Zoan Andrea, the two winged sphinxes supporting the sphere on which the obese and androgynous figure of blind ignorance is enthroned have a contrary significance:

their meaning ultimately derives from the anonymous third-century Greek *Tabula Cebetis*, where the sphinx was equated with ἀφροσύνη (senselessness). Even more pejorative is the symbolism recorded by Topsell. The Theban sphinx, in his view, was a kind of evil Amazon. Because of the Greek myth concerning her, Alciatus in one of his emblems "deciphered that her monstrous trebleformed-shape signified her lustful pleasure under a Virgins face, her cruel pride under the Lions claws, her winde-driven levity under the Eagles or Birds feathers." Topsell's account also placed the sphinx in the animal kingdom:

The *Sphinx* or *Sphinga* is of the kind of Apes, having his body rough like Apes, but his breast up to his neck, pilde and smooth without hair; the face is very round yet sharp and piked, having the breasts of women, and their favour or visage much like them: In that part of their body which is bare without hair, there is a certain red thing rising in a round circle like Millet seed, which giveth great grace and comliness to their colour, which in the middle part is humane. Their voice is very like a mans but not articulate, sounding as if one did speak hastily with indignation or sorrow. Their hair is brown or swarthy colour. They are bred in India or Ethiopia . . . . They carry their meat in the storehouses of their own chaps or cheeks, taking it forth when they are hungry and so eat it . . . . The name of this Sphinx is taken from binding, as appeareth in the Greek notation, or else of delicacie and a dainty nice loosness (wherefore there were certain common strumpets called Sphinctae, and the Megarian Sphingas, was a very popular phrase for notorious harlots).

Gesner, whom Topsell translated, suggested that the sphinx of art, woman in front and lion behind, was merely the representation of a kind of ape. This simple explanation has not satisfied later writers who classify her with Lamia, Lorelei, witches, vampires, sirens, and the like. The sphinx's riddle, in particular, has been the subject of intensive investigation by Laistner, Reik, and others, with inevitably "Freudian" results. Róheim considered that it belonged to the group of riddles which had to do with the father and mother in bed, with the observer first seeing four legs (the man on all fours), then the two outstretched legs of the woman, and finally the third leg which, in most variants of the riddle, mysteriously disappears. The question has its basis in the anxiety associated with infantile experiences: the questioner, who dies when the answer is found, is herself the object of the riddle, the father and mother in one person, who awakens Oedipal tendencies in the child:

In very truth only "Swollen Foot" Oedipus can solve this riddle of the feet; for he is the victorious hero of the Oedipus tragedy of all mankind.

Iconographically, as Réau observes, the sphinx often appears to be the equivalent of a female centaur, but whereas the centaur is always represented in movement, the sphinx is characterized by extreme immobility. Not without significance is the fact that sphinx means strangler, deriving from the same Greek root as sphincter, the circular muscle.

Chastel, p. 180; Isidore, xii.ii.32; Panofsky and Panofsky, *Pandora*, fig. 23; Pico, pp. 152, 154; Réau, 1.120; Róheim, p. 22; Tervarent, pp. 363–64; Topsell, p. 14 (1658 ed.).

Tiger

When advertisers conducted a campaign to make the tiger a symbol of power, they had no difficulty in captivating the popular imagination. People were apparently only too ready to believe that a certain brand of gas "put a tiger in their tanks," and that a detergent whitened their wash with "tiger power." Before the campaign was over, the tiger no longer had to appear in a television advertisement; all that was necessary to convey the meaning was a gigantic roar.

That the tiger should be associated with energy was not new. What was unusual and, in fact, totally opposed to Western tradition, was that it should be represented

as a benign force, for the "good" tiger belongs mainly to the Orient. In China, for example, it was the symbol of power, especially of supernatural power, and of money. The Taoist god of wealth rode on a tiger, and the tiger watched over a magic money chest. Gamblers set up images of the tiger holding gold in its paws and burned incense to it. Because of its association with force and courage, the tiger was formerly painted on the shields and on some of the robes of the military. According to their color, tigers defended the spatial order against the forces of chaos. The black tiger reigned in the north, where his season was winter and his element fire. Similarly, the blue tiger prevailed in the east amid spring and vegetation, and the white tiger in the west, amid autumn and metals. At the center where the emperor had his chief palaces was the yellow, imperial, solar tiger. In India, on the other hand, the tiger was the symbol of fire.

In the West the swiftness and fierceness of the Hyrcanean tiger, which was described by Pliny and other natural historians, became proverbial. Although Sir Thomas Browne queried the validity of the first attribute, the two qualities were associated with the animal over the centuries.

While the tiger thinks that the face reflected in the glass sphere is its offspring, the wily hunter steals the cub.

Tigers were also said to have drawn the chariot of Bacchus when he crossed the Tigris river, and they came to symbolize the ferocity and inhumanity occasioned by overindulgence in the product of the god. In some representations, tigers are either devouring clusters of grapes or drinking the liquor pressed from them. Richard Payne Knight considered these tigers to be symbols of the powers of destruction in general; he cited as a further example a cameo, possessed by the Duke of Marlborough, on which a tiger sucked the breast of a nymph, representing the same power of destruction, "nourished by the passive power of generation."

By medieval times the tiger was firmly entrenched as the epitome of inhumanity. Among exegetical writers and later among secular writers it was identified with the Devil. Rabanus Maurus and Garnerus, when commenting on Job iv.11, likened the tiger to Satan because of its astuteness. Garnerus also regarded the tiger as a symbol of hypocrisy. Ulyssis Aldrovandi in the sixteenth century described how the tiger deceived its victims because of its attractive coloring; it was a symbol of Satan because of its guile. Both secular and religious writers saw the tiger as the image of wrath and lust, the irascible and concupiscent passions. Spenser used the tiger as a symbol of lawlessness in a fallen world when he metamorphosed Adicia into a tiger; it was the force that despoiled the pastoral and typified the evil which might erupt in man and his environment.

The tiger looking at its reflection in a glass sphere is the tiger of the fable. According to a story given in Ambrose's *Hexaemeron* and popularized by the bestiaries, a tiger pursuing a robber who has stolen her cubs is deceived by a trick. The robber throws down a glass sphere; the tiger, seeing her reflection in it, believes that it is the stolen cub and settles down to nurse it. The story did not lend itself very readily to religious allegorical interpretation, but the emblem writers saw the tiger as a symbol of man deceived by imitation. Other writers dealt less with the deception than with the revenge which, according to some versions, the tiger took when she finally pursued the hunter and tore his horse to pieces on the seashore. Revenge might diminish pain, said the moralists, but man should leave such punishment to God.

Little seems to have been known about the tiger in medieval times, and it was rarely used in heraldry. The animal which appears on the arms of Sir John Norwich, a fourteenth-century knight, is supposed to be a tiger, but it looks like a lion with a handlebar moustache at its nose. Yet the duplicity which characterized it, according to Aldrovandi, not only appears to be a fact of natural history but was also known in the Middle Ages. In Chaucer's *Squire's Tale*, a talking bird, describing her unhappy love affair to a princess, alludes to her false lover as "this tigre, ful of doublenesse" (543). In the jungle, deceit is the very quality which the tiger exemplifies. According to Wood,

> the tiger never appears to employ openly that active strength which would seem sure to attain its end, but creeps stealthily towards the object, availing itself of every cover, until it can spring upon its destined victim . . . . The tiger has, besides, a curious habit of drawing in its breath and flattening its fur, so as to reduce its bulk as far as possible.

It is, presumably, this ability for dissimulation that Robert Greene refers to in *The Groatsworth of Wit Bought with a Million of Repentence*, in a passage thought to allude to Shakespeare:

> For there is an upstart crow, beautified with our feathers, that with his tiger's heart wrapped in a player's hide, supposes he is as well able to bombast out a blank verse as the best of you: and being an absolute *Johannes fac totum*, is in his own conceit the only Shakescene in a country. (XII.144)

Shakespeare himself, while he most frequently uses the tiger as a symbol of inhumanity and ferocity, seems to have been mindful of the less popular symbolism. York, after his son has been murdered, addresses Queen Margaret, "the she-wolf of France," thus:

> O tiger's heart wrapped in a woman's hide!
> How could'st thou drain the life-blood of the child,
> To bid the father wipe his eyes withal,
> And yet be seen to bear a woman's face?

In the same scene (*Henry VI*, Pt. III, I.iv) York also uses Pliny's concept:

> But you are more inhuman, more inexorable—
> O, ten times more!—than tigers of Hyrcania.

The traditional values are also inherent in much later literary tigers, in Blake's "Tyger! Tyger! burning bright" as well as in "Christ the Tiger" in T. S. Eliot's *Gerontion*. Such ambivalent symbols particularly emphasize the power with which the animal is still popularly associated.

Aldrovandi, pp. 111–12; St. Ambrose, *PL*, XIV, col. 265; Browne, III.xxviii; Garnerus, *PL*, CXCIII, col. 113; Greene (ed. Grosart), XII.144; Knight, *Priapus*, pp. 148–49; Pliny, VIII.18.25; Rabanus Maurus, *PL*, CXI, col. 219; Spenser, *FQ*, v.viii.49; Wood, II, 130–31.

Unicorn

The fabulous unicorn of ancient folklore still turns up in poetry, popular song, and psychoanalysis as a symbol of both good and evil. Its most essential feature is, of course, its single horn, which from earliest times has been associated with curative and generative powers. In China the unicorn was the emblem of perfect good: the noblest of the animals, it lived one thousand years and symbolized longevity, grandeur, felicity, illustrious offspring, wise administration. Throughout the East it was a symbol of miraculous energy.

The animal was first described by Ctesias, a Greek physician at the court of Darius II of Persia in the fifth century B.C. It was exceedingly swift and powerful, and no creature—"neither the horse nor any other"—could overtake it. This description as well as that of Pliny's and other early historians seems to rely partly on the Indian rhinoceros. But the medieval unicorn was usually smaller and looked like a long-haired goat or a white horse; its horn, often convoluted, conical, and always sword-like, was as long as its body. Its reputation for great strength and fierceness may have been due to the fact that the Hebrew Re'ēm, in Numbers xxiii.22, Deuteronomy xxxiii.17, and Job xxxix.9–10, appeared in the Septuagint as μονόκερως, in the Vulgate as *unicornis* or *rhinoceros*, and in the Authorized Version as *unicorn*.

In an account of the hunt for the Abyssinian unicorn, the animal is rendered helplessly ecstatic by the amorous gesture of a female monkey. But its partner in the hunting episode is usually a woman naked to the waist.

The girl here is a beautiful virgin sent out into a forest

The unicorn can be captured only by a virgin.

or desert to decoy the unicorn. Attracted, so some versions state, by her smell, or, as others suggest, by the sight of her uncovered bosom, the unicorn loses its fierceness, crouches in her lap, plays with her, and then falls asleep, with the result that it can be taken by the hunters. Most explications in the bestiaries agree that the unicorn is

153

Christ who, descending into the Virgin's womb, is incarnate, captured, and condemned to death. The horn symbolizes Christ's unity with his Father; the unicorn's fierceness, the inability of any power to contain him; its smallness, Christ's humility; its kid-like appearance, His incarnation in the likeness of sinful flesh. The huntsmen stand variously for the angel Gabriel, the Jews, or God the Father pursuing the unicorn until it takes refuge in Mary's womb. The phallic nature of the symbolism is particularly obvious in a fifteenth-century German engraving of the Annunciation described by Evans. Gabriel, as a huntsman, blows the angelic greeting on a hunting horn. The unicorn, pursued by dogs, flees to the Virgin, who is sitting in a state of ecstasy with upturned eyes and her hands folded across her breast as the horn is plunged in her lap. God the Father blesses the pair from above. Here the unicorn clearly represents the fertilizing breath of the Holy Ghost or *Logos*, the Word of God made flesh.

In secular terms this figure offered further possibilities of interpretation. In miniatures, medallions, tapestries, and engravings of the fifteenth and sixteenth centuries in particular, it represented variously the triumph of chastity, a state of courtship and marriage, or the wiles of woman, including those having to do with sorcery.

In some representations, religious and secular symbolism occurs simultaneously. In the so-called Unicorn Tapestries at the Cloisters, in New York City, five of which were probably made for Anne of Brittany to celebrate her marriage to Louis XII in 1499, themes of the Incarnation, courtship, and marriage are simultaneously depicted in a richly decorative contemporary hunt. The tapestries are crowded with sniffing alaunts in spiked collars, prancing greyhounds, grim-faced, gesticulating huntsmen and courtiers, brocaded ladies, timid rabbits, a squirrel on a hazel-nut tree, birds clearly identifiable as pheasant, European goldfinch, and swallow. The figures give a compelling authenticity to scenes which culminate in the agony of the strange equine beast rearing up its long horn as three huntsmen spear its head and breast and hounds fix their teeth in its back and flanks. A concluding tapestry of slightly later date shows the unicorn sitting alone, its wounds exposed, chained to a single tree enclosed in a garden which is rich with flowers. Here the unicorn is the risen Christ; the garden is the *hortus conclusus* (enclosed garden) of the *Canticum* and symbolizes both the church and the Blessed Virgin; the pomegranate tree is the Cross, its fruit Christ.

Psalters also depicted the unicorn as symbolizing death. A parable, originally from the *Legend of Barlaam and Josaphat*, and subsequently incorporated in the *Golden Legend*, stated:

> They that desire the delights corporeal and suffer their souls die for hunger, be like to a man that fled before a unicorn that he should not devour him and in fleeing he

fell into a great pit, and as he fell he caught hold of a branch of a tree with his hands and set his feet upon a sliding place and then saw two rats, the one white and other black, which without ceasing gnawed the root of the tree and had almost gnawed it asunder. And he saw in the bottom of this pit, an horrible dragon casting forth fire and who had his mouth open and desired to devour him. . . . Then he lifted up his eyes and saw a little honey that hung in the boughs of the tree and thereupon he forgot the peril that he was in and gave himself entirely to the sweetness of that honey. The unicorn is the figure of Death, which continually followeth man and desireth to seize him. The pit is the world which is full of wickedness. The tree is the life of every man, who, by the two rats that are day and night, and the hours thereof, incessantly has been wasted and therefore approached to the cutting or gnawing assunder. . . . The horrible dragon is the mouth of hell which desireth to devour all creatures. The sweetness of the honey in the boughs of the tree is the false deceivable delectation of the world, by which man is deceived so that he takes no heed of the peril in which he is.

Death rides a unicorn in a miniature of Jean Colombe in the second part of the *Hours of Chantilly* (1485), according to Van Marle. In Dürer's Rape of Persephone, a unicorn is Pluto's mount as he carries off his bride to the underworld.

What of Spenser's "prowd rebellious unicorn," or more recently, Dylan Thomas' "unicorn evils" that run through hapless humanity? The wicked unicorn has always existed alongside the good. In an early bestiary edited by Max Goldstaub and Richard Wedriner from a manuscript in the Biblioteca Communale at Padua, the unicorn is a symbol of violent and cruel people who can only be subdued and rendered gentle by the grace of God. This unicorn of wrath appears in the twelfth-century *Ancrene Riwle*, a rule book for nuns, which includes in English for the first time a discussion with various animals associated with the Seven Deadly Sins. Here it is in the company of the lion of pride, the serpent of envy, the bear of sloth, and other evil beasts.

More commonly, however, the chastity, solitariness, and nobility of the unicorn are aspects subsequently stressed in heraldry, representations of saints, and emblems. Among the saints the unicorn became associated with St. Justina for purity and with St. Boniface as a symbol of solitude or the monastic life. For obvious reasons it was the symbol of Queen Elizabeth I. It also appeared early in the Scottish royal arms, but its origin is uncertain. Seton suggests that it may have been introduced as a supporter on James I's marriage to Jane Beaufort, the Beauforts as dukes of Somerset having used it. At the Union the unicorn became incorporated in the royal arms of both England and Scotland in a motif of great antiquity, once seen on the walls of ancient Persepolis itself, where the unicorn confronted its traditional enemy, the lion. Reusner in his *Emblems* (1581) chose the unicorn for the emblem *Victrix casta fides* (spotless faith victorious).

The therapeutic powers attributed to the unicorn gave rise to special symbolism. Aelian said that the horn of the unicorn was an antidote against poison. The bestiaries elaborated and popularized the idea. They told of a stream which had been poisoned by a dragon. Just when all the animals of the forest were gathering to drink, a unicorn entered the stream, made the sign of the cross, and purified the waters. Here the unicorn was Christ; the animals were sinners seeking salvation.

The miraculous properties of the unicorn became widely known. For centuries there was a brisk trade in drinking cups, salt cellars, and spoons believed to have been fashioned from the horn of the unicorn but, in fact, made from narwhal. Many cathedrals and rich men possessed an entire prophylactic horn. Queen Elizabeth I had one in her bedroom at Windsor valued at nearly ten thousand pounds. Even as late as 1789, instruments of "unicorn's horn" were used to test the royal food for poison in the court ceremonial of France. In a fifteenth-century Italian manuscript by Pope Gregory I, a unicorn illustrates an incident in the life of St. Benedict. The story has nothing to do with the unicorn but tells how the saint, because of his purity, was able to detect poison in a loaf of bread which had been sent him by an enemy. The parallel could be readily understood.

In the Renaissance, emblem writers referred to the curative properties of the unicorn. Bartholomew Alviano, hero at the Battle of Marignan, took it as his emblem because, according to Camerarius, he routed out his enemies just as the unicorn routed out poison. The unicorn also served as a mark for various printers and as an apothecary's sign.

In modern times there have been attempts to "explain" the unicorn. Zeckel, noting the phallic significance of the horn and various discrepancies in the legend of the virgin and the unicorn, questions whether the unicorn can be equated with the son in an Oedipal situation, castrated by his father (the hunter) for his sexual rivalry. He concludes that the unicorn does not basically represent the son but the totem animal, which is the father:

> This seemingly contradictory conclusion will prove to be closer to the truth than we have been before. The hunt now means the killing or castration of the father with the help of the mother. Those who are the delegates of the king, the huntsmen, are the group of sons who will take the trophy, the totem animal, alive or dead, to the king who will own its horn. Why to the king? He is the symbol of the father. It is obvious that the father was slain while having intercourse with the mother.

Suhr, observing the ancient and widespread belief in a composite creature which was solitary, ambivalent, much sought after, and which essentially possessed a single magical horn, suggested that in primitive times the unicorn was a symbol of a total solar eclipse.

Aelian, III.xli, IV.lii, XVI.xx; *Ancrene Riwle* (ed. Day), p. 89; Camerarius, xii, xiii, xiv; Ctesias, *PG*, CIII, col. 226; Dürer, *see* Panofsky, *Studies*, fig. 63; *Golden Legend*, p. 816, CLXXX; Ley, *passim*; McCulloch, pp. 179–83; Morgan, p. 8; Petti, p. 73; Pliny, VIII.21.31; Reusner, iv; Rorimer, *passim*; Seton, p. 274 n.; Shepard, *passim*; Spenser, *FQ*, II.v.10; Suhr, pp. 91–109; Thomas, "And Death Shall Have No Dominion"; Valeriano, II, s.v. "De rhinoceronte"; Van Marle, II.256; Zeckel, p. 356.

Viper

St. Ambrose in his *Hexaemeron* found a lesson in marital relations in the viper. This creature, he said, indulged in unnatural coupling. It went down to the seashore and with its hiss summoned a muraena, a kind of vicious sea eel. The female muraena, being very highly sexed, came at once to embrace it. Often, declared St. Ambrose, the married man tried to behave like a viper by seeking a lady friend.

The she viper's married life is short and painful.

There was some justification for the male viper's behavior: the female viper was very peculiarly constituted. According to one of the oldest versions of the bestiary, the male viper had the appearance of a normal man, but the female viper was only a woman to the waist: below

157

the navel she had a crocodile's tail and no place to conceive. When the male injected his seed into her mouth, she cut off his member and he died. According to Pliny, amorous vipers entwined so closely that they might be taken for a single animal with two heads. The male viper put its head into his spouse's mouth, and the female was so enraptured with pleasure that she bit it off: *viperae mas caput inserit in os, quod illa abrodit voluptatis dulcedine.* Retribution followed. The resultant progeny, having no place through which to be born, tore open their mother's side and killed her.

Pliny's account appears to have been known to the Egyptians, if we are to believe the statement of Horapollo. Horapollo said that the viper symbolized the woman who hated her husband. She wanted to kill him and was complaisant only during intercourse. Young vipers, gnawing through the belly of their mother, symbolized children plotting against their parents.

Misogynists were naturally attracted to the viper for the opportunities it afforded for symbolism. If the Pharisees and Sadducees were a generation of vipers to St. John the Baptist (Matthew iii.7), all women were vipers according to medieval antifeminists. Even in the sixteenth century the viper signified "a common woman or harlot lying in the way, to sting men with the contagion of her wantonness and lust."

The viper was also a very early symbol of envy and was frequently used as such in the Renaissance. Tervarent cites numerous engravings employing the symbol. A striking example of its use occurs in the book trade. On the mark of Theodore Reinsart, bookseller in Rouen (1576–1612), Fortune, a naked woman, stands on another woman, who has vipers in her hair. The motto is *Fortuna domat invidia* (Fortune overcomes envy).

St. Ambrose, *PL*, xiv, cols. 227–28; Ferne, ii.40; Horapollo, ii.lix, lx; McCulloch, pp. 183–84; Pliny, x.62.82; Tervarent, cols. 405–406.

Weasel

Although the weasel was credited with the ability to kill basilisks and with the knowledge of the herb of life, it has had an unsavory reputation in almost every country since early times. It was the symbol of a young woman, usually a bad one, and was basically associated with trickery. Aelian said that the weasel was once human but was transformed by Hecate, and there are innumerable folktales of the weasel as a shape-shifter. A weasel may become a beautiful girl in order to marry, but at the wedding feast she reverts to her animal nature and pursues a mouse. Various proverbs indicate that young women and weasels have lust and craftiness in common. *Si une fois une fille a fait l'amour*, runs the French proverb, *j'aimerais mieux garder un pré rempli de belettes* (once a girl has made love, I would rather look after a meadow full of weasels).

The weasel was associated with many forms of supernatural evil. In ancient Greece an assembly would break up if a weasel suddenly appeared in its midst. Artemidorus, who wrote a dream book in the second century A.D., regarded the weasel as a token of death or evil-doing. At the same time, in Apuleius' *Golden Ass*, witches transformed themselves into weasels. Even in modern folklore the sight of a weasel foretells misfortune, although disaster can sometimes be averted by throwing stones or making the sign of the cross.

In ancient Egypt, according to Horapollo, a weasel depicted a woman who performed the works of a man (ἄνδρος ἔργα πράττουσαν). Horapollo added the explanation that the weasel had a male pudendum, like a little bone. Plutarch, on the other hand, said that the ancient Egyptians took the weasel as a symbol of speech. He stated: "There are still many people who believe and declare that the weasel conceives through its ear and brings forth its young by way of the mouth, and that this is a parallel of the generation of speech."

The weasel's peculiar mode of conception and parturition was found by the medieval bestiarists to lend itself to moralization. Well aware that in the Bible the weasel was

The weasel revives its young with the herb of life.

classified as an unclean animal (Leviticus xi.29), they took it as a symbol of the unfaithful, of those men who received the seed of the Divine Word, the spiritual and celestial bread of the church, only to cast it from their hearing.

159

There was also a tradition, however, that the Virgin conceived through the ear—*Deus per angelum loquebatur et Virgo per aurem impregnabatur* (God spoke through the angel and the Virgin was impregnated through the ear)—and some writers noted the parallel.

As a magic animal the weasel was not, of course, always a pejorative symbol. Very ancient is the belief that it was able to intercede with the gods and that it used rue or the herb of life to restore life. In the *Gesta Romanorum*, the weasel typifies St. John and the other prophets who predicted the coming of Christ. As the enemy of the basilisk or serpent, it also became the symbol of Christ himself. Aldrovandi summed up the tradition when he observed that Christ was the weasel because he saved mankind and fought against the serpent, who was the Devil. In secular terms, emblem writers saw the weasel as a symbol of prudence and advised the cautious man to similarly fortify himself against his enemies.

What of the weasel that goes pop? The phrase is from a music-hall song of an extravaganza popular in the 1840s.

> Up and down the City Road,
> In and out the Eagle,
> That's the way the money goes,
> Pop goes the weasel.

The City Road, according to the *Westminster Magazine*, was haunted by "rouged and white-washed creatures with painted lips and eyebrows, and false hair." The Eagle was the local tavern. Partridge suggested that the phrase regarding the weasel may be of "erotic origin," but he did not explain. James Barke in his prefatory essay to *The Merry Muses* added another stanza beginning "Long and Thin goes too far in," which he said was sung in the school playgrounds of West Fifeshire. The weasel itself has been variously interpreted as a tailor's instrument to cut cloth, a hatter's iron to press felt, and a skin purse which popped open. *Pop* could mean to "hock" or "pawn."

There is also a song-dance which is a kind of kitchen version of the usual theme:

> Half-a-pound of two-penny rice,
> Half-a-pound of treacle,
> Mix it up and make it nice,
> Pop goes the weasel.

Here the use of the weasel may be easier to interpret: the dancer is supposed to imitate the darting, sinuous movement of the animal. Another version about the monkey chasing the weasel seems to support the contention of an erotic origin.

Aelian, xv.xi; Aldrovandi, p. 321; Apuleius, ii.xxv; Artemidorus Daldianus, iii.xxviii; Barke, p. 28; Duncan, *passim*; *Gesta Rom.* (ed. Oesterley), clxxii; Horapollo, ii. xxxvi; McCulloch, pp. 186–88; Meier, pp. 34–54; Pliny, viii.27.41; Réau, i.100 "Wald. Phys.," p. 408.

Wolf

Today the term *wolf* carries vague sexual connotations and a hint of derision. The human wolf, whether he actively pursues or simply whistles, has a predatory interest in girls. But he is a humorous figure because his proclivities have been exposed.

The early Christians in the catacombs used the same symbolism to illustrate the apocryphal story of Susanna and the Elders. Susanna was often depicted by Renaissance artists as a voluptuous blonde, with a very white skin, bathing in a pool in her garden while two rabbis peered lustfully through some bushes. (Afterward, because she repulsed them, they accused her of adultery.) Such was the economy of early Christian art that she was represented in the catacombs as a lamb between two wolves.

Many of the early associations of the wolf are paradoxical: a murderous beast of prey, the natural symbol of night and winter, and even of death itself, its fierceness and swift movement also caused it to be identified with the sun, the life-giver, and with life. In Greece the wolf was associated with both Apollo and Zeus. At Lycopolis, according to Macrobius, the Egyptians worshipped the wolf as Apollo. Osiris appeared as a wolf when he returned from the dead to help Horus take vengeance on

The wolf bites its paw because, by treading on a branch, it has aroused the guardians of the sheepfold.

Set. The Nez Perces in America believed that the human race was descended from a wolf. Romulus and Remus, according to ancient belief, were not only suckled by a wolf but born of one.

Associated with such ideas is the totemistic fantasy concerning the werewolf, a constant and general superstition existing from Scandinavia to the Mediterranean in the Middle Ages, though refuted much earlier by Herodotus:

It appears that the Neuri are sorcerers, and such they are confidently held to be both by the Scythians and by the Greek settlers in Scythia, who relate that once each year each Neurian becomes a wolf for a few days,

161

and then resumes his original form. This, however, they will never persuade me to believe, although they assert it roundly and confirm their statement by a solemn oath.

The antiquity and continuity of the belief establishes the eminence of the wolf as a universal baleful beast and helps to account for the persistence of its pejorative symbolism.

In Egypt there was an animal known as Ap-uat, the wolf-god, which acted as a psychopomp leading through death to bliss. In this figure of the wolf, death and lust were closely linked, as they are in primitive fantasies about coition. In Richard Payne Knight's *The Worship of Priapus* is an illustration from a temple of Bacchus at Puzzuoli in which a wolf is devouring grapes, the symbol of life or, more specifically, of the male genitals. In Celtic mythology, Lok was represented under the form of a wolf as the great destroying power of the universe. In Nordic mythology the monstrous wolf Fenris was destined ultimately to devour the sun.

The typical representation of Mars, god of war and death, in paintings, sculpture, tapestries, enamels, and miniatures until the end of the fifteenth century, is of a fierce-looking armed god of battle mounted on a chariot or cart. Almost invariably he is accompanied by a wolf, an acknowledgment of the indivisibility of war and lust. For similar reasons, the symbolism occurs much later in Shakespeare's *Troilus and Cressida*, where rapacity, particularly sexual rapacity, and martial violence become interchangeable metaphors. The end of both, says this play over and over, is self-annihilation. War within results in war without and, like Thersites' "wenching rogues," Troilus and Cressida, they swallow one another, or, as Ulysses says:

> . . . appetite, an universal wolf, . . .
> Must make perforce an universal prey,
> And last eat up himself.
>
> (I.iii)

More commonly the wolf was a symbol of any kind of rapacity. A man was a wolf, according to Boethius as translated by Chaucer, if he were "ardaunt in avarice, and . . . a ravynour by foreyn richesse" (IV, pr. 3). Ripa used the wolf in the company of an old hag to denote avarice: Aldrovandi referred to the frequent use of the wolf as an emblem of voracity, particularly with the inscription *Homines ab gulam in belluas* (men becoming beasts on account of greed).

The concept which appears to have especially stirred the imagination in medieval times stems from Matthew vii.15: "Beware of false prophets, which come to you in sheep's clothing, but inwardly they are ravening wolves." Used to denounce delinquent clergy or heretics, the wolf in sacerdotal garb found its way on to misericords and pillars of churches. Odo of Ceriton in the twelfth century

162

applied the idea to Cistercian monks to denounce their rapacity and hypocrisy. Monks were called wolves because they seized land so that they could entertain the nobility lavishly. The appellation was particularly apt because ancient authorities such as Pliny declared that wolves even ate earth when hungry. Pardoners, who had the power to sell "pardons" to contrite sinners, and heretical teachers with their "false turning of Holy Scripture" were called wolves by medieval preachers. Time after time negligent priests were scolded for handing over their flocks to wolves of uncertain identity. Chaucer's parson denounced those who "been the develes wolves that stranglen the sheep of Jhesu Crist" (*Parson's Tale*, 767); Wycliffe was scathing about the curate who would leave his sheep unguarded among the "wolves of helle" and ride "with grete cost to ferre placis for pride."

The wolf was also used as a symbol to denounce any person who misused his power, whether religious or secular. Dante applied the symbol both to the clergy and to his acquaintances in Florence. In the fourteenth-century allegory of love called *Le Roman de la rose*, the wolf not only represented false prelates but usurers, tax-collectors, coiners, bailiffs, magistrates, accountants, and others.

In the stories of the Reynard cycle, the wolf symbolized the brutal force of the aristocracy; the fox, the astuteness and resilience of the plebeians. While the king, more distant from his people, might pass for a lion, the baron in his castle, dominating the plain, was a wolf, an immediate power for evil. In the Reynard fables, the wolf, as the symbol of the baron, used forced labor from asses, cheated old she-goats with kids, was treacherous to neighboring wolves, and committed many other crimes. In some situations he was outwitted, but there was never any sympathy for him; he was a frequent victim of malice and bad luck, but he deserved whatever punishment he received.

There are a few instances in the literature of the Middle Ages where the wolf was portrayed sympathetically. Dante symbolized Count Ugolino and his sons as the wolf and his whelps when they were hunted across the mountain by Archbishop Ruggieri, who had betrayed them. In saints' lives the animal sometimes behaved in such a way as to suggest that it was really a sheep in wolf's clothing. Wolves guarded saints' bodies, guided them through forests, plowed their fields. Giraldus tells how a priest in a forest was approached by a polite wolf who wanted sacrament for his dying wife. He led the man of God to a hollow tree, where his expiring spouse unzipped her hide to reveal that both she and her husband were natives of Ossory, forced to assume the wolf-skin as the result of a curse.

But, in general, the concept of the wolf which exercised the imagination was not that of a desperate and pathetic quarry, the creature which, so modern zoologists tell us, has been much maligned. Alfred de Vigny in a romantic

163

age could present the wolf as the symbol of stoicism whose arduous life and silent, solitary death were matters for human emulation. But that was several centuries after wolves had ceased to roam the woods. Even in the early years of the fifteenth century wolves penetrated by night into European towns, including Paris, and throughout the Middle Ages the wolf's destruction as a beast of prey was authorized and rewarded. According to forest law, it was hunted from Christmas to March 25, but it was also taken by various snares and poisons and was probably hunted all the year. An old Welsh law said that everyone was free to kill a wolf and fox and various other animals which only did mischief. Of the criminal who abjured the realm, it was said that he "took the wolf's head." If, on his way out of the country, he turned aside from the main route, he might be slain, like vermin, by anyone who encountered him. A similar law existed among the Anglo-Saxons, and in the laws of Canute an outlaw was designated a *verevulf*; in other words, he was a man transformed into a wolf because of his antisocial behavior.

The wolf was popularly believed to have no joint in its neck and was therefore unable to turn it. To bestiarists it could thus symbolize a stiff-necked people, stubborn in sin. The bestiarists also remarked that the word *wolf* meant "ravisher," and for this reason the term was applied to the prostitute. From earliest times *lupa* did, in fact, mean "prostitute" as well as "she-wolf." The Lu-

percal temples became brothels, and in the vocabulary of brothel-keeping in ancient Rome were many related words: *lupanar*, *lupanarium*, *lupanus*, *lupariae*, and *lupor*. In Elizabethan times Topsell remarked:

> *Lupa* and *lupula* were the names of noble devouringe harlots, and from thence commeth *Lupanar* for the stewes. It is doubtful whether the nurse of Romulus and Remus were a harlot or she Wolfe, I rather thinke it was a harlot then [than] a Wolfe that nursed those children.

When the Latin satirist Plautus scoffed at young men who could not keep away from the brothels, he called the inmates wolves and their victims sheep. A similar sexual significance occurs in a scathing twelfth-century poem attributed to the satirist Walter Map. A worldly abbot in fur coat and fine linen goes into his church. He stops not by the altar but by a woman to whom he says, "Thou alone art my joy: thou shalt lie with me tonight." The angry poet continued:

> Does the woman consent? Yes, truly, nor can we be surprised since there is no wretch so poor that she may soon flaunt gold on all her fingers, if a monk pays a pound for that which the clerk gets for a halfpenny or for love. Of foul and preposterous thing, that turns God's temple into a brothel; for hither come the she-wolves daily.

164

Folklore reinforced the symbolism of the she-wolf. According to the *Romance of the Rose*, and *The Master of Game* and other works, particularly from the twelfth century onward, the she-wolf had peculiar mating habits and would eschew the most worthy suitor for the worst in the pack. Chaucer's Manciple uses the illustration to make the point that women have a natural taste for sexual depravity:

> A she-wolf hath also a vileyns kynde.
> The lewedeste wolf that she may fynde,
> Or leest of reputacioun, wol she take,
> In tyme when hir lust to han a make.
> (*Manciple's Tale*, 183–86)

The idea may have arisen by analogy to the prostitute and her pimp. It may also have a zoological basis: the male wolf fights with many rivals for its mate and may indeed be an unprepossessing sight by the time he wins her; moreover, as Earle Birney, the Canadian poet and Chaucer scholar, observes, mating takes place in the fall when wolves have old, tattered pelts. The she-wolf which, with the leopard and the lion, blocks Dante's path to the Mountain of Joy in the first canto of the *Inferno* is usually taken to symbolize either incontinence or fraud. Homilists warned men about women in similar terms. "If you approach a beautiful woman" said Odo of Ceriton sternly, "she will devour you like a wolf."

At the same time the Devil himself, frequently termed "the wolf of hell," was lying in wait to have sexual relations with any woman, either young or old. Angela de Labarethe was fifty-six when she had intercourse with the Devil and gave birth to a monster that had the head of a wolf and the tail of a snake. The monster, which fed only on human flesh, subsequently disappeared, but not before Angela, in 1275, was burned alive in La Place Saint Etienne in Toulouse.

Poor Angela "saw the wolf" and lost her life. In ancient times, however, there was a superstition that you lost only your voice if a wolf had the advantage of eyeing you first. "Has the wolf seen you?" is the question put to a silent party girl in the ninth eclogue of Theocritus, and it simply means, "Have you lost your tongue?" In medieval times various schoolmen testified to the truth of the superstition and offered explanations and precautions: the sign of the cross might act as a deterrent; the mute man might regain his voice by removing his top clothing.

The phrase is still proverbial in France but the meaning is specialized; the girl who *n'a jamais vu le loup* is a virgin; the girl of whom one says *elle a vu le loup* has been deflowered.

The emblem writers often made use of the fables to moralize about the wolf. In one fable the wolf and the ass saw a log of wood together. The ass stands on the log and saws from above while the wolf works from below, hoping that the ass will tumble and that he can then devour him. Instead, the wolf is accidentally hit on the head and killed. In *Apologi Creaturarum*, printed in Antwerp in 1584, the fable emblematizes *scelesti hominis imago et exitus* (the image and end of a wicked man). The moral is:

> Who for the innocent spreads snares,
> Himself shall perish unawares.

Camerarius shows the wolf tearing a lamb as a device for *hominibus piis et probis* (men devout and honorable). Such virtuous men, by reason of their blameless life and zeal for truth, are subjected to all manner of perils and torments in this life. Nevertheless, they offer themselves as acceptable sacrifices to God.

According to Horapollo, the ancient Egyptians depicted a mare kicking a wolf to symbolize a woman who miscarried, the belief being that a mare miscarried if she trod in the footsteps of a wolf. Aldrovandi repeated the symbolism and added that the Egyptians also used a sheep and a wolf to signify discord. Ferne in his book on heraldry gave the symbolism of discord as well as that of greed and guile. The enmity between the sheep and the wolf was such that if the entrails of a sheep were used as the strings of an instrument, one string from the entrails of a wolf would produce discord:

> . . . Be the musician never so cunning in his skil, yet can he not reconcile them to an unity & concord of sounds: so discording alwayes is that string of the wolfe.

The "wolf" string in an instrument has thus come to mean an untrue note.

Although *wolf* was anciently used as a suffix to denote praiseworthy fierceness, as a personal designation the wolf customarily implied cruelty. The she-wolf of France was Isabella, wife of Edward II, reputed to have murdered her husband by searing his bowels with a hot iron or tearing them out with her own hands. Wolf, duke of Gascony, one of Charlemagne's knights, was said to be the originator of the device of tying wetted ropes round the temples of prisoners to make their eyeballs start from their sockets.

What of the wolf in *Little Red Riding Hood*? The symbolism, according to modern psychoanalysis, is the same as that of the Elders in the story of Susanna. Our heroine, whose hood denotes menstruation and indicates that she has just become a mature woman, strays from the path of virtue and is punished. As Fromm points out, the wolf's cannibalism, in which the male devours the female, not only represents the hostile feminine view of the sexual act but an attempt of the male to usurp the role of the female by having living beings in his belly.

His punishment is primitive and apt. He is killed by stones, the symbol of sterility.

Aldrovandi, p. 160; *Apologi Creaturarum, see* Green, pp. 54–55; Camerarius, lxxii; Du Cange, s.v. *lupae, lupor,* etc.; Dante, *Inf.,* xxxiii.29; *Purg.,* xiv.50; *Parad.,* ix.127–32; Ferne, ii.41; Fromm, pp. 235–41; Giraldus, *Top. Hibern.,* ii.xix; Herodotus, iv.cv; Horapollo, ii.xlv; Knight, *Priapus,* pl. xvi, fig. 1; Lowrie, p. 64; Macrobius, *Saturnalia,* i.xvii.40–41; Map (ed. Wright), p. xliii; *Master of Game,* pp. 55, 256; McCulloch, pp. 188–89; Odo of Ceriton, iv. 216, 230–31; Owen, p. 358; Plautus, *Truc.,* iii.i.656–57; Pliny, viii.22.34; Ripa, p. 520, s.v. "Voracita"; *Roman de la rose,* iii.7764–66; Seznec, figs. 74-77; Topsell, p. 734; de Vigny, "La Mort du loup"; Whitney, p. 162; Wycliffe, *Engl. Works* (ed. Matthew), p. 32; White, B., p. 43.

Selected Bibliography

(See Bibliographical Note, pp. xviii–xix)

Adolf, Helen. "The Ass and the Harp." *Speculum*, xxv (1950), 49–57.

Agnel, Emile. *Curiosités judiciaires et historiques du moyen âge*. Paris, 1858.

Albertus Magnus. *De animalibus*. Venice, 1495.

Alciatus, Andrea. *Omnia Andreae Alciati V.C. emblemata cum commentariis . . . per Claudium Minoem*. Paris, 1583.

Aldrovandi, Ulyssis. *De Quadrupedibus Digitalis Viviparis*. Bonn, 1645.

d'Alviella, Goblet. *The Migration of Symbols*. London, 1894.

Analecta Hymnica medii aevi, ed. G. M. Dreves and Cl. Blume. Leipzig, 1886–1922.

Ancrene Riwle, The English Text of, ed. M. Day. EETS, OS 225. London, 1952.

———, ed. J. Morton. Camden Society, 57. London, 1853.

Anderson, M. D. *Drama and Imagery in English Medieval Churches*. Cambridge, England, 1963.

———. *The Mediaeval Carver*. Cambridge, England, 1935.

———. *Misericords*. London, 1954.

Aneau, Barthélemi. *Picta poesis*. Lyons, 1552.

Appleton, LeRoy H., and Stephen Bridges. *Symbolism in Liturgical Art*. New York, 1959.

Artemidorus Daldianus. *Onirocriticon*, ed. Rudolph Hercher. Leipzig, 1864.

Audsley, W. J., and G. A. Audsley. *Handbook of Christian Symbolism*. London, 1865.

Barke, James, and Sidney Goodsir Smith (eds.). *Robert Burns: The Merry Muses of Caledonia*. 1959; 1st Amer. ed., New York, 1964.

Bartholomaeus Anglicus, *see* Trevisa, John.

Bartholome, Batman Uppon. His Booke De Proprietatibus Rerum. London, 1582.

Berchorius Petrus. *Reductorium Morale super totam Bibliam*. Nuremberg, 1517.

Beza (Théodore de Bèze). *Icones*. Geneva, 1580.

St. Birgitta. *Revelationes Caelestes*. Munich, 1680.

Bloomfield, Morton W. *The Seven Deadly Sins*. 1952; rpt., East Lansing, Mich., 1967.

Boas, George. *The Happy Beast.* 1933; rpt., New York, 1966.

Bode, G. H. (ed.). *Scriptores rerum mythicarum Latini.* 1834; rpt., Hildesheim, N. Y., 1968.

Boissard, J. J. *J. J. Boissardi emblematum liber . . . a T. de Bry sculpta . . . .* Frankfort, 1593.

Boutell, Charles. *English Heraldry.* London, 1902.

Brand, John. *Observations on Popular Antiquities.* Newcastle, 1777.

Brant, Sebastian. *Das Narrenschiff Faksimile der Erstausgabe von 1494,* ed. Franz Schultz. Strasbourg, 1913.

Brewer, E. Cobham. *Dictionary of Phrase and Fable.* London, 1900.

Brieger, Peter. *English Art 1216–1307.* Oxford, 1957.

Briffault, Robert. *The Mothers: A Study of the Origins of Sentiments and Institutions.* 3 vols. New York, 1927.

Brunetto Latini. *Li Livres dou Trésor,* ed. F. J. Carmody. Berkeley, 1948.

Bunker, Henry Alden. "The Voice as (Female) Phallus." *Psychoanalytic Quarterly,* III (1934), 391–429.

Burns, Robert, *see* Barke, James.

Burriss, Eli Edward. "The Place of the Dog in Superstition as revealed in Latin Literature," *Classical Philology,* XXX (1935), 32–42.

Burton, Maurice. *The Hedgehog.* London, 1969.

Busch, Harald, and Bernd Lohse. *Romanesque Sculpture.* London, 1962.

Camerarius, Joachim. *Symbolorum et Emblematum.* Nuremberg, 1590.

Campbell, Joseph. *The Hero with a Thousand Faces.* New York, 1949.

Carcopino, J. *Daily Life in Ancient Rome.* 1941; rpt., Harmondsworth, Middlesex, 1962.

Carroll, William Meredith. *Animal Conventions in English Renaissance Non-Religious Prose (1550–1600).* New York, 1954.

Chastel, André. "Note sur le Sphinx à la Renaissance." *Archivo di Filosofia . . . Università di Roma.* Rome, 1958. Pp. 179–82.

Chew, Samuel C. *The Pilgrimage of Life.* New Haven and London, 1962.

Ciarrocchi, Arnoldo. *Italian Votive Tablets.* Udine, Italy, 1960.

Clausen, Lucy W. *Insect Fact and Folklore.* 1954; rpt., New York, 1962.

Cokaygne, The Land of, ed. W. Heuser. *Bonner Beiträge zur germanischen und romanischen Philologie,* XIV (1904), 145–50.

Colonna, Fra Francesco. *Hypnerotomachia Poliphili.* Venice, 1499.

Conger, Jean. *The Velvet Paw: A History of Cats in Life, Mythology and Art.* New York, 1963.

Cook, A. S. (ed.). *The Old English Elene, Phoenix and Physiologus.* New Haven, 1919.

Cornelius a Lapide. *Commentariis in Josue, Judicum, Ruth, IV Libros Regum et II Paralipomenon.* Antwerp, 1687.

Coulter, Cornelia C. "The 'Great Fish' in Ancient and Medieval Story." *Transactions of the American Philological So-*

ciety, LVII (1926), 32–50.

Creuzer, Georg Friedrich. *Religions de l'antiquité . . . de Dr. Frédéric Creuzer*, ed. J. D. Guigniaut. 4 vols. Paris, 1825–1841.

Crooke, W. *An Introduction to the Popular Religion and Folklore of Northern India*. Allahabad, 1894.

Curtius, E. R. *European Literature and the Latin Middle Ages*, trans. W. R. Trask. New York, 1963.

D'Ayzac, Félicie. "De la zoologie composite . . . ." *Revue de l'art chrétien*, ser. 4, IV (1886), 13–36.

Dent, A. A., and D. M. Goodall. *The Foals of Epona. A History of British Ponies from the Bronze Age to Yesterday*. London, 1962.

Dio Cassius. *Dio's Roman History*, tr. E. Cary. 9 vols. London, 1914.

Ditchfield, P. H. *Symbolism of the Saints*. London, 1910.

Drake, Maurice, and Wilfred Drake. *Saints and Their Emblems*. London, 1916.

Drimmer, Frederick. *The Animal Kingdom*. 3 vols. New York, 1954.

Druce, G. C. "An Account of the μυρμηκολέων or Ant-Lion." *The Antiquaries Journal*, III (1923), 347–64.

———. "The Amphisbaena and its Connexions in Ecclesiastical Art and Architecture." *Archaeological Journal*, LXVII (1910), 285–317.

———. "The Elephant in Medieval Legend and Art." *Archaeological Journal*, LXXVI (1919), 1–73.

———. "Some Abnormal and Composite Human Forms in English Church Architecture." *Archaeological Journal*, LXXII (1915), 135–86.

———. "The Symbolism of the Crocodile in the Middle Ages." *Archaeological Journal*, LXVI (1909), 311–38.

Duchaussoy, Jacques. *Le Bestiaire Divin*. Paris, 1958.

Dulaure, J. A. *Histoire Abrégée de differens cultes*. Vol. II. *Des Divinités Génératrices chez les anciens et les modernes*. Paris, 1825.

Duncan, Thomas Shearer. "The Weasel in Religion, Myth and Superstition." *Washington University Studies*, XII, Humanistic Series no. I. (Oct. 1924), 33–66.

Durandus, William. *The Symbolism of Churches and Church Ornaments*, ed. J. M. Neale and B. Webb. London, 1906.

Epiphanius, *see Physiologus*.

Ettlinger, E. "The Hildburgh Collection of Austrian and Bavarian Amulets at the Wellcome Historical Medical Museum." *Folklore*, LXXVI (1965), 104–17.

Evans, E. P. *Animal Symbolism in Ecclesiastical Architecture*. New York, 1896.

Faerno, Gabriel. *Fabulae*. Rome, 1564.

Farinator, Mattias. *Lumen animae*. Augsburg, 1477.

Ferne, John. *The Blazon of Gentrie*. 2 pts. London, 1586.

Ficino, Marsilio. *Opera*. 2 vols. Basle, 1576.

Flinn, John. *Le Roman de Renart dans le littérature française et dans les littératures étrangères au moyen âge*. Toronto, 1963.

Fournival, Richard di. *Li Bestiaires d'Amours di Maistre Richart de Fornival e li Response du Bestiaire*, ed. Cesare

Segre. Milan, 1957.

Franc, Helen M. *The Animal Kingdom*. New York, 1940.

Frazer, Sir James G. *The Golden Bough: A Study in Magic and Religion*. Abridged ed., London, 1959.

Freitag, Arnold. *Mythologia Ethica*. Antwerp, 1579.

Fromm, Erich. *The Forgotten Language, An Introduction to the Understanding of Dreams, Fairy Tales and Myths*. New York, 1951.

Gesta Romanorum, ed. Herman Oesterley. Berlin, 1871.

————, ed. Sidney J. H. Herrtage. London, 1879.

Ginzberg, L. *Legends of the Jews*. Vol. I. Philadelphia, 1909.

Giraldus Cambrensis. *Opera*, ed. J. F. Dimock. Vols. V and VI. London, 1867–1868.

Golden Legend, The, see Jacobus de Voragine.

Goldsmith, Oliver. *A History of Earth and Animated Nature*. 2 vols. London, 1876.

Gower, John. *The Complete Works*, ed. G. C. Macaulay. 4 vols. Oxford, 1899–1902.

Graves, Robert. "Mother Goose's Lost Goslings." *Hudson Review*, IV (1951–1952), 586–97.

————. *The White Goddess*. London, 1948.

Gray, Minna. "St. Mary-church Parish Church Font." *Torquay Directory and South Devon Journal*, Dec. 30, 1905.

Green, Henry (ed.). *Shakespeare and the Emblem Writers*. 1870; rpt., New York, 1964.

Gubernatis, Angelo de. *Zoological Mythology*. 2 vols. London, 1872.

Guillaume, le Clerc. *Le Bestiaire, das Thierbuch des normanischen Dichters Guillaume le Clerc*, ed. Robert Reinsch. Leipzig, 1890.

Guillim, John. *A Display of Heraldry*. London, 1679.

Haeckel, Willi. "Das Sprichwort bei Chaucer." *Erlanger Beiträge*, II, viii, 1890.

Hassell, James Woodrow, Jr. *Sources and Analogues of the Nouvelles Recreations et Joyeux Devis of Bonaventure des Periers*. Athens, Ga., 1969.

Havelok, ed. W. W. Skeat, rev. K. Sisam. Oxford, 1915.

Hazlitt, W. C. (ed.). *Fragmenta Antiquitatis. Antient Tenures of Land, and Jocular Customs*. London, 1874.

Heckscher, William S. "Bernini's Elephant and Obelisk." *Art Bulletin*, XXIX (1947), 155–82.

Highet, Gilbert. *The Classical Tradition*. London, 1949.

Holbrook, R. T. *Dante and the Animal Kingdom*. New York, 1902.

Hollstein, F. W. H. *German Engravings, Etchings and Woodcuts, 1400–1700*. Amsterdam, 1954–.

Horapollo. *The Hieroglyphics of Horapollo Nilous*, ed. Alexander Turner Cory. London, 1840.

Hulme, F. E. *The History, Principles and Practice of Symbolism in Christian Art*. London, 1892.

Hunt, Leigh. *The Political Examiner*, DCLXIV (Sept. 17, 1820).

Isidore of Seville. *Etymologiarum sive originum libri XX*, ed. Wm. Lindsay. 2 vols. Oxford, 1911.

Jacob's Well, ed. A. Brandeis. Pt. I. EETS 115. London, 1900.

Jacobus de Voragine. *Jacobi a Voragine Legenda Aurea . . . ,* ed. Th. Graesse. 1846; 3rd ed. rpt., 1965.

Jameson, Anna. *Sacred and Legendary Art.* 2 vols. London, 1848.

Janson, H. W. *Apes and Ape Lore in the Middle Ages and the Renaissance.* London, 1952.

Jennison, George. *Animals for Show and Pleasure in Ancient Rome.* Manchester, England, 1937.

Jewett, Llewellyn. "Scolds . . . ." *Reliquary,* I (1860–1861), 65–78.

————. ". . . some additional examples of pranks, or scolds' bridles." *Reliquary,* XIII (1873), 193–94.

John of Sheppey. *Les Fabulistes Latins,* ed. Leopold Hervieux. Vol. IV. 1896; rpt., Hildesheim, N. Y., 1970.

Jones, Ernest. *Essays in Applied Psychoanalysis.* 1912; new ed., Vol. II, London, 1964.

Katzenellenbogen, Adolf. *Allegories of the Virtues and Vices in Mediaeval Art.* 1939; rpt., New York, 1964.

Kidson, P., and V. Parker. *Sculpture at Chartres.* London, 1958.

Klingender, Francis. *Animals in Art and Thought to the End of the Middle Ages,* ed. Evelyn Antal and John Harthan. London, 1972.

Knight, Richard Payne. *A Discourse on the Worship of Priapus.* 1786; rpt., New York, 1957.

————. *The Symbolical Language of Ancient Art and Mythology.* 1818; new ed., New York, 1876.

Krappe, Alexander Haggerty. "Ἀπόλλων Σμινθέυς." *Classical Philology,* XXXVI (1941), 133–41.

————. "Guiding Animals." *Journal of American Folklore,* LV, 228–46.

————. *The Science of Folklore* (1942). New York, 1964.

"Lai d'Aristote." *Recueil général et complet des fabliaux des XIIIe et XIVe siècles,* ed. Anatole de Montaiglon and Gaston Raynaud. Vol. V. Paris, 1883.

Lanoe-Villène, Georges. *Le livre des symboles.* Vols. I–III. Paris, 1926–1929.

Layard, John. *The Lady of the Hare.* London, 1944.

Leach, Maria. *God Had a Dog: The Folklore of the Dog.* New Brunswick, N. J., 1961.

Lewysohn, L. *Die Zoologie des Talmuds.* Frankfort, 1858.

Ley, Willy. *The Lungfish, the Dodo and the Unicorn.* New York, 1948.

Les livres du roy Modus et de la royne Ratio, ed. Gunnar Tilander. Paris, 1930.

Loomis, C. G. *White Magic.* Cambridge, Mass., 1948.

Lowrie, Walter. *Art in the Early Church.* 1947; rev. ed., New York, 1969.

Ludus Coventriae, ed. K. S. Block. EETS, ES 120. London, 1922.

McCulloch, Florence. *Mediaeval Latin and French Bestiaries.* 1960; rev. ed., Chapel Hill, N. C., 1962.

McDermott, W. C. *The Ape in Antiquity.* Baltimore, 1938.

Mâle, Emile. *L'Art Religieux de XIIe siècle en France.* Paris, 1922.

————. *L'Art Religieux du XIIIe siècle en France.* Paris, 1925.

Mandeville's Travels, ed. P. Hamelius. EETS, OS 153–54. 2 vols. London, 1919–1923.

The Master of Game by Edward, Second Duke of York, ed. Wm. A. Baillie-Grohman and F. Baillie-Grohman. London, 1909.

Matheolus. *Les Lamentations de Matheolus*, ed. A. G. Van Hamel. 2 vols. Paris, 1892–1905.

Meier, Harri. "Flink wie ein Wiesel." *Lebende Antike: Symposion für Rudolf Sühnel*, ed. H. Meller and H-J. Zimmerman. Berlin, 1967. Pp. 34–54.

Merlin, ed. H. B. Wheatley. EETS, OS 10, 21, 36. London, 1865–1869.

Morgan, H. T. *Chinese Symbols and Superstitions*. S. Pasadena, Calif., 1942.

Nares, Robert. *A Glossary*. 1822; new ed. 2 vols., London, 1867.

Neckam, Alexander. *De naturis rerum, libro duo*. London, 1863.

Necker, Claire. *The Natural History of Cats*. New York, 1970.

Needham, G. B. "New Light on Maids 'Leading Apes in Hell.'" *Journal of American Folklore*, LXXV (1962), 106–19.

Nordenfalk, Carl. *Romanesque Painting from the Eleventh to the Thirteenth Century*, Part II. Pt. I, mural painting by Andre Grabar; pt. II, book illumination by Carl Nordenfalk; trans. Stuart Gilbert. New York, 1958.

Oakeshott, W. *The Sequence of English Medieval Art*. London, 1951.

Odo of Ceriton. *Les Fabulistes Latins*, ed. Léopold Hervieux. Vol. IV. 1896; rpt., Hildesheim, N. Y., 1970.

Owen, A. *Ancient Laws and Institutes of Wales*. London, 1841.

Owst, G. R. *Literature and Pulpit in Medieval England*. 2nd ed., Oxford, 1961.

Panofsky, Dora and Erwin. *Pandora's Box*. 1956; rev. ed., New York, 1962.

Panofsky, Erwin. *Studies in Iconology*. 1939; rpt., New York, 1962.

Partridge, Eric. *Dictionary of Slang and Unconventional English*. London, 1949.

————. *Dictionary of the Underworld*. London, 1950.

Paston Letters, The, ed. J. Gairdner. 4 vols. Edinburgh, 1910.

Patrologia Graeca, ed. J. P. Migne. 166 vols. Paris, 1857–1866. [Cited as *PG*.]

Patrologia Latina, ed. J. P. Migne. 221 vols. Paris, 1844–1864. [Cited as *PL*.]

Petti, Anthony G. "Beasts and Politics in Elizabethan Literature." *Essays and Studies*, XVI (1963), 68–90.

Philippe de Thaon. *Le bestiaire de Philippe de Thaün, see* Wright, *Popular Treatises . . . ,* London, 1841, pp. 74–131. *Li Livre des creatures, see* Wright, *Popular Treatises . . . ,* pp. 20–73.

Physiologus (attributed to Epiphanius), ed. D. Gonsali Ponce de Leon. 1587; another edition, Antwerp, 1588 [ed. cit.].

"Physiologus Latinus Versio Y," ed. F. J. Carmody. *University of California Publications in Classical Philology*, XII (1941), 95–134.

Picinelli, F. *Mondo Simbolico*. Venice, 1678.

Picot, E. "Le cerf allègorique dans les tapisseries et les miniatures." *Bulletin de la soc. franc. de reproduction de manuscrits à peintures*, III (1913), 57–67.

Pierre de Beauvais. "Bestiaire en prose de Pierre le Picard," ed. Charles Cahier and Arthur Martin. *Mélanges d'archéologie, d'histoire et de littérature*. Paris, II (1851), 85–100, 106–232; III (1853), 203–88; IV (1856), 55–87.

Pricke of Conscience, The, ed. Richard Morris. Berlin, 1963.

Prudentius. *Psychomachia*. London. British Museum. Cot. Cleo MS. CVIII.

Réau, Louis. *Iconographie de l'art chrétien*. 4 vols. Paris, 1957.

Reusner, Nicholas. *Emblemata—partim ethica et physica*. Frankfort, 1581.

Ripa, Cesare. *Iconologia*. 1603; rpt., Hildesheim, N. Y., 1970.

Robbins, Rossell Hope. *The Encyclopedia of Witchcraft and Demonology*. New York, 1959.

———. *Secular Lyrics of the XIV and XV Centuries*. 1952; rev. ed., Oxford, 1955.

Robertson, D. W., Jr. *A Preface to Chaucer*. Princeton, 1962.

Robin, P. Ansell. *Animal Lore in English Literature*. London, 1932.

Robinson, F. N. (ed.). *The Works of Geoffrey Chaucer*. 2nd ed., Boston, 1957.

Robinson, Philip Stewart. *The Poet's Beasts*. London, 1885.

Róheim, Géza. *The Riddle of the Sphinx*, trans. R. Money-Kyrle. London, 1934.

Le Roman de la Rose, ed. Ernest Langlois. 5 vols. Paris, 1920–1924.

Le Roman de Troie, ed. Léopold Constans. Paris, 1904.

Rorimer, James J. *The Unicorn Tapestries at the Cloisters*. New York, 1962.

Ross, A. S. C. "The Middle English Poem on the Names of a Hare." *Proceedings of the Leeds Philosophical and Literary Society*, III (1932–1935), 347–77.

Rowland, Beryl. *Blind Beasts: Chaucer's Animal World*. Kent, Ohio, 1971.

———. "Forgotten Metaphor in Three Popular Children's Rhymes." *Southern Folklore Quarterly*, XXXI (1967), 12–19.

———. "'Owles and Apes' in Chaucer's *Nun's Priest's Tale*, 3092." *Mediaeval Studies*, XXVII (1965), 322–25.

Ryan, L. V. "Some Czech-American Forms of Divination and Supplication," *Journal of American Folklore*, LXIX (1956), 281–85.

Sambucus. *Emblemata*. Antwerp, 1584.

Secreta Secretorum, Three Prose Versions, ed. R. Steele. EETS, ES 74. Vol. I. London, 1898.

Seton, George. *The Law and Practice of Heraldry in Scotland*. Edinburgh, 1863.

Seznec, Jean. *The Survival of the Pagan Gods*. 1953; rpt., New York, 1961.

Shepard, Odell. *The Lore of the Unicorn*. 1930; rpt., London, 1942.

Sillar, F. C., and R. M. Meyler. *The Symbolic Pig*. Edinburgh, 1961.

———. *Elephants Ancient and Modern*. New York, 1968.

The South English Legendary, ed. Charlotte D'Evelyn and

Anne J. Mill. EETS 235, 236. London, 1956.

Spies, Joseph R. *The Compleat Cat*. Englewood Cliffs, N. J., 1966.

Suhr, Elmer G. "An Interpretation of the Unicorn." *Folklore*, LXXV (1964), 91–109.

Szövérffy, Joseph. "*Et conculcabis leonem et dracone*, embellishments of Medieval Latin Hymns: Beasts in Typology, Symbolism and Simile." *Classical Folia*, XVII (1963), no. 1, 1–4; no. 2, 66–82.

Taylor, Archer. "The Proverb 'The Black Ox has not Trod on His Foot' in Renaissance Literature." *Philological Quarterly*, XX (1941), 266–78.

Tervarent, Guy de. *Attributs et symboles dans l'art profane, 1450–1600*. Geneva, 1958.

Theobaldus. *Physiologus of Theobaldus*, ed. Richard Morris in *An Old English Miscellany*. EETS 49. London. 1872.

Thiébaux, Marcelle. "The Mouth of the Boar as Symbol in Medieval Literature." *Romance Philology*, XXII (1969), 281–99.

Thynne, Francis. *Emblemes and Epigrames*, ed. F. J. Furnivall. EETS, OS 64. London, 1876.

Tindall, William York. *The Literary Symbol*. Bloomington, Ind., 1955.

Topsell, Edward. *The Historie of Foure-Footed Beasts and Serpents* . . . . 1607 [ed. cit.]; rev. ed., 1658; rpt., with new introd. W. Ley, New York, 1967.

The Towneley plays, ed. by G. England and A. Pollard. EETS, ES 71. London, 1897.

Trevisa, John. *Trevisa's Englishing of Bartholomaeus de proprietatibus rerum, libri*. XVIII. London, 1495.

Trachtenburg, Joshua. *The Devil and the Jews*. New York, 1966.

————. *Jewish Magic and Superstition*. Cleveland and New York, 1961.

Twici. *La Vénerie de Twiti*, ed. Gunnar Tilander. Uppsala, 1956.

Twining, Louisa. *Symbols and Emblems of Early and Medieval Christian Art*. London, 1885.

Utley, F. L. "The Equine Subconscious in Ireland." *American Anthropologist*, LXVI (1964), 418–20.

Valeriano. *Hieroglyphica . . . Ioannis Pierii Valeriani*. Basel, 1575.

Van Marle, Raimond. *Iconographie de l'art profane au moyen âge et à la renaissance*. 2 vols. La Haye, 1931–1932.

Varty, K. *Reynard the Fox*. Leicester, 1967.

————. "Reynard the Fox and the Smithfield Decretals." *Journal of the Warburg and Courtauld Institute*, XXVI (1963), 347–54.

Veale, Elspeth M. *The English Fur Trade in The Later Middle Ages*. Oxford, 1966.

Verstegan, Richard. *Restitution of Decayed Intelligence in Antiquitie*. London, 1652.

Vincent de Beauvais (Pseudo). *Speculum Morale*. Douai, 1624.

Vogel, Sister Mary Ursula. *Some Aspects of the Horse and Rider, Analogy in The Debate Between the Body and the*

Soul. Washington, D.C., 1948.

"Der waldensiche Physiologus," ed. Alfons Mayer. *Romanische Forschungen*, v (1890), 392–418.

White, Beatrice. "Medieval Beasts." *Essays and Studies*, xviii (1965), 34–44.

White, T.H. *The Book of Beasts*. London, 1954.

Whitney, Geoffrey. *Whitney's "Choice of Emblemes,"* ed. Henry Green. London, 1866.

Whittick, Arn. *Symbols, Signs and Their Meaning*. London, 1960.

Willet, Andrew. *Sacrorum emblematum centuria una*. Cambridge, England, n.d.

Wimberly, Lowry C. *Folklore in English and Scottish Ballads*. New York, 1959.

Wittkower, R. "Eagle and Serpent." *Journal of the Warburg and Courtauld Institute*, ii (1939), 293–325.

Wood, J.G. *Animate Creation*. 5 vols. New York, 1898.

Woodruff, Helen. "The Physiologus of Bern." *Art Bulletin*, xii (1930), 226–53.

Wright, Thomas (ed.). *A Contemporary Narrative of the proceedings against Dame Alice Kyteler*. London, 1843.

————. *A History of Domestic Manners and Sentiments*. London, 1862.

————. *Popular Treatises on Science*. 1841; rpt., London, 1965.

————. *The Worship of the Generative Powers*. 1886; rpt., New York, 1957.

Yorkshire Writers: Richard Rolle of Hampole and His Followers, ed. Carl Horstmann. New York, 1896.

Zeckel, Adolf. "The Totemistic Significance of the Unicorn." *Psychoanalysis and Culture*, ed. G.B. Wilbur and W. Muensterberger. New York, 1951. Pp. 344–60.

Zeydel, Edwin H. (tr.). *The Ship of Fools by Sebastian Brant*. New York, 1944.

Zimmer, Heinrich. *Myths and Symbols in Indian Art and Civilization*. New York, 1946.

Zircle, Conway. "Animals Impregnated by the Wind." *Isis*, Belgium, 25 (1936), 95–130.

Index

The Author

In *Animals with Human Faces*, Beryl Rowland provides answers—some whimsical, all erudite—to questions relating to the animal as symbol. For centuries Man has regarded animals as representations of qualities which he himself possessed. Ideas concerning the wiliness of the serpent, the faithfulness of the dog, and the industry of the ant are universal, and we are still reluctant to believe that the wolf, so long the symbol of rapacity, is actually a rather admirable creature. In this book Dr. Rowland discusses the fascinating symbolical and allegorical meanings of forty-seven animals from earliest times to the present. Unlike previous studies, her evidence is drawn from primary works and from all periods. Over fifty illustrations, gathered largely from medieval manuscripts, add a delightful dimension to this study.

Beryl Rowland is Professor of English at York University; she holds a Ph.D. from the University of British Columbia. In addition to many contributions to scholarly journals, Prof. Rowland is the author of *Blind Beasts: Chaucer's Animal World*, and is the editor of the *Companion to Chaucer Studies* and of *Chaucer and Middle English Studies in Honor of Rossell Hope Robbins*.

Animals with Human Faces was cast on the Linotype in eleven-point Granjon with one-point spacing between the lines. Handset Garamond was selected for display.

The Granjon type design came into being in 1924 through the hands of George W. Jones, one of England's great printers. Granjon continues to meet the most exacting requirements for fine books, which is a tribute to the honest design and legibility distinguishing this type.

This book was designed by Jim Billingsley and manually composed at Heritage Printers, Inc., Charlotte, North Carolina. It was printed by offset lithography at Thomson-Shore, Inc., Ann Arbor, Michigan and bound by John H. Dekker & Sons, Grand Rapids, Michigan.

THE UNIVERSITY OF TENNESSEE PRESS / KNOXVILLE